Origins of
Mental Illness

To Hans Eysenck
who first pointed me towards the problem

Origins of Mental Illness

Temperament, Deviance and Disorder

Gordon Claridge

Basil Blackwell

© Gordon Claridge 1985

First published 1985

Basil Blackwell Ltd
108 Cowley Road, Oxford OX4 1JF, UK

Basil Blackwell Inc.
432 Park Avenue South, Suite 1505,
New York, NY 10016, USA

British Library Cataloguing in Publication Data

Claridge, Gordon
 The origins of mental illness: temperament,
 deviance and disorder.
 1. Mental illness
 I. Title
 616.89'001   RC454

 ISBN 0-631-14198-7
 ISBN 0-631-14473-0 Pbk

Library of Congress Cataloging in Publication Data

Claridge, Gordon.
 Origins of mental illness.

 Bibliography: p.
 Includes index.
 1. Mental illness—Etiology. 2. Temperament.
 3. Mental illness—Genetic aspects. I. Title.
 [DNLM: 1. Mental Disorders—etiology. 2. Mental
 Disorders—familial & genetic.   WM 100 C59350]
 RC454.4.C56 1985   616.89'071   85-8383
 ISBN 0-631-14198-7
 ISBN 0-631-14473-0 (pbk).

Typeset by Saxon, Derby.
Printed in Great Britain by Billing & Sons Ltd, Worcester.

Contents

Preface

The exact origins of this book are, I must confess, lost to me, though I do recall that in its present form it began to take shape in the waiting-room of a car body repair shop just north of Oxford. If that seems too casual a beginning, I should explain that my melancholic visit to that establishment eventually led to a more sanguine encounter with Philip Carpenter of Blackwell's. After seeing an early version of the manuscript he suggested to me that, with some revision, it might make a publishable book. Among other things I am grateful to him for articulating what was wrong with the original version and for focusing my mind on the laborious task of reshaping it. The book now conveys as well as it can, I believe, the ideas I meant to impart, at least to the audience for whom it was intended: students of psychology, psychiatry, and allied disciplines, inquisitive professionals in other specialties, and even those members of the general public interested in what an academic (*alias* clinical) psychologist has to say about mental illness.

The last remark gives a clue to the kind of book this is. What I have tried to do is to air – hopefully in an inhalable form – some ideas about mental disorder that are rarely ventilated outside the laboratories of psychologists and other scientists like myself who are interested in clinical phenomena, yet committed to a search for an understanding of them based on experimental study. Bridging the gap between these two aspects of psychopathology – the clinical and the experimental – is bound to be fraught with controversy: speculation can often run too far ahead of the facts; the facts themselves, though numerous, may on occasions be ambiguous; and particular interpretations can arouse antipathy, disbelief or other strong emotions. That being so, I anticipate that some of the ideas presented here will seem contentious – though for different reasons to different people. For example, the book lays considerable stress on the biological basis of behaviour and on the need to relate our explanations of mental illness to the brain. Those readers with a similar conviction might, at first glance, delight in the emphasis but, on closer inspection, disagree with what is a central theme of the discussion; that psychiatric disorders – even their most severe forms – are not 'brain diseases' in the generally accepted sense, but rather abnormal manifestations of temperamental and personality characteristics which we all possess to a greater or lesser degree and which happen to have interesting correlates in the central nervous system. The connection implied here – between the healthy and the pathological – is, of course, by no means a novel idea, though it has usually been discussed from another perspective, that associated with the humanistic tradition in psychiatry. I, on the other hand, have chosen to draw more heavily on a different school of thought, one emerging more out of abnormal psychology than psychiatry, and one seeking part of its explanation for personality (and hence disorder) in the ways in which individual central nervous systems can vary. There may be other readers therefore who, while sharing my own distaste for some conventional disease concepts of mental illness, will find my insistence on referring constantly to the biology of behaviour an awkward juxtaposition. I can only invite them to consider without prejudice the arguments put forward in the book.

Although content to let most of these arguments emerge of their own accord during the book itself, there are two points which I feel are sufficiently open to misinterpretation to require further comment here, even though I do return to both in the final chapter. The first refers to the fact that the biological theories of personality which I frequently draw upon almost all contain in their conception of Man the idea that genetic influences on brain structure and function make some contribution to differences in human individuality. Unfortunately, any such mention of hereditary factors in behaviour almost invariably evokes accusatory comment from some critics who wrong-headedly wish to impute the writer in question certain sociopolitical motives. I have to say that I strongly deplore such tendencies and hope that the following pages will dispel the myth that a concern with the genetics of personality and mental disorder is anything other than a legitimate part of the genuine search for their origins.

The second related (though slightly different) point I would like to emphasise here concerns the possible implication that books of this kind necessarily lead us towards a crudely reductionist, deterministic theory of human personality. Again I would firmly deny this. Several times during the course of the discussion I draw attention to the fact that one of the major tasks facing abnormal psychology is the need to find ways of integrating factual evidence about biological differences between people with a view of the person that pays proper regard to those aspects of human individuality that are irreducible to brain processes and which, even if ultimately capable of being shown to have correlates in the higher nervous system, nevertheless have status in their own right. In trying – inadequately I fear – to offer a perspective on that question, I have suggested that we need to look outwards from the rather narrow theories of temperament with which I open the book, towards several other kinds of material and sources of ideas. These include introspection, clinical observation, and what nowadays are fashionably labelled 'cognitive' theories in psychology.

As intimated earlier, the thoughts conveyed in this book represent an attempt to formulate a view of personality and mental illness that combines an interest in the clinical with a concern for the scientific. The struggle to consummate such an uneasy marriage is of many years standing and has occurred in several places with the help and guidance of a large number of people, both students and colleagues. These are too numerous to name individually, though one does deserve special mention: my friend and former colleague, Gordon Mangan, who, during his stay in the Oxford Department of Psychology, was a constant source of inspiration and encouragement and a fund of knowledge about East European research on temperament which I drew upon unashamedly in preparing certain parts of this book.

If any particular group of people merit a special word of thanks for helping me order my thoughts, it is that generally unacknowledged band of individuals, the undergraduate students who came (and still come) to pick my brains about abnormal psychology. Dreary though the experience may come to seem for all concerned at the end of a long day, the Oxford tutorial has the retrospective advantage (for the tutor, that is) that years of experience of constantly confronting basic issues – some of which one hasn't thought of before – have an accumulating effect, until one becomes aware of having learned a great deal from the students themselves. Some of the ideas in this book are therefore theirs – or, at the very least, an articulation of thoughts that pervaded the air during hours of discussion with them.

I am also grateful to my undergraduates – and one in particular – for influencing the layout of chapters in the book. The student in question once said to me that having tutorials with me was like peeling an onion. At the time I assumed that what she was implying was that they unfolded knowledge in layers. (It was only afterwards that it occurred to me that what she may really have meant was that they simply made her weep!) At any rate I took the remark in its more complimentary sense and, guided by it, have arranged the discussion here in a similar layer-by-layer fashion. That is to say, I have opened the book with several chapters that lay the groundwork of ideas about the biology and genetics of temperament and suggest how these can provide a basic model for understanding the nature of mental illness and why people are predisposed to develop different forms of illness. In two subsequent chapters I consider how this model can be applied to the most straightforward examples of deviance and disorder we encounter, namely less severe forms such as the psychoneuroses. Then in the second half of the book I tackle the more difficult problem of the severe psychotic disorders from a similar point of view, before returning to what for me at any rate is the most intriguing question of all: how normal temperament, psychological deviance and manifest mental illness appear on occasions to form an unbroken continuum, the frankly psychotic merging into the unbalanced and the unbalanced into the merely unhappy, and how throughout there often seems to run a thread of psychological process which is not only compatible with health, but sometimes even necessary for great achievement. If there is a single message I would wish the book to impart it is that.

Finally, on a practical, but important, note I would like to acknowledge the valuable assistance of those who helped in the actual production of this book. Apart from Philip Carpenter, whom I have already mentioned, his colleagues at Blackwell's are to be congratulated on the speed and efficiency with which, once the manuscript had been accepted, they expedited its publication. Thanks are also due to Mrs Valerie Mitchell for typing endless revisions of the manuscript and, once the word-processor took me over, giving me patient instruction in its mysteries.

Gordon Claridge

1

Health, Aberration and Disease

The *British Journal of Psychiatry* recently published a fascinating article entitled 'Self-shooting of a phantom head'[2]. It describes the case of a man who, believing that he had two heads, tried to get rid of his alien head by shooting it off with a revolver. Surviving this self-inflicted wound, the man explained that the reason for his action was that the head had been talking to him, taunting him with disturbing suggestions. The patient was diagnosed as schizophrenic.

The same issue of the journal carried a review of a book by the journalist Richard Whitmore about Mad Lucas, a celebrated nineteenth-century hermit whose peculiar behaviour was an object of public curiosity, and considerable controversy, in late-Victorian England[195]. The hermit in question was James Lucas, a son of wealthy Hertfordshire parents, who after the death of his mother in 1849, barricaded himself in the family home together with his mother's corpse. Only after three months were police able to break into the house to remove the body, but Lucas himself remained there until his death 25 years later, living in a state of personal neglect and domestic squalor – as Whitmore puts it, 'a wild biblical figure sitting amid the trappings and fast-decaying elegance of an upper-class Victorian household'. Lucas's fame quickly spread and throughout his life he received a steady stream of visitors who came to stare, taunt him, argue with him, or sponge on his generosity:

> The clergyman who sought to convert him. The thousands of tramps to whom he gave gin and money. Men, good and bad, whom he sent packing with a blast from his shotgun. One who tried to kill him. There were the medical men – the most prominent experts on mental illness of the time – who interviewed him and tried to analyse him, and there were the London 'swell mob' who brought their womenfolk out to Hertfordshire for a perverted afternoon of hermit-baiting. There was also Charles Dickens, who attempted to interview him in what turned out to be a verbal cat-and-mouse duel, which caused the great author to return to London and pen a vicious critical portrait of Lucas that succeeded in attracting even bigger crowds. Finally, there were the children,

particularly the little girls, to whom the hermit gave sweets and ginger beer. To them he was 'The Squire' and, in the case of close friendship, 'Uncle Jimmie'. To the majority he was 'Hermit Lucas' but to those who lived around him he became known as 'Mad Lucas' – 'Mad' because they were convinced he was mad, but also because they felt they needed to set him well apart from the highly-respected members of another Lucas family – devout Quakers – who farmed and brewed beer in the same district of North Hertfordshire and to whom James Lucas was not related.

According to those who knew him well and engaged him in serious conversation the hermit was an intelligent, articulate man, able – and only too willing – to argue on social, religious, and political matters; though his views were certainly somewhat unconventional. For example, declaring himself a fervent supporter of the long-lost Jacobite claim to the English royal succession, Lucas persistently refused to recognise the monarchy of Queen Victoria and to sign any legal documents that contained stamps or seals acknowledging her authority! This aberration added even further to the already complicated financial and legal difficulties of managing the extensive family estates which James had inherited. In exasperation his brother George twice applied to the Commissioners of Lunacy to get James certified insane – and twice they refused, on the grounds that despite his 'eccentricities and dirty way of life' the hermit was basically of sound intellect. However, that view is not one with which all contemporary expert observers agreed. For example, the eminent Victorian psychiatrist, Daniel Hack Tuke, writing after the hermit's death, considered Lucas to have been insane, an opinion with which Richard Whitmore's psychiatric advisor concurred: he retrospectively diagnosed Mad Lucas as a case of paranoid schizophrenia.

Set side by side the two examples of abnormal behaviour just described illustrate a dilemma that continues to bedevil psychiatry in its attempts to define and understand the nature of mental disorder. Part of the dilemma concerns the connection between those disturbances of psychological functioning which we have come to recognise as signs of mental disease and those features of the personality or temperament which we are more likely to regard simply as an expression of human individuality, however deviant that expression might be. Often the borderland between these two ways of describing abnormality seems blurred, and it is only in extreme cases that we feel able to separate one from the other, apparently confident that we can explain the behaviour without reference to the personality of the individual in whom it occurs. The man with two heads is a case in point. His experiences were so dissonant from the familiar, his behaviour so bizarre, that it seems convincing enough to regard them as signs of illness, better understandable as an imposed change in mental functioning than as a transformation or outgrowth of the man's normal personality.

Mad Lucas, however, presents a more difficult problem. He too was described as schizophrenic (or its nineteenth-century equivalent), if not unanimously, at least with confidence by expert observers. Was it simply a case of misdiagnosis? Or was Mad Lucas an example where there seems to be a genuine connection between the merely aberrant and the frankly insane, such that it is possible to visualise them both stemming, in some sense, from the same roots? And if that is true can we, by the same token, extend the connection to encompass the normal and the socially adjusted as well, so that there is a continuous, or nearly continuous, progression from the healthy to the aberrant and from the aberrant to the mentally ill?

The manner of answering those questions brings us to another part of the dilemma posed by the two examples of psychological abnormality just quoted. It concerns the explanation of the *causes* of mental disorder. With a few dissenting voices, psychiatry has traditionally sought that explanation in the nervous system, on the assumption that only a serious malfunctioning of the brain could possibly account for extraordinary disturbances of the mind like thinking that you have two heads. In the latter case the assumption seems reasonable enough: the brain, after all, is just as likely to go wrong, or be the subject of disease, as any other part of the body. But what, in that case, do psychiatrists mean by mental 'disease', if they are also prepared to put the same label on someone whose behaviour was merely odd? Was Mad Lucas's brain also malfunctioning, albeit to a lesser degree? And, if so, does not that imply – since our definition of eccentricity is arbitrary – that even the normal brain has within it the capacity for madness?

Outside orthodox psychiatry, the conclusion that things are otherwise will appear trite, though those who, as professional antipsychiatrists or in the literature of the novel, have taken it for granted that the mind's instabilities are an essential expression of Man's nature, have rarely made reference to the brain: usually their thoughts on the matter have been couched in the language of psychodynamic or existentialist psychology. Orthodox psychiatry – supported by the basic sciences of neurophysiology and neurochemistry – has, on the other hand, given considerable prominence to the nervous system, vigorously searching the brain for the causes of mental disorder.

Unfortunately, neither of these perspectives has entirely resolved the dilemma with which I opened this chapter. Although the psychological analysts have given us considerable insight into the extremes to which the normal mind can go when in conflict or under stress, their formulations seem unconvincing when applied to aberrations which, because of their sheer magnitude, seem to point to brain dysfunction. Organic psychiatry, despite its inexact knowledge, certainly appears to be on the right course towards explaining such dysfunction, but its preference for focusing on the *pathology* of the brain leaves it uncomfortable with the idea that in all psychiatric disease – including the most severe – there may be a thread of continuity with the normal.

The purpose of this book is to present a third alternative view of mental illness, derived neither from the psychodynamic nor from the narrow organic tradition. It is one which, despite a long and respectable scientific history, is relatively unfamiliar, the evidence upon which it draws – mainly from experimental psychology – being little quoted in either the popular or the academic literature about mental disorder. Yet I believe the arguments to be developed here come closest to answering not only the questions already raised, but also several others that we are constantly forced to confront in our search for a complete understanding of human individuality, such as its immense variability, its resistance to and potential for change, and its differing susceptibility to the catastrophic alterations in function that are the signs of mental disorder.

Four major themes will run through the book. The first, and perhaps the least contentious, is that individuals differ fundamentally in the kinds of nervous system they possess, just as they differ in facial features and physique. These differences can be observed or inferred to exist as variations in many aspects of the functional organisation of the brain; for example, in the reactivity or sluggishness of the circuitry controlling emotion, in the responsiveness to environmental stimuli (including externally imposed agents, such as drugs), in the form of interaction between the two cerebral hemispheres, and so on. It will be suggested that the existence of such individual differences in central nervous function is now beyond reasonable doubt: indeed it is inconceivable that it could be otherwise, given the wide variability to be observed elsewhere in Man's biology.

The second, and somewhat more controversial theme, is that the differences in brain organisation just referred to become overtly manifest in the individual as variations in his or her behaviour and psychological activity. Included here are both cognitive, or intellectual, as well as emotional functions; but in its most generally stated form the argument refers to the notion that temperament or personality has biological roots that reflect the type of nervous system the individual possesses. Incidentally, in making use of this idea the term 'tempera-ment', rather than 'personality', will often be preferred, at least to begin with and as a starting-point for illustrating certain central principles of the theory. This is because the former term has, through historical usage, come to take on a meaning that is better able to capture the inherent physiological quality of certain basic characteristics which seem to differentiate one person from another. Thus, some people have anxious temperaments, some irritable, others calm, yet others depressive temperaments which, both intuitively and from experimental evidence, appear to represent the fundamental style or tempo of their nervous systems. The examples just quoted are, of course, fairly straightforward, but later in the book I shall have occasion to elaborate the idea. In particular, I shall develop the theme that psychotic or 'schizotypal' forms of personality structure – and therefore brain organisation – can also be observed in normal people. That suggestion, we can anticipate, will raise a number of intriguing questions about the nature of the more serious forms of mental disorder, including their relation to human individuality.

A third, and very important, theme running through the discussion will be that the biologically based traits of temperament described above are synonymous with predispositions to differing forms of mental illness. In other words, it will be argued that, in most cases, people develop the kind of psychiatric disorder or form of aberration to which their basic temperament makes them susceptible: the anxious develop anxiety neuroses; the impulsive become psychopathic; depression is more common in those of melancholic temperament; the schizophrenic is already predisposed to breakdown because of his schizotypal nervous system. By the same token it will be argued that the obverse is true. By no means everyone with these various forms of temperament will become mentally ill, a fact which will raise several issues. These include: the mechanisms whereby temperamental variation gets translated into illness; how and why we distinguish one form of illness from another; whether it is always possible to do so; and the reason some people are more susceptible to psychological disorder than others.

The fourth, and final, theme of the book will address the last of these issues. It will be argued that some of the most important influences responsible for temperamental variations, and hence predispositions to deviance or mental illness, are genetic in origin; not in a crudely deterministic sense, but by helping to define certain broad limits on the capacity for change in an individual, whether away from or towards disorder. The serious and the less serious disorders will not be considered to differ very much in this respect nor in the way in which genetic factors exert their effect. There a central idea will loom large: that temperamental dispositions of all forms are inherited as continuously variable characteristics, giving rise to shades of difference that only become evident as such at the extremes, especially when disposition is translated into illness.

Before developing these four themes in detail and applying them to specific forms of mental disorder, let us first try to judge their credibility against opinion about a more general topic of concern, one which over the years has been the subject of bitter controversy. I am referring to the debate about whether the concept of disease has any place in psychiatry or whether psychological illnesses are, by their very nature, set apart, somehow different from diseases encountered elsewhere in medicine; different, that is, except in the obvious sense that the brain, as the organ of *all* behaviour, is necessarily involved. In a sense I have already pre-empted part of my conclusion by implying earlier, when discussing the man with two heads, that at least in cases like his, describing the condition as a disease seems very reasonable. Nevertheless, it will be instructive to try to disentangle some of the threads in the argument about disease, for two reasons. First, it will help to clear away some of the misunderstandings about the meaning of the term 'disease', at the same time countering some of the wilder statements that have occasionally been made about its usefulness in psychiatry. And secondly, it will allow us to see how, despite a basic sympathy with a brain-centred approach to psychological disorder, the ideas to be presented later in this book diverge, at certain important points from the disease models currently in vogue in orthodox organic psychiatry.

It has sometimes been said that it is only for historical reasons that the question 'Are there such things as psychological diseases?' ever came to be posed at all; that it arises as a debatable issue only because care of the mentally, as well as of the physically, sick fell by tradition into the hands of medically trained doctors, accustomed to thinking of all abnormality – including psychological abnormality – as forms of disease. The observation is not merely captious, for it has stimulated serious and seriously intended objections to the disease concept in psychiatry. Before considering these objections, let us look more closely at the notion of disease itself and how it has influenced thinking about psychological abnormality.

It is important first to recognise that even in physical medicine it has not been all that easy to agree precisely what the term 'disease' means, since it has proved difficult, if not impossible, to arrive at a set of defining criteria covering all of the complaints that take people to their doctors. Criteria such as personal distress, statistical rarity, biological disadvantage, threat to life and evidence of physical pathology have all been tried and found wanting: there is always some exception that can be quoted. Nevertheless, in physical medicine the issue has now become one of mainly academic interest: physicians, on the whole, tend to be tolerant of its ambiguity, content that they cannot define 'disease' exactly but sure they know what it is when they see it.

There are three reasons why doctors in physical medicine can go about their business with such confidence. One is that the characteristic features of different bodily diseases – their overt signs and symptoms – can be fairly readily agreed upon. Another is that description of the superficial signs of most diseases can be supplemented by more precise information of a biological nature. This may range from a simple change in, say, body temperature to the results of complex laboratory analyses – of the blood or urine, for example, or of samples of body tissue obtained from biopsy. And sometimes the exact cause of a disease, perhaps in the form of a micro-organism or recognisable change in some bodily function, can be identified.

A third difference between psychiatry and physical medicine is that, generally speaking, the latter deals with abnormalities of function that are relatively *localised*: the patient complains of pain in the abdomen or displays tenderness or swelling in some part of his anatomy, signs which allow the possibility of disease to be recognised and understood without reference to the whole behaviour of the individual. Of course, it is true that any form of sickness will have effects that go beyond the local disability it causes, just as the management of all physical disease involves, or should involve, the whole person: the adjustment of life-style after heart attacks is a good example. However – and this is the important point – in physical medicine both the actual *definition* of disease and its *diagnosis* in the individual case can be arrived at uncomplicated by such considerations. In psychiatry, on the other hand, the situation is quite different. There the very signs of illness are themselves, of necessity, behavioural or psychological, and our decision about whether a person is sick or not is often difficult to disentangle from judgements based on interpersonal, cultural, legal and even political criteria. Exceptions are the fairly rare instances where the disordered behaviour can be definitely traced to gross changes in the nervous system – caused, for example, by a tumour, a virus, or structural anomalies of the brain.

Several interpretations have been placed on these differences between psychiatry and physical medicine. One view is that since the brain is a complex organ, psychiatry cannot be expected to have made the same progress as, say, cardiology. Those who hold this opinion would maintain that some progress *has* been made, pointing to cases of mental disorder which, previously of unknown origin, have now been shown to have a definite physical causation. An example would be dysfunction of the temporal lobes of the brain, which is known to produce behaviour that mimics schizophrenia. In that instance it might further be argued that continued research on that same area of the brain could help to explain all forms of the illness.

A slightly more cautious version of this argument is that at least it applies to the more serious types of mental illness. Thus it might be admitted that psychiatry's understanding of the milder forms of illness – the neurotic disorders – will always place less reliance on knowledge about any disturbances in the nervous system that accompany them: such disorders, after all, appear to be more within our psychological reach and they are therefore less likely to be entirely explained in purely organic terms. But severe disorder, so the argument goes, certainly *looks* organic – recall the man with two heads – and continuing to seek its causes in the brain seems to be worth a try, even if progress so far has been rather limited.

Violently opposed to both of these viewpoints is the opinion of the so-called 'radical psychiatrists', especially Thomas Szasz[172, 173]. With polemic fury he has attacked conventional psychiatry for what he considers to be its fruitless pursuit of psychological 'diseases', arguing that psychiatrists were simple seduced by one of their early successes, namely the discovery at the beginning of this century that one form of madness common at that time, general paralysis of the insane or GPI, is due to syphilis. Since then, according to Szasz, psychiatry has continued along the same path of research on the brain, in the misguided belief that other major mental illnesses would yield comparable secrets. Their lamentable failure to do so, he says, is a clear sign that the disease model borrowed from physical medicine is irrelevant to our understanding of psychiatric disorders, which he considers are more 'failures in living', better construed from a socio-psychological than from a biological standpoint.

None of the perspectives on the disease issue considered so far seems entirely satisfying, least of all that offered by Szasz. Although, like his fellow antipsychiatrists, he properly calls attention to the psychosocial element in serious mental disorder (for he chooses schizophrenia as his main platform for debate), his outright rejection of brain research in psychiatry is absurd, on two counts. First, because there is overwhelming evidence for some form of brain malfunction in psychiatric illness, the point at issue, being the way it is interpreted. And secondly, because, even setting aside questions about the nature of illness, any attempt to give an account of Man's behaviour that totally ignores the central nervous system is necessarily incomplete.

The more conventional psychiatric viewpoint can also be criticised, however. As Szasz quite rightly points out (albeit for the wrong reasons), psychiatrists have commonly relied on a model for disease that is ill suited to explain most mental disorder; that is, they have tended to look for discrete causes for entities of illness that have been defined without much reference to normal behaviour. What Szasz and some of his opponents in orthodox psychiatry have equally failed to recognise is that even in physical medicine not all illnesses are alike and there are other disease models that might be more appropriate.

Physical diseases can be broadly divided into two types. There are, on the one hand, some diseases characterised by a clearly discontinuous change in bodily functioning and traceable to some discrete cause, often external in origin; the infectious illnesses are examples. But other diseases have a different quality. These are the *systemic* diseases, which have their origins in the internal state of the organism and arise as a transformation and ultimate breakdown of otherwise normal functions. A good example is essential hypertension, in which sustained high blood pressure eventually brings about irreversible signs of disease, not only in the cardiovascular system, but in other organs as well, including the eyes, the brain and the kidney. It is worth examining these systemic diseases (especially essential hypertension) in some detail because they have a number of interesting features that can find a parallel in mental disorder. They therefore, I believe, offer a good template for the latter, helping to resolve some of the difficulties inherent in the disease model currently in vogue in psychiatry.

One property of the systemic diseases is the necessity to define them with reference to the normally functioning organism; indeed, the impossibility of doing otherwise. They are not imposed on the body: they arise intrinsically from it, and our understanding of their causation draws as much upon knowledge of the normal (the cardiovascular system in the case of essential hypertension) as it does upon the study of the pathological state. Implied in this first feature is a second important quality: that of *continuity* between the healthy and the diseased. It may be genuinely difficult to decide where one shades into the other, so that the criteria for diagnosing mild forms of systemic disease become quite arbitrary. In essential hypertension, for example, the only guide to its early signs may be persistently raised blood pressure which, of course, is measured on a continuous scale: the cut-off point for clinical diagnosis is therefore a matter of conventional usage rather than absolute rule. Even where advancing hypertension begins to produce detectable structural changes of a pathological nature these, to begin with, may also have a pseudo-continuous appearance, only becoming truly discontinuous, and apparently irreversible, in chronic disease. In other words, in essential hypertension, as in other systemic disorders, there is a *spectrum* of function – from health, through mild aberration, to severe illness.

A third feature of these diseases concerns their causes, which are often multiple. It is well recognised that the development of essential hypertension is associated with a number of environmental factors, such as smoking, lack of exercise, diet, obesity and stress. An additional important element, however, is the individual's genetic susceptibility.

This is manifest as a variation – continuous throughout the population – in measured blood pressure which, though normal in itself, at the high end of the range helps to define a person's predisposition to essential hypertension. Blood pressure can therefore be looked at from three points of view: as a measure of individual differences in physiological make-up; as an index of disposition to illness; and as a potential sign of illness itself. A similar observation can be made about other systemic disorders which, like essential hypertension, frequently have their roots in biological processes which may otherwise merely appear to describe individual variability.

The conception of *mental* disease towards which we are moving in this book is perhaps now clear. Let me state it here in a rather bald form, leaving it to be elaborated in later chapters. It will be argued that the equivalent, in the psychological domain, to the blood pressure in essential hypertension – or similar processes in other systemic physical diseases – is the genetically influenced variations in brain organisation which underlie temperamental and personality differences; that the latter can, simultaneously, be construed as dispositions to varying forms of mental disorder; and that the emergence of such disorder is, in essence, a transformation of these biological dispositions into signs of illness. As in the physical systemic illnesses, the transformation may be mild or incomplete. This may be for a variety of reasons: a relative weakness of the temperamental qualities in question, the degree to which modifying influences during the person's life have afforded protection against severe disorder, and an absence of triggering factors in the individual's immediate environment. Because it *is* sometimes incomplete, translation of normal function into disorder gives rise to a genuine spectrum of abnormality which corresponds to the distinction between mild and serious mental disorder. It is only at the extremes that the disease 'entities' of psychiatry become clearly definable.

The writer who, in the recent literature, has come closest to the view of mental disorder I have just summarised (and who indeed partly inspired it) is Eysenck[46]. As we shall see in the next chapter, his biological theory of individual differences, and its historical antecedents, have formed an important starting-point for the arguments to be developed here about the nature of psychological illness. That is also true of his contribution to the study of another aspect of abnormality, its description and classification. Here, too, there has been considerable controversy, the position adopted by different discussants usually dictating their views on the disease issue. For example, Eysenck drew attention quite early on to some of the continuities between normal personality and mental disorder, thus emphasising features largely ignored in the classic psychiatric literature: in so doing he helped to bridge a crucial gap in our understanding of how, at a descriptive level, the normal and the abnormal may be related.

As a personality theorist and experimental psychologist, Eysenck came to the problem of classification through a route that began as an attempt to define the ways in which *normal* individuals differ. This entailed using statistical techniques to isolate the major dimensions or continua along which people vary and which, in differing combinations, are said to describe their relative weightings towards such characteristics as emotionality, sociability, impulsivity, psychotic tendency and so on. The people who occupy the furthest extremes of these continua have naturally also been of interest to Eysenck, who considers them to be heavily represented among the mentally ill. In other words, for Eysenck mental illness consists of an extreme deviation along one or more of his personality dimensions, the emphasis here therefore being on the *continuity* of behaviour, rather than its discontinuity.

When tackling the same question psychiatrists have traditionally adopted a quite different approach. As clinicians they have, perhaps understandably, focused more on the data before them, on the behavioural and psychological indicators of what they have perceived to be states of illness in their patients. And in attempting to distinguish between those states they have looked for clusters of signs which differentiate illness from health and one illness from another. The early psychiatrists, of course, did this on the basis of simple observation: more recently statistical methods have been used to achieve the same end. But in both cases the emphasis has been on a search for sharp *discontinuities* in behaviour.

As mentioned earlier, the difference between these contrasting approaches to the recognition and description of various forms of abnormality has naturally had a profound influence on opinion about the usefulness of the idea of disease in psychiatry. Psychiatrists themselves, both because of their medical background and because of their focusing on relatively discontinuous signs of abnormal behaviour, have naturally considered it of value; though, in doing so, they have sometimes been deluded into a false sense of reality about the exclusiveness of different illness categories and have hence been led rather too easily towards the version of the disease model which I earlier criticised as ill-suited to most mental disorder.

The kind of approach to classification advocated by Eysenck, on the other hand, has caused him to reject the medical model altogether, though it must be said that his work has not fully addressed the issue because the type of descriptors with which he has been mainly concerned – personality and temperamental characteristics – have more to do with the *predispositions* to various forms of mental illness, than with illness itself. Nevertheless, his emphasis on abnormality as something that has an essential connection with the normal helped to redress a serious imbalance in the classic psychiatric viewpoint.

Eysenck's notion of dimensionality in behaviour is also entirely consistent with the suggestion earlier that at the *biological* level there seems to be a similarity between mental disorder and physical systemic disease, with its elements of continuity of physiological function. It is instructive to consider further how far that parallel at the biological level is continued in the *overt* manifestations of psychological abnormality.

The relevant material here is contained in discussions about the supposed distinction between *traits*, on the one hand, and *symptoms*, on the other, and about whether either of these alone can provide a complete description of mental disorder. A writer who contributed thoughtfully to that debate was the late Graham Foulds[56]. Foulds started out by arguing that only symptoms can be validly used to delineate states of disorder, in this respect agreeing with most psychiatric opinion. Foulds also clearly distinguished symptoms from traits. The latter, he suggested, are universal, frequently observed, adjustive and continuously variable descriptors of the personality: symptoms, on the other hand, are signs of maladaptiveness, usually distressing for the person, rare both within and across individuals, and have a discontinuous quality about them. However, Foulds was eventually driven to recognise that there are some human characteristics that appear to fall midway between symptoms and traits: he called these 'deviant traits'[57]. Deviant traits, he said, have many of the qualities of 'normal' traits but, unlike the latter, in their extreme form indicate that the person is seriously malfunctioning, though without showing strong symptoms in an entirely discontinuous sense. He admitted, in other words, that it is not at all easy to base a description of abnormality on a clear distinction between symptoms and traits.

Foulds confined his own use of the idea of deviant traits to the description of individuals with so-called 'personality disorders' – psychopaths and others of similar disposition whose behaviour is profoundly abnormal but who are difficult to classify as ill. However, it is doubtful whether this exclusive usage of the term is realistic. It seems merely to reflect the way society reacts to the behaviour of such people. Psychopaths, after all, are a considerable nuisance to others, and their apparent lack of suffering evokes little tolerance for their kind of departure from the norm. But other forms of deviant trait are equally recognisable and, at their extremes, are difficult to distinguish from clearly formed symptoms. Excessive anxiety or obsessiveness are examples where trait merges imperceptibly into symptom but, because the suffering is directed internally, society simply has a higher threshold for distinguishing one from the other. Throughout the range of disorder, therefore, there seems to be a series of 'boundaries of uncertainty' at the meeting-points between illness and normal behavioural variation.

A similar conclusion can be reached from formal studies by statistically minded psychiatrists attempting to decide between two possible methods of classifying mental disorder: that based on discrete categories of illness and that, following Eysenck, based on the idea of continuously variable dimensions. It turns out that neither is entirely adequate, even when analysis is confined to people who are already self-selected as being psychiatric patients. Some characteristics show a definite dimensionality: these include features like anxiety and depression, which are often difficult to distinguish from personality traits and which only in extreme form break into discontinuous symptoms. Other signs show a clear discontinuity – hearing voices, for example. The overall picture that emerges is that the more severe the general clinical state the greater the appearance of discontinuity in behaviour[113]. In other words, the serious mental disorders are clearly recognisable as distinct illnesses, but only by virtue of their progression from their milder forms.

Let me now try to summarise some of the main points introduced in this chapter. I have argued that mental disorders can validly be regarded as diseases, though in a sense rather different from that on which most psychiatric opinion is based. Using physical systemic disease as a model, I have suggested that mental illness similarly arises from a pre-existing tendency to disorder, the tendency manifesting itself as a variation in normal function – in the psychological realm as those characteristics which we refer to the temperament or personality. In some cases deviation from the norms of behaviour in a particular sphere may be difficult to distinguish from a simple aberration of temperament, though it becomes progressively easier to identify discontinuous states of illness in more extreme or more complete forms of mental disturbance. This parallel with the systemic diseases is not merely evident at a superficial, behavioural level: there is reason to believe that it can also be carried down to the biological level, represented as potentially discoverable processes in the brain which, in principle, are comparable to those giving rise to disorder elsewhere in the body. Such processes, I suggest, might be found to follow similar rules, including: the tendency, in health, to subserve a normal function; the capacity, nevertheless, to be translated into dysfunction; and a gradation of breakdown which, at the extreme, is irreversible, or relatively so.

Drawing this analogy with physical systemic disease carries a number of implications and perhaps stimulates some objections, most of which will hopefully be resolved for the reader in later chapters. However, two questions deserve some attention here. One refers back to a comment made earlier concerning the essential difference between physical and psychological disease in the criteria used to define abnormality. Try as we may we cannot avoid applying social and cultural standards to our judgements about mental health, and it could be argued that this would remain so even if we had complete knowledge of the neurophysiological basis of behaviour. In other words, psychiatry and abnormal psychology can never be in the position of having entirely objective criteria by which to judge sickness; even criteria which – as in the example of essential hypertension quoted earlier – may be arbitrary in their application. This is true, though it is difficult to imagine that growing understanding of brain function will not lessen our reliance on non-biological criteria for defining sickness. Less severe or intermediate forms of disorder will always be a problem, of course, but it is worth noting that this is also true in physical medicine: the mild diabetic, for example, might not wish to consider himself ill, any more than his doctors would.

The most difficult cases of aberration for psychiatry, however, are those that arouse strong emotions in others – outrage, irritation, fear, or even admiration – but where the individual experiences little personal distress. Indeed, he or she may feel a right to deviate from the norm, a claim which society may either condone or condemn, depending on the social context: the psychopathic personality may seek his fortune in crime or in big business depending on where Fate and opportunity situate him. And Mad Lucas may well have been hospitalised for schizophrenia had he been alive today. It is less easy here to find a parallel in the physical domain (though anorexic fashion models might qualify!) and psychiatry will probably have to live with this ambiguity in its definition of disorder. But these reservations do not detract from the central argument here: that if we are to adopt a disease view of mental illness – as I believe we must – then the medical systemic diseases offer, in several important respects, the closest working model.

A more serious objection, perhaps, to the parallel being drawn here is that the brain, as the organ of mind and behaviour, is unique, incomparable to the physiological systems that underlie other forms of disease. In a deeper philosophical sense that criticism cannot be met by reference to the sorts of argument and evidence to which we shall have recourse in this book. But I suspect that what is usually meant by uniqueness in this context is *complexity*. And while even that cannot be brushed aside, the questions it raises are, at least, more manageable.

At the moment the biological sciences are able to given only the crudest account of nervous function, a fact that generally seems to evoke one of two opposite reactions. On the one hand, there are those who express pessimism, even hostility, towards the idea that it will ever be possible to bridge what from our present standpoint is an enormous gap between our knowledge of the brain and the marvellous intricacy of human mentality. Others, however, see this lack of knowledge as a sign of the huge amount of understanding still to be attained. Needless to say, the present writer veers towards the second of these attitudes, conscious nevertheless of the complexity of the problem. In attempting to disentangle part of that complexity – and with respect to only one of its aspects, personality and mental disorder – it is obviously necessary to start somewhere. The point chosen here is a *general principle*, one that seems to work well in the explanation of some forms of physical disease. The fact that in the latter case the physiological systems involved are simpler does not in itself mean that the principle is entirely inapplicable to mental disease and certainly it should not deter us from exploring the possibility.

In doing so here I will not, perhaps surprisingly, refer very much to the 'palpable flesh' of the brain, in the sense that this book is not written from a strictly neurophysiological perspective. The intention instead is to show how certain ideas that have arisen – mainly out of experimental psychology – about the 'conceptual nervous system' can be applied to temperament and personality and, by extrapolation, to an understanding of both mild and serious mental disorder. This emphasis arises because much of the evidence to be referred to has been obtained from studies of human subjects, in whom the brain can rarely be examined directly. Drawing a hypothetical picture of the possible brain mechanisms involved can therefore only be done by inference; though of course the veracity of the design arrived at can be, and is, constantly tested against evidence available from studies of the 'real' nervous system.

The central aim of the book is, in a sense, to address a paradox: how illness can flow from health, normality become abnormality. It is therefore fitting that I should close this opening chapter with an earlier statement of the paradox, taken from the writings of the American physiologist W.B. Cannon, whose studies earlier this century made an enduring contribution to our understanding of the psychology of emotion. In his classic monograph, *Bodily Changes in Pain, Hunger, Fear, and Rage*, Cannon devoted a whole chapter to the question of how mechanisms that normally have *utility* for the organism can nevertheless bring about a derangement of function. He was of course concerned with physical disease, but his comments, I believe, have a considerable relevance here. He wrote as follows:

> There are many systems in the body which, because of misuse or misfortune, may have their services to the organism as a whole so altered as to be actually harmful. Thus vicious circles of causation

become established which may lead to death . . . The development of pathological functions in a system is quite consistent with its usual performance of normal functions . . . The problem is presented of attempting to learn under what circumstances the transformation occurs. And so, in an examination of the bodily changes which characterise the strong emotions, we may admit the common utility of the changes as preparations for action, we may admit also that such changes may become so persistent as to be a menace instead of a benefit, and we may also be stimulated by this contrast to attempt to understand how it may arise[19].

2

Dimensions of Temperament

In the previous chapter I outlined an approach to psychiatric disorder grounded in the study of the biology of normal personality. Distinguishing between factors of predisposition and factors of illness, I argued that individual susceptibilities to different disorders can be traced to, indeed are synonymous with, temperamental variations that have their origins in the central nervous system. Only when we know what these variations consist of, and how they arise, can we begin to understand how predisposition translates into illness, deviation becomes disorder. Over the next three chapters, therefore, I will discuss the biology of personality, before returning, in chapters 5 and 6, to consider illness itself.

The first part of the book will concentrate on aspects of personality that define the predispositions to *milder* forms of disorder, including the neurotic disturbances. The reason is that these provide the least ambiguous examples of the analogy previously drawn between systemic disease and mental illness. In the neuroses, for example, there is a quite clear connection between normal and abnormal, the jump between predisposition and illness thus being conceptually easy to make. Furthermore, the normal temperamental characteristics to which the mild disorders relate have been reasonably well defined by psychologists, who have also been able to point to some variations in central nervous activity that underlie them. And, finally, the variations in question can be referred to *actual* brain systems which, comparatively speaking, are fairly low-level and well understood, hence making it easier to see how, at the biological level, normal temperament and behavioural aberration may be joined together.

While concentrating here on the milder disorders, it is important nevertheless to bear in mind that the distinction between mild and severe is somewhat arbitrary. Indeed, for reasons already discussed, the possibility of aberration becoming serious mental illness, being a halfway stage towards it, or having brain mechanisms in common with it, is part and parcel of the model for psychiatric disorder adopted in this book. As we shall eventually see, the model finds a parallel in the fact that some ideas that have grown up around the study of temperament in relation to mild disorder are now finding increasing relevance to the understanding of more serious forms of mental illness, like schizophrenia: that is particularly so at the boundary between the psychotic conditions and some forms of 'personality disorder'. We can therefore anticipate that a number of questions will gradually emerge which we shall not properly be able to address until later in the book and the reader should be warned that it will be necessary, in the meantime, to carry forward certain half-formed ideas that it will be impossible to avoid introducing here but which can be best elaborated in later chapters.

Returning to the main theme of this chapter, it should not be necessary to justify the general idea that human personality has some of its roots in the biological make-up of the individual. It is almost inconceivable that the nervous system is unique in showing none of the idiosyncrasy of structure and function that characterises other features of the living organism. It is equally inconceivable that such idiosyncrasy would fail to manifest itself as the variations in action and reaction which partly help to define the personality. This perspective on personality has a venerable history, first as an astute piece of observation and then as a valid scientific concept. In its classic form – the ancient 'humoral' theory of temperaments – the idea that we are as we are because we are made up of varying mixtures of blood, phlegm and bile turned out to be nonsense; though it did leave us with some usefully evocative adjectives for describing our fellow men.

In modern times the most influential version of the same theory has been been the notion of 'nervous types' proposed by the Russian physiologist Pavlov[131]. He arrived at his theory during the course of his famous experiments on the conditioned reflex in dogs. Noting that dogs differed markedly in the rate at which they acquired and lost such responses, he proposed that the differences are due to variations in the kind of nervous system each animal possessed, and that this nervous type corresponded to the observed temperament of the dog. Later Pavlov applied his theory to human personality and to the explanation of abnormal mental states, both of which, for him, represented ways in which some fundamental properties of the nervous system could combine to influence differences in behavioural and psychological tendencies. This basic theoretical viewpoint has, in some degree, coloured the thinking of most subsequent writers on the topic, both in the West and in Eastern Europe, and such is the importance of the Pavlovian origins of the ideas to be discussed here that the whole of the next chapter will be devoted to them.

There are, however, other reasons for considering strict Pavlovian theory separately. The reasons can be variously considered historical, conceptual and geographical, and arise because the evolution of biological theories of personality (or temperament) during this century has proceeded somewhat unevenly, and along several different lines. The most obvious division is geographical, the fact that Pavlov's original theory of nervous types has continued, long after his death, to have a direct impact on psychology in Eastern Europe. Writers there who have made use of the theory – revising and updating it – have naturally stayed closer than those in the West to Pavlov's original ideas. That is particularly true of the kind of terminology they have used to describe the properties of brain activity which, they believe, underlie temperamental variations. In other words, their design for a 'conceptual nervous system' has differed somewhat from that used in the West. Recently, with increasing exchange of ideas, the gap between East and West has lessened considerably but, even so, by spreading our discussion of the theory of nervous types across two chapters it will be easier to show how, despite differing interpretations, it has been possible to reach a remarkable amount of agreement about the biological influences in human personality.

Here in the West the most important single contribution has undoubtedly come from the work of Eysenck. Indeed, it is in his early writings that one finds the first attempt by a Western psychologist to apply the idea of nervous types to human personality[45]. He did so by making use of a very fundamental principle in Pavlovian theory, one which we shall frequently come across in these pages and which is crucial to our understanding of many aspects of nervous activity. This is the notion that the nervous system, at all levels and in all aspects, is constantly under the control of two active, but opposing processes – one of *excitation*, the other of *inhibition*. Pavlov referred constantly to this idea in defining the properties of individual nervous systems, though Eysenck himself took it over in a much simplified form. He merely argued that individual brains differ intrinsically in their relative balance of excitation and inhibition, some showing a greater tendency towards excitability, others being more easily inhibitable. Later we shall examine this theory and some developments of it in more detail.

Another important growth point in the study of the biology of personality, especially in the West, has been the influence of the scientific discipline of psychophysiology, a somewhat mongrel branch of learning halfway between psychology and physiology. As its name implies, psychophysiology aims to give an account of the neurophysiological correlates of mental activity; but, because it tries to do so by studying the intact human subject, it relies on taking 'soundings' of the nervous system from outside. Its experimental techniques consist of procedures like studying brain-waves (EEG) recorded from the scalp; or, alternatively, the reactions of the autonomic nervous system, such as heart rate and the 'sweating' (galvanic skin) response beloved of, though much abused by, practitioners of lie detection. From the pattern of responses shown by the subject under defined conditions the psychophysiologist tries to infer the nature of the underlying brain activity: indeed, it is probably here that the term 'conceptual nervous system', already used several times here, has its most direct application. Psychophysiology is very much in the business of trying to construct hypothetical models of the brain, and in so doing constantly seeks support for its ideas from its nearest neighbour, neurophysiology.

A great deal of academic psychophysiology has been concerned, of course, with the problem of devising *general* conceptual models of the nervous system. But it has obviously also been well placed to incorporate the idea that nervous systems differ in certain fundamental respects, and this application to individual variations has made a contribution in its own right to the study of the biological basis of personality, sometimes independently of the strict Pavlovian tradition. Even so, we can discern two historically distinct trends in Western research on the psychophysiology of individual differences. One is the relatively recent attempt, mainly by psychologists, to examine the psychophysiological basis of personality, mainly in normal subjects, though sometimes in abnormal states. The other is in a much older tradition – that of 'experimental psychopathology' – which originated in the late 19th century as an attempt to find objective psychophysiological indicators of psychiatric disorders. (Indeed, one of the very first studies of the galvanic skin response – carried out by the Frenchman Charles Féré, who discovered the phenomenon in the late 1800s – had that purpose.) Continuing subsequent research, often by psychiatrists, has involved trying to differentiate patients of various diagnoses according to such measures as EEG or galvanic skin response; or alternatively, trying to describe in psychophysiological terms a specific feature of psychiatric disorder, such as anxiety or depression.

One of these various influences on Western thought about the biological basis of personality must, of necessity, be chosen as the starting-point for more detailed discussion. I am referring, of course, to Eysenck, whose early theory referred to above set the scene for much of what has followed in the past thirty years. However, Eysenck's borrowing of Pavlov's notion of nervous types is only one of the reasons his work is important here. As we saw in the previous chapter, he has made an equally salient contribution to the analysis of the *descriptive* features of personality. Even before, and as a prelude to, considering the possible *biological* reasons why people differ, Eysenck carried out a number of studies utilising more superficial tests of personality traits, including questionnaires. From these experiments he concluded that it is possible to identify three independent, continuously variable dimensions of personality: introversion-extraversion, neuroticism, and psychoticism. These factors, he says, can be visualised as a three-dimensional 'space' in which an individual can be located at any one of an infinite number of positions, according to his or her weighting on each. It is thus possible, Eysenck suggests, to encompass the great variety of human personality structure, yet at the same time reduce to manageable proportions the number of parameters needed to describe it.

As we saw in the previous chapter, this descriptive framework for normal personality was, in addition, intended as a scheme for classifying psychiatric disorder, Eysenck himself making no clear distinction between these two applications of his dimensional theory. Thus, his two dimensions with 'psychiatric' labels – neuroticism and psychoticism – were deliberately identified as such because the extreme positions on them are occupied, he argues, by individuals diagnosed as, respectively, neurotic and psychotic. According to Eysenck, variations *within* each of these broad diagnostic categories can be accounted for by referring to the third dimension of introversion-extraversion: in different combinations, therefore, the dimensions can provide a nosological scheme for classifying the main varieties of mental illness.

It is worth noting here that Eysenck's way of conceptualising mental illness – including his linking of it to normal personality – drew upon some earlier ideas in psychiatry, the descriptive scheme he arrived at representing the application of scientific method to theories based on clinical observation that had been around for some time. For example, in considering the more severe, psychotic, disorders he was influenced by the writings of the German psychiatrist Kretschmer, who earlier this century proposed that schizophrenia and the cyclical disorder, manic-depressive psychosis, really represent only the extremes of a continuum of personality, which he named 'schizothymia-cyclothymia'[95]. I will return to that idea in a later chapter. In the case of neurosis, some influence on Eysenck's thinking came from Jung's view that introverted and extraverted personality traits characterise individuals who show different forms of neurotic symptomatology[88]. The extravert, according to Jung, is more likely to develop hysterical neurosis, whereas the introvert shows a greater tendency towards what, in the terminology of the time, was described as 'psychasthenia'; that is, symptoms associated with chronic anxiety, such as phobias and obsessional reactions. Eysenck advocated a similar association between introversion-extraversion and neurotic type, though he substituted the term 'dysthymia' for 'psychasthenia'.

Conceived originally as a three-dimensional model, Eysenck's theory nevertheless for many years remained effectively a two-dimensional scheme, concerned solely with introversion-extraversion and neuroticism and with the milder disorders to which they are related. However, even in its earlier, incomplete form the theory offered a prototype for studying personality and hence the predispositions to some of the less severe varieties of psychiatric illness. That possibility crystallised when Eysenck, convinced that the behavioural dimensions he had identified have a constitutional basis, took the next step of joining his ideas about personality *description* to the Pavlovian theory of nervous types. As noted earlier, he did this initially by taking over directly from Pavlov the idea that individuals differ in the relative influence of excitatory and inhibitory processes on their nervous systems. In particular, Eysenck suggested that the introvert has a more excitable nervous system with weakened inhibitory mechanisms: the extravert was considered to be physiologically less responsive because of a greater tendency to generate inhibition that damps down brain activity.

Later Eysenck completely revamped this biological theory, in two respects[47]. First of all, he brought it more into line with Western ideas about the nervous system, or at least couched it in a language more familiar to readers in the West. Here he drew heavily upon the ideas of psychophysiologists and the conceptual nervous system models which they, in the meantime, had generated. A key concept in those models is that of 'arousal', the notion that the level of alertness in the higher nervous system is dependent upon a constant, upwardly directed stream of impulses from lower down in the brain and originating in the so-called 'ascending reticular formation'. Eysenck, by this time in common with a number of other psychologists, suggested that the reticular formation is more active in introverts, causing them to be more arousable than extraverts. In revising his theory Eysenck also further elaborated it by drawing on another contemporary idea in psychophysiology: that there is a *second* source of arousal or activation in the brain, additional to that emanating from the reticular formation. This involves the limbic system or 'emotional brain' which, as the name implies, is responsible for integrating events in the nervous system that signal emotion and for acting as a kind of emotional power house. It is from there, according to Eysenck, that the arousal associated with anxiety arises: which means that some individuals – neurotic introverts and anxiously neurotic patients, or dysthymics – have a double tendency to become highly aroused.

In moving away from the original Pavlovian theory Eysenck clearly put more emphasis on properties of the nervous system that have to do with individual differences in the brain's 'excitability'. However, it should also be noted that he did remain loyal to some extent to the idea that *inhibitory* processes also constitute an important feature of nervous activity. Thus, supported by a good deal of evidence from neurophysiology, he perceived both of the circuits responsible for the brain's state having built into them inhibitory feedback loops which, like a thermostat, are capable of constraining or actually damping down excitability if the latter gets too high. Later we shall several times come across the principle of homeostasis contained in this idea and discuss its significance in a number of different contexts.

Testing Eysenck's theory has made use of a very wide range of experimental techniques. Indeed, most pieces of behaviour that can be said to reflect differences between people in their level of arousability have come under scrutiny. I will give some examples in a moment. But first let us look at the overall strategy employed, of which there have been two main versions. The first has involved making a comparison, on some test of arousability, between groups of *normal* subjects, selected for their scores on the introversion-extraversion and neuroticism scores of an appropriate questionnaire – usually one of the family of personality inventories devised by Eysenck himself. The other strategy has been to compare *neurotic patients* with different diagnoses, on the grounds that they represent, albeit in a more extreme form, the same varieties of 'nervous type' that are being identified by questionnaire among normal subjects. In the case of patients the appropriate comparison is between those diagnosed as hysterical and those with anxiety disorders who, as noted earlier, Eysenck labelled 'dysthymic'.

Comparing the strategies just described, it is obvious that two crucial requirements need to be met if the arguments being put forward by Eysenck can be considered to have any force. First of all, there should be some predictable differences in the biological status of the individuals studied, whether they are selected as psychiatric patients or on the basis of their questionnaire scores. And secondly, the *direction* in which they differ should be generally similar in the two kinds of sample: for example, dysthymic neurotics should resemble normal subjects who rate themselves as both introverted and neurotic. So much for the theory. What of the evidence?

In a previous book, *Personality and Arousal*, I brought together the results of a series of experiments which set out deliberately to test Eysenck's theory, comparing clinically diagnosed dysthymic and hysterical neurotics, as well as normal subjects, on a wide range of measures of 'arousability'[22]. Almost without exception the two patient groups were found to differ markedly in the expected fashion. Let me illustrate this with a few examples.

One technique we made extensive use of was a procedure called the 'sedation threshold'. This involves administering a depressant drug, usually a barbiturate, by continuous injection, and determining the amount an individual needs before he or she can be considered sedated. The point of sedation can be judged in several ways: according to psychophysiological criteria – a change in the EEG or galvanic skin response – or by behavioural signs, which in our studies consisted of a measure of the individual's ability to do a simple arithmetical task, namely multiplying by two a series of numbers to which the person listened while receiving the injection. The expectation here, of course, is that individuals whose nervous systems are highly arousable should require a greater amount of drug before appearing sedated – that is, have higher sedation thresholds – than people who are less arousable. Related to diagnosis we would expect dysthymic neurotics to have higher sedation thresholds than hysterics. This indeed turns out to be the case. Both in our own work, and in similar experiments by other investigators, the sedation threshold proved to be very good at distinguishing dysthymic and hysterical neurotics. The former tend to have extremely strong tolerance of barbiturates, indicative of their high levels of arousability: hysterics, on the other hand, are just the opposite – they have poor drug tolerance, are very easily sedated, and appear to have very low levels of arousability. Incidentally, the interpretation here that the sedation threshold is measuring differences in actual *physiological* arousability is supported by the fact that drugs like the barbiturates, while having a widespread effect on the nervous system, bring about loss of consciousness by damping down activity in precisely that part of the brain – the ascending reticular formation – which, as we have just seen, is thought to be important in determining certain aspects of temperament.

A rather less drastic procedure we used in these same experiments, but one which can also be said to reflect arousal differences, was to examine subjects' ability to perform on tasks of sustained attention, or vigilance. Here the individual is required to pay attention, over a relatively long time, to a boringly monotonous set of repeated stimuli, the task being to detect salient 'signals' occurring very infrequently. It has been known for a long time that performance on this kind of test is related to personality – indeed, ever since serious failures of observation by radar watchers during World War II caused the problem to be investigated. Our own comparison of neurotic patients confirmed this. Using a task which involved trying to pick out certain combinations of digits from an otherwise randomly arranged stream of numbers, we found that dysthymic patients had a very much higher rate of detection than hysterics. Again it seemed possible to put this down to a basic difference in their respective degree of arousal during the test, a conclusion confirmed by the fact that the patients' heart rates, measured while they were performing the task, were also markedly different. Dysthymic patients had very high heart rates, hysterics very low.

Measuring heart rate during vigilance performance was only one of a number of psychophysiological procedures we used in our studies. Another method was to examine various features of brain-wave activity as reflected in the EEG recorded under several conditions. Here again we found that dysthymics were more aroused and more arousable than patients given a diagnosis of hysteria. This was especially evident in the 'alpha rhythm', an EEG waveform known to be an especially good index of the brain's level of alertness. The alpha rhythm of dysthymic patients was of faster frequency and of lower amplitude than that found in hysterics; it also tended to be blocked more easily by visual stimulation and to be replaced by the faster wave-forms that are indicative of increased cortical arousal.

How do the results obtained on these various psychophysiological measures line up with the differences observed in *normal* people? In the research just quoted our sample of normal subjects tended to show moderate degrees of arousability, falling midway between the two neurotic groups on most of the experimental measures. Of more interest here, however, is the fact that variations *within* the normal group were related to descriptive features of personality in a predictable fashion. Individuals who were introverted and high in neuroticism behaved exactly like dysthymic neurotics, whereas normals with high questionnaire scores on both extraversion and neuroticism resembled diagnosed hysterical patients. This was especially true on our most powerful measure – the sedation threshold – where there is a now considerable amount of evidence for the similarity[30]. It was therefore possible in these experiments, and others like it, to establish a clear continuity between normal personality and psychiatric disorder with respect to certain basic properties of the nervous system that reflect its degree of arousability.

Although Eysenck's theory formed a useful starting-point for research of the kind just described, there have been lingering doubts in the minds of some psychologists that the personality dimensions he made use of are not sufficiently fundamental, and do not map directly enough on to the underlying properties of the brain which define various nervous types. Introverted and extraverted personality traits, for example, represent complicated socially contextual pieces of behaviour which, while certainly resting on a biological base, seem intuitively rather distant from the nervous system. The observation refers back to a point made right at the beginning of this book (and reflected in the title of this chapter): that the term 'temperament', rather than 'personality', has a connotation which comes closest to describing the kinds of variation in nervous system style that appear to differentiate people. Others, thinking along similar lines, have therefore recently tried to redefine the questions raised by Eysenck and to seek the biological basis of behavioural characteristics that have a more temperamental feel about them.

One such investigator is Gray, who has suggested that 'anxiety', for example, is a much more fundamental dimension of personality (or, as I would prefer to call it, temperament) than either of Eysenck's neuroticism and introversion-extraversion dimensions[68]. In practice, of course, at a purely descriptive level the two ways of describing individual differences are actually interchangeable. As Gray rightly points out, this is because anxiety can be visualised as a kind of fusion of introversion and neuroticism. Which means that people who achieve high scores on a questionnaire designed to measure anxiety will be the very same people who, on Eysenck's personality scales, emerge as introverted and very neurotic. Correspondingly, in the psychiatric domain dysthymic neurotic patients will represent the very extremes of anxiety. Nevertheless, Gray's argument is that by concentrating on anxiety as such it is possible to get nearer to the brain mechanisms that underlie this important dimension of temperament. Gray himself has literally been able to do so because his own research has enabled him to go somewhat beyond the designs for the nervous system proposed by psychophysiologists and into the study of the 'real' brain. Admittedly this has been in animals, mainly the rat, but it has thereby been possible to examine directly parts of the brain which serve similar functions in Man and which in all species seem to mediate between certain basic features of anxiety. As it happens, Gray's proposed 'conceptual nervous system' for anxiety is not all that different from that arrived at, by inference, from data on human subjects, though it is naturally able to point to some of the actual brain structures involved.

Gray's model starts from the assumption that what characterises the highly anxious (human or animal) is a biologically determined tendency to react more strongly to events in the environment that signal punishment. From his research on the rat brain Gray has been able to identify neural structures that seem to be uniquely responsible for this increased sensitivity to punishment. Some of the structures in question – the ascending reticular formation and the limbic system – we have already come across. These, together with parts of the frontal cortical areas of the brain, form a closed-loop circuit which, according to Gray, operates at varying levels of reactivity in different individuals and, in the rat, can actually be seen to do so, depending on the animal's state of anxiety. An important feature of the circuit – referring back to an earlier part of the discussion here – is that its various components are considered to be in a relationship of negative feedback due to reciprocally acting excitatory and inhibitory influences. The excitatory impulses come, in the manner suggested earlier, from the ascending reticular formation, which may be more or less active in different people. But arousal is opposed by downward inhibition from part of the limbic system – the hippocampus – which, if reticular activation gets too high, has the capacity to suppress any ongoing behaviour. It is this 'behavioural inhibition' which, Gray suggests, is responsible for many of the avoidant, phobic or withdrawal reactions seen in highly anxious individuals. The idea contained in his model – that the circuit he proposes can have different 'setting-points' of arousal in different people – of course also explains, and gives further physiological reality to, our own psychophysiological findings described earlier. Indeed, we can be confident that dysthymic neurotics represent the very extreme of Gray's anxiety dimension.

Of course, anxiety is not the only dimension of temperament along which people can be distinguished. Another receiving some attention has been impulsivity, a characteristic that has been of interest because it seems to relate to forms of aberration very different from those associated with anxiety, namely psychopathic and other types of antisocial disorder. Unfortunately, the neurophysiological basis of impulsivity is less well understood, though Gray, neatly counterbalancing his theory of anxiety, has suggested that it may reflect a high degree of sensitivity to environmental signals of *reward*, rather than punishment. Individuals who are constitutionally so predisposed might thus be actively driven to carry out positively reinforcing acts; in an extreme form this might issue as antisocial behaviour.

The same general idea, though in a slightly different guise, is to be found in the concept of 'sensation seeking', recently popularised by the American psychologist Zuckerman[201]. He has argued that individuals differ intrinsically in the extent to which they are motivated by the need to seek out stimulation, or variety, in the environment. The characteristic has sometimes been termed 'stimulus hunger' or the need for 'arousal jag' and has appeared in several forms throughout the history of psychology. One writer who, in the 1960s, made considerable use of the idea was Berlyne, in an a notable book called *Conflict, Arousal, and Curiosity*[6]. As the title indicates, Berlyne suggested that organisms are constantly driven to try to maintain an optimum level of arousal; but in seeking this they are often – like the horror movie fan – caught in a conflict between anticipated trepidation and fascination engendered by their curiosity.

Zuckerman's own interest in the phenomenon stemmed initially from work he was carrying out on the effects of sensory deprivation. Noting wide individual differences in the tolerance of that experience he coined the name 'sensation seeking' to refer to what he perceives as a basic temperamental trait describing the varying need for stimulation. A questionnaire subsequently developed to measure the trait, explores various aspects of sensation seeking, such as the individual's susceptibility to boredom, like or dislike of physicallly dangerous activities, such as hazardous sports, and tendency to prefer unorthodox life-styles. Using his questionnaire to select high and low sensation seekers Zuckerman has demonstrated differences between them on a wide range of psychological and biological measures. Let us look at just one example which illustrates the physiological nature of the trait particularly well.

The experiment in question examined a phenomenon that has received considerable attention in recent years, both from psychologists interested in normal individual differences and from psychiatrists looking for objective ways of describing certain features of mental illness. The phenomenon – known as 'augmenting-reducing' – refers to the fact that individuals appear to vary in the extent to which their nervous systems either amplify or diminish the effects of stimulation. This tendency can now be quantified using the EEG, by looking at the change in the amplitude of a specific wave-form brought about by increasing the intensity of a stimulus to which the subject attends. Usually the method involves presenting light flashes at several different intensities and then determining the rate at which the amplitude of the EEG response changes. (In practice many flashes at each intensity are presented to the subject, the wave-forms then being averaged in order to get a more reliable measure of the typical response to a given level of stimulation.)

Using this technique Zuckerman found that high sensation seekers tended to be 'augmenters'; that is, the amplitude of their EEG response simply became larger as the intensity of the flash was increased. Zuckerman took this as evidence that such individuals can either tolerate unusually high levels of stimulation or had nervous systems which actively amplify its effects. Low sensation seekers, on the other hand, showed quite the opposite, a 'reducing' type of reaction; in their case very high intensities caused the EEG response to become paradoxically *smaller* in amplitude, indicating that the nervous system in these self-confessed sensation avoiders literally turns away from strong stimulation. Incidentally, that might be seen as an example of an effect discussed earlier when describing how inhibition in the nervous system helps to modulate its activity if arousal or the stimulation impinging on the brain gets too high; some individuals seem to more susceptible to the effect than others.

Speculating further about the biological basis of sensation seeking, Zuckerman has considered, as one possibility, the idea that the anatomical substrate of the trait may lie in the so-called reward centres of the brain, located in the limbic system. Here there is an interesting comparison to be made with the explanation of *impulsivity*, considered earlier; namely, that it is has something to do with individual differences in the sensitivity to events in the environment that signal reward. The parallel is not coincidental of course, since, given the similarities in the two ideas, it is doubtful whether sensation seeking and impulsivity can be regarded as entirely independent of each other. But it is important to note that both seem to be separable from anxiety. Thus people who are high sensation seekers, or very impulsive, are *not*, as one might be tempted to think, merely individuals who are lacking in anxiety and consequently less likely to avoid arousing situations. Instead there seems, in both traits, to be an element of *active* search for stimulation. This means that people can be high in both anxiety *and* sensation seeking (or impulsivity) – or show various mixtures of the two. Even such an arrrangement, based on just two temperamental dimensions and referred to quite low-level structures in the brain, could therefore give rise to a number of different variations in observed behaviour.

It may be asked how these more temperament-like dimensions we have just been discussing relate to the dimensions contained in Eysenck's original description of personality. We already know that anxiety is very similar to a combination of introversion and neuroticism: in fact it is almost certainly a basically anxious form of temperament that gives rise, secondarily, to the kinds of unsociable, emotionally sensitive traits associated with those two sets of characteristics. Similarly, impulsivity and sensation seeking probably help to determine the outgoing patterns of behaviour found in the extravert – and, in more extreme form, in some pleasure-bent psychopaths. There is, however, a slight complication here. As mentioned earlier, Eysenck's theory actually consists of *three* dimensions, the third, psychoticism, being intended to encompass the controversial suggestion that traits can be observed in the normal population which appear to be associated with the predisposition to the more severe, *psychotic* mental states. It is therefore worth noting, in passing, that many of the behavioural traits found by Eysenck to define 'psychoticism' are identical to those used to describe impulsivity and sensation seeking. This raises some very interesting questions, which we have already touched upon and will return to later, about the overlap between mild and severe dysfunction and the relationship of each to certain kinds of temperamental disposition, especially those that give rise to what are euphemistically called 'disorders of the personality'.

Some readers, contemplating the drift of the discussion in this chapter, might feel inclined to comment that even if what has been described here were the whole story about temperament (which of course it is not), the account it offers is oversimplistic, bearing in mind the complexity of the human personality. It is perhaps therefore worth re-emphasising the aim of the kind of research discussed. Its intention – and indeed success – has been to establish with some degree of certainty that there are fundamental differences in the style in which individual nervous systems can be organised. The fact that these differences appear to represent variations occurring fairly low down in the brain is both a cause for delight (in making the problems for future research more manageable) and a reason for modesty. For it would certainly be wrong to claim that the kinds of theory that have so far guided research on *temperament* can hope to give a complete account of *personality*, as we normally understand that term – or, by the same token, the disorders that arise from it. As will be increasingly emphasised here, to achieve that purpose requires us to make reference to much more complex psychological functions and to the higher nervous system mechanisms that mediate them. Nevertheless, the ideas discussed so far do illustrate the general utility of working from the bottom upwards, as it were; of starting by first trying to define, under the heading of temperament research, what can best be regarded as fairly basic biological restraints on individual behaviour – or, looked at another way, as neurophysiological templates which determine the broad direction in which personality, in its fuller sense, develops. Put more concretely, the theories described merely try to articulate, in a scientific form, some everyday observations about people: like the fact that few of us would ever be judged calm enough (even if we were fit enough) to become an astronaut or a deep sea diver, and the greater tendency of some to enjoy the thrills of swings and roundabaouts.

Another advantage of the 'bottom-up' approach to research on temperament is that it enables us to discern more clearly the continuity between normal and abnormal and to appreciate the possibility that beneath various forms of mental breakdown there are directing tendencies of temperamental origin which, as in their normal expression, help to dictate the nature of illness if it occurs. But these tendencies must always be regarded merely as *predispositions*, to be realised or not depending on the presence or absence of other influences that arise from the life-long interaction between the individual and his environment.

The origins of these ideas, as we saw at the beginning of this chapter, go back into the remote history of psychology. But an important step forward in understanding their significance came from Pavlov's investigations of animal temperament at the beginning of this century, his pioneer work then inspiring some later psychologists in Eastern Europe to continue research on the theory of 'nervous types'. To begin with they did so independently, but in recent years there has been an increasing convergence between East and West in the kind of approach adopted to research on the biological basis of temperament, considerably strengthening the theoretical and experimental base of the ideas introduced here. Quite apart from that, however, Pavlov himself, though formulating his theory in the animal laboratory, made some unique insights, which are worth recalling, into the nature of human temperament. We shall look at all of these topics in the next chapter.

3

Nervous Types

To illustrate how human nervous systems differ in their responsiveness to environmental events, I described in the previous chapter a recently developed procedure, based on the EEG, for measuring people's differing tendencies either to accept and amplify external stimulation or, alternatively, to reject and diminish its effects. As part of the research on the neurophysiological mechanisms of this 'augmenting-reducing' phenomenon some psychologists have also examined it in animals – for example in cats[106]. It turns out that there, too, wide individual differences can be demonstrated and, furthermore, that the variations observed are related to the judged temperament of the animal. Thus, cats whose brain reaction is the equivalent to that of 'augmenting' in the human tend to be behaviourally more active and responsive, to be more aggressive and generally emotional, and to explore the surrounding environment much more inquisitively. They are, in other words, the sensation seekers of the feline world, compared with their 'reducing' fellows who, in the experiment referred to, were altogether more timid and inactive.

The observation that cats, like other animals, differ in their temperamental disposition will come as no surprise to admirers of that species; but what is of interest here, of course, is the similarity between Man and animal in the way observed temperament correlates with brain activity. The similarity is important because it confirms a point brought out in the previous chapter; namely, that certain rather basic features of human personality can probably be referred to quite low-level brain structures shared by Man with other species. Reflecting this view, the American authors of the study just described conclude their report by noting that 'future animal research may provide a model system for understanding the relations between cortical functioning, augmenting-reducing, and individual differences in personality'.

Interesting though the comment is, it is sobering to realise – and illustrative of the time-lags occurring in research – that an essentially similar view was being aired some three-quarters of a century ago, in the laboratory of the Nobel Prize-winning physiologist, I. P. Pavlov. To those who know his name Pavlov is probably most familiar because of his famous experiments teaching dogs to salivate to the sound of a bell. Even in psychology it is his work on conditioning that has been most widely recognised, through its influence on the growth of behaviourism which, in its most extreme form, argued that the conditioned reflex could be used as a building block to construct a complete, and entirely objective, science of human activity having no need to take account of such things as thoughts, feelings, memories and other internal processes that are difficult to get at experimentally. Nothwithstanding the important contribution of that brand of psychology, few people would now adopt such a simplistic view of Man. But unfortunately the tendency to associate Pavlov's name exclusively with that narrow form of behaviourism has obscured those of his other interests that were equally important and can now be seen to have at least as much significance for human psychology.

From the very beginning of his work on the conditioned reflex Pavlov took seriously the question of individual differences, the fact that not all of his animals behaved in the same way but, instead, varied in the extent to which they acquired and could be made to lose their learned responses. Slowly in his laboratory a theory was formulated to explain these differences, based on the observation that they probably had something to do with the temperamental disposition of his subjects. Two things helped to draw Pavlov towards that conclusion. One was the evident fact that dogs – even more than cats – show very wide variations in such temperamental characteristics as aggressivity, fearfulness, gentleness and sociability. The other derived from the manner in which Pavlov and his students conducted their research. The nature of the work required that they study the same animal for very long periods, often years. Thus they became very familiar with, and were able to describe in great detail, the temperamental qualities of each dog, qualities they were able to relate quite precisely to the behaviour of the animal during conditioning. It was from these painstaking observations that Pavlov developed what was to become the first rational 'conceptual nervous system' to explain the physiological basis of temperament.

Pavlov's theory of animal nervous types went through many revisions, some of which were not always consistent with others. In addition, it was – and in its modern version still is – couched in a terminology that is rather unfamiliar to Western readers. Here I shall not attempt to disentangle the intricacies of the theory, but merely try to draw out its main themes in order to demonstrate its historical importance as the root from which many later ideas, including some already discussed, have sprung. Readers wishing to delve more deeply can do no better than consult the writings of two of my former colleagues: Jeffrey Gray who gives an eminently readable account of Pavlov as a scientific figure[70] and Gordon Mangan whose book, *The Biology of Human Conduct*, analyses in detail the evolution of the Pavlovian theory of nervous types up to the present day[111].

In formulating his original theory of nervous types Pavlov drew upon the idea that brains differ in certain basic properties. One of the most important properties, he suggested, is that of *strength*, defined as the capacity of the nervous system to endure, that is to tolerate the action of very strong stimulation. According to Pavlov, some nervous systems can maintain a high level of responding over a relatively long time and can tolerate the effects of ultra-strong stimuli: others (weak or sensitive nervous systems) respond much more strongly even to mild or moderately intense stimuli, but exhaust rapidly. An important indicator of the difference between a 'weak' and a 'strong' nervous system was said to be what happens to its response at very high levels of stimulation. Strong nervous systems will continue to react. Weak systems, on the other hand, will show a paradoxical *reduction* in the size of the response, an effect which was considered to be due to the intervention of an active inhibitory process that protects the nervous system against further stimulation – what has literally sometimes been referred to as 'protective inhibition'.

It is worth noting in passing that this part of Pavlov's theory has an obvious relevance to the understanding of 'augmenting-reducing' discussed earlier. Indeed, the 'reducing' mode of responding to stimulation seen in some individuals in contemporary studies of that phenomenon have often been explicitly interpreted as evidence for some process like 'protective inhibition', occurring more readily in those with sensitive nervous systems. Thus, Pavlov can be said to have anticipated in a quite specific sense the suggestion by more recent writers that it is feasible to model in animals such signs of human individual variation as those measured by 'augmenting-reducing' techniques. It is interesting, however, that this possibility of extrapolating across species is now construed as a strategy whereby researchers are urged to test out in animals ideas formed on the basis of experiments with human subjects. Pavlov, of course, moved in the opposite direction – from animals to Man – and in that respect can be said to have been particularly far in advance of contemporary thinking on the question of cross-species similarity.

Returning to his theory, as indicated above Pavlov assigned an important role to *inhibition*, which was also considered to vary in strength, quite independently of the variations in the strength of excitation that give rise to the overall sensitivity of the nervous system. For Pavlov, therefore, nervous systems could show differing combinations of weakness or strength of *both* excitation *and* inhibition. Thus some may show strong excitatory tendency but weak inhibition, others strong excitation and strong inhibition, and so on. This idea implied a further property of nervous systems: that they vary in the degree of *equilibrium* or balance between the two opposing processes of excitation and inhibition. In some the former, and in others the latter, will predominate: in yet others the two processes will be equally matched in power.

We can now begin to see the origins of some of the important ideas introduced in the previous chapter. The differences in 'arousability' according to which Western workers have characterised people correspond to what Pavlov referred to as variations in the property of strength of excitation: nervous systems that are 'weak' in that respect are more arousable, more sensitive to stimulation, and in response to very intense stimuli tend to withdraw from it. We also saw how most contemporary conceptual nervous models contain, in one form or another, the concept of feedback between excitatory or arousing influences and regulating, or inhibitory, influences in the brain. Again, that was fundamental to Pavlov's thinking and surfaced very early on in Eysenck's first attempt to account for the biological basis of personality: it will be recalled that, borrowing from Pavlov, he too emphasised the *balance* between excitatory and inhibitory processes when trying to explain differences in the human trait of introversion-extraversion. Subsequent elaborations of that theory, elucidated by increased knowledge of the real brain, have stayed close to the same idea. The thread linking current views of the conceptual nervous system with the original Pavlovian formulation has therefore been remarkably tenacious, especially if we recall that Pavlov himself did not have the benefit of being able to draw upon the findings of modern neurophysiological research. Nor did he, incidentally, directly study the nervous system itself very much. Despite working with animals his studies were mainly behavioural, and his model of the brain almost entirely based on inferences drawn from experiments manipulating various features of the conditioned reflex.

Inferring the nervous properties that might account for individual differences in the behaviour of his dogs was, of course, only one of Pavlov's insights. The other was to relate these properties to the temperamental variations he observed among his animals. Here, in the tradition of his time, he made use of the ancient theory that it is possible to recognise, even in humans, four temperamental 'types': phlegmatic, choleric, sanguine and melancholic. Pavlov argued that dogs with each of these types of temperament differed in behaviour during his conditioning experiments because their nervous systems were con-structed differently with respect to the properties of brain function he

had defined. Two of the temperamental types – sanguine and
phlegmatic – he considered to have 'strong' nervous systems. In these
cases the nervous system was also judged to be relatively 'balanced', in
the sense that it did not show a tendency to veer either towards
increased excitability (arousal) or towards increased inhibition.
According to Pavlov the 'weaker' – and unbalanced – types of dog were
those of choleric or melancholic temperament. These types themselves
differed, he said, depending on the direction which the lack of central
nervous equilibrium took. Choleric animals tended to lack inhibition
and therefore shift very easily towards high excitability; in contrast,
melancholic animals showed a predominance of inhibition.

Even at the very early stage of his theorising about animal behaviour
Pavlov saw its possible relevance to the understanding of human
personality and occasionally drew colourful parallels between his
favourite dogs and the varieties of temperament he observed among
his fellow men:

> The melancholic is evidently an inhibitory type of nervous
> system. To the melancholic, every event of life becomes an
> inhibitory agent; he believes in nothing, hopes for nothing, in
> everything he sees only the dark side, and from everything he
> expects only grievances. . . . The choleric is the pugnacious type,
> passionate, easily and quickly irritated. . . . The phlegmatic is
> self-contained and quiet – a persistent toiler in life. The sanguine
> is energetic and very productive, but only when the work is
> interesting, i.e. if there is a constant stimulus. When he has not
> such a task he becomes bored and slothful, exactly as seen in our
> sanguine dogs, as we are accustomed to call them[130].

Of course, Pavlov was fully aware of the important differences
between animals and Man – particularly with respect to language –
and, as we shall see later, he eventually elaborated his views accordingly
in speculating about human personality differences. Nevertheless, he
was convinced – as we now see quite rightly – that different species do
have sufficient in common, so far as certain basic features of nervous
activity are concerned, to allow rough and ready models of human
temperament to be constructed from animal data. Here Pavlov was
referring not merely to the normal but also to the pathological,
especially to the way temperamental variations might determine the
differing susceptibility to mental breakdown. Indeed, one reason for
him developing his theory of nervous types was in order to explain the
reactions of his dogs studied during the course of investigations of
'experimental neurosis'.

In a series of studies dating back to the first decade of this century,
Pavlov and his colleagues showed that it was possible to produce

functional pathological behaviours in dogs by subjecting the nervous system to stress. While it was not claimed that all of these experimentally induced states were simplified versions of human diseases, Pavlov in many cases did succeed in establishing laboratory models of disorder which, to some extent, were analagous to human neuroses and, occasionally, psychoses. Several methods were employed to induce these reactions, such as the use of ultra-strong stimuli or subjecting the animal to conflicting stimuli, a frequently quoted example of the latter being one of the earliest experiments in which a dog, trained to make finer and finer discriminations between a circle and an ellipse, was finally unable to make the appropriate response – at which point its behaviour collapsed into signs of 'neurotic' disturbance.

These various procedures for producing disordered reactions in animals were considered by Pavlov to cause what was interpreted as a 'collision' between excitatory and inhibitory processes in the brain or, more generally, to overstrain the nervous system. Here it was supposed that the precise behaviour observed depended on the particular nervous property that was most affected. It was also eventually noticed that the form of reaction varied in dogs of different temperament, the response of some being quite opposite to that of others, according to the natural make-up of the animal. In general, it was found that dogs whose nervous systems were naturally most unstable, or unbalanced – those recognised by Pavlov as melancholic or choleric – were, in their different ways, more susceptible to 'nervous breakdown'.

Towards the end of his life Pavlov took an increasing interest in human psychopathology, frequently leaving his laboratory to visit psychiatric clinics and attempting to apply his ideas about the nervous system to the explanation of a wide variety of mental disorders. Although always strongly committed to his original theory of nervous types he was, as already mentioned, well aware of its limitations when applied to Man and in his later theorising he developed a view of human types which differed radically from the earlier animal model. He did so by introducing the notion of 'signal systems'. These referred to the mechanisms that mediate the way organisms analyse the environment. His 'first signal system', which he suggested is present in all creatures, was concerned with relatively primitive forms of analysis, responsible for very basic, automatic reactions such as emotional responses; or simple forms of learned connection, like the conditioned salivary reflex that had formed the cornerstone of his animal studies. But in Man, he said, it is necessary to recognise a higher form of environmental analysis, occurring at the level of speech and thought and consisting of an abstracting system that is capable of symbolic representation of primary signals from the environment. This Pavlov described as the 'second signal system'. As might be expected, Pavlov argued that the two signal systems he had postulated had their physiological basis at different levels in the brain. The first, simpler mechanism, according to him, involves fairly primitive structures, situated below the level of the cortex. The second signal system, on the other hand, he referred to the very highest levels of the brain which are only fully developed in Man.

Elaborating this revised theory of individual differences, Pavlov considered that the activity of and relationship between the two proposed signal systems play a crucial role in human personality and human neurosis. He argued that people differ in the relative degree of balance between the first and second signal systems or in the extent to which one predominates over the other. Most humans, he proposed, fall into a middle category but two other, more extreme, types could also be recognised. One he called the 'bohemian' or 'artistic' type, whose emotional life is to a degree not subject to the regulating influence of ideas and in whom the first signal system was considered to predominate. The other, in whom the second signal system was said to be predominant, was named the 'intellectual' type, in whom abstract thought is not enlivened by imagery and emotions.

Pavlov then went on to associate these two extreme personality types with the major forms of neurosis, hysteria and psychasthenia – or what, as we saw in the previous chapter, would now be called 'dysthymia'. Psychasthenia was regarded by him as the neurosis of the 'intellectual' type, being characterised by excessive rationality, weak emotions, and high levels of social inhibition which, according to Pavlov, indicated a morbid predominance of the second over the first signal system. Hysteria, on the other hand, was considered to be the general neurosis of the 'artistic' personality, its features being rash and impulsive actions, imaginative, emotionally toned thinking, and a tendency to substitute fantasy for reality – due, Pavlov said, to a pathological tendency for the primitive impulses mediated by the first signal system to gain control over the higher brain centres that normally regulate emotional expression.

Although Pavlov's personality characterisations now seem rather quaint, and his physiological speculations are certainly very archaic, his later clinical observations do serve to reinforce an important point which, although mentioned several times here, might have been lost in the intervening discussion. So far the greater emphasis has been placed on the notion of *continuity* between animal and human temperament and the possibility of finding common brain mechanisms, of relatively low order, that underlie that continuity. This idea is still essentially correct, I believe: indeed we have already come across some of the evidence for it. And Pavlov himself, while feeling the need to revise his theory when trying to explain human variability, in so doing did not entirely abandon his earlier model of animal temperament. On the contrary, he argued that the fundamental nervous properties identified in his animal research will, even in the human, determine the individual's basic temperamental 'style'. However, what Pavlov did implicitly recognise – though he did not exploit the idea in a way which would satisfy most modern psychologists – is that these features alone do not constitute *personality* in its fullest sense. They merely represent a ground-plan from which it develops; in neurophysiological terms a set of tendencies, probably mediated low down in the nervous system, and finding a particular kind of expression in Man because of his unique possession of brain structures that are responsible for higher mental functions such as self-awareness, symbolic thought, and language. The theme is one that will become increasingly prominent in this book and I will return to it again briefly at the end of this chapter. First, however, let us complete our look at Pavlov's influence on psychiatry and psychology and at some contemporary developments of his theory.

Pavlov died in 1936 after a career that spanned more than half a century. It was a career, too, which coincided almost exactly in time with that of the other great thinker of the period, Sigmund Freud. Freud's writings are, of course, the better known, at least in the Western world, and have captured the imagination much more. One reason for this is no doubt geographical or, perhaps more strictly, geopolitical: it was only very slowly that an awareness of Pavlov's work trickled through to the West and began to be translated from the Russian. But probably a more significant reason is that conditioned reflexes, or even nervous types, do not fire the soul in the manner of Oedipal conflicts, oral-erotic fixations, and the dark world of dreams and the unconscious. It is understandable that a vision of Man carved in Freudian images should have had more appeal for psychiatry and for the popular psychology that trailed behind it.

Naturally this was not true in the Soviet Union, where the form of Pavlovian theory made it reasonably acceptable from an ideological viewpoint and, after a period of disfavour following his death, Pavlov's writings continued, and to some extent still continue, to have an impact on clinical psychiatry there. Thus treatments based on Pavlov's theory were evolved, such as prolonged sleep therapy, intended to facilitate recovery of the patient's nervous system, which was seen as being 'overstrained' in the manner of Pavlov's dogs in whom experimental neuroses had been induced. And Pavlov's own explanations of psychological disorders like hysteria and schizophrenia were further elaborated on the basis of his principle of nervous properties, such as 'strength' and 'protective inhibition'. Often these accounts were obscurely stated, over-general, and only loosely related to Pavlov's original theory, but they helped to maintain an essentially biological approach to mental disorder and counteract what was perceived as the philosophical idealism of psychoanalytic and comparable 'mentalistic' conceptions of Man.

Of course, even in the West by no means all psychiatrists have embraced Freudian theory or diluted or bastardised versions of it. But those organically inclined clinicians who rejected psychoanalysis equally studiously ignored Pavlov. Again the reasons are not difficult to find. By the time Pavlov's ideas had begun to be known, Western neurophysiologists had already established a science of brain function upon which psychiatry could draw. In any case Pavlovian conceptions of the nervous system were difficult to understand, as well as being, from a strictly physiological point of view, probably wrong. Only rarely did psychiatrists seeking an alternative to Freud turn to Pavlov.

A notable exception was the English psychiatrist William Sargant, probably one of the most 'organic' clinicians of his generation. In his autobiography Sargant describes how he discovered Pavlov's work towards the end of World War II. He was immediately struck by the remarkable parallel between the experimental neuroses Pavlov had induced in dogs and the acute battle neuroses which he himself had frequently seen during the war. In both cases he noted common elements of traumatic shock to the nervous system and subsequent 'collapse' which Pavlovian concepts like 'strength' and 'protective inhibition' helped him to understand. Seeking an alternative to Freudian theory, which he found repugnant, Sargant saw a possible solution in Pavlov's work. Recalling this in 1967 he notes:

> As we know, Russian psychiatry, and even Russian general medicine, has now for many years been dominated by the Pavlovian experimental approach. The Russians tend to scoff at the unprovable philosophic theories of Freud, Adler and others, so popular in the Western world – where the Russians were sometimes equally despised for daring to suggest that human beings had any psychological affinities with dogs. Yet our acute war neuroses, and some of the canine neuroses studied by Pavlov, showed such pronounced points of similarity that I found it harder than ever to swallow the current Western psychoanalytic theories about the origin of abnormal behaviour patterns in human beings – unless it were conceded that Pavlov's dogs, too, had their own little subconscious minds, their own psyches, their own egos, super-egos and ids[146].

In addition to considering how Pavlovian principles could be used to *explain* certain forms of very acute neurotic reactions Sargant also used the theory to provide a rationale for some of the treatments commonly employed in wartime psychiatry. These included the method of 'abreaction' in which the patient was encouraged, often with the aid of drugs, to relive and 'blow off' the emotion surrounding the traumatic experience that originally led to his neurotic symptoms: the mal-adaptive behaviour could often be successfully extinguished with that form of treatment. The mechanism of abreaction had previously been discussed from the viewpoint of psychoanalytic theory, but Sargant reinterpreted it along Pavlovian lines, seeing it as an example of how 'protective inhibition' could be deliberately induced for therapeutic purposes.

These pioneering observations by Sargant in the 1940s sank virtually without trace in professional psychiatric circles and he is probably better known for his book *Battle for the Mind*, where he discussed some more general applications of Pavlov's ideas to such things as brain-washing, religious conversion and other experiences in which profound psychological changes are brought about by inducing a condition of heightened emotional disturbance[145]. Fascinating though these topics are they have only marginal relevance to a serious understanding of Pavlov's work, at least within the present context. In any case, Sargant made little formal reference to the question of individual differences and Pavlov's theory of nervous types.

That in itself contains an interesting (and ironic) twist because, contemporaneously with Sargant's appeal that psychiatrists take more notice of Pavlov, that other arch-enemy of Freud, Hans Eysenck, was also incubating his biological theory of personality, based on Pavlovian principles. Eysenck, of course, was doing so from the standpoint of experimental psychology and was rapidly to become himself the *bête noire* of British psychiatry. The more substantive research tradition he took over from Pavlov, and which we traced in the previous chapter, therefore developed quite independently of Pavlov's fleeting appear-ance in the clinical psychiatry of postwar Britain. Even when Eysenck did begin to exert an influence on psychiatry, in the mid-1960s, it was mainly through his work on the application of learning theory principles to treatment and his contribution to the development of the methods of 'behaviour therapy' for removing neurotic symptoms, such as phobias. But Eysenck's writings on the biological origins of personality – especially where they referred to explanations of mental illness – remained quite isolated from the mainstream of psychiatric thinking.

Western academic psychologists have, on the whole, been equally indifferent to biological theories of personality and to the Pavlovian model of temperament from which they sprang. As we saw at the beginning of this chapter, Pavlov's work is mostly known for having been taken up by those psychologists persuaded by the ideas of behaviourism. A notable feature of the behaviourist movement, which

originated and especially flourished in the United States, has been its
studied disregard of individual variations between people, except in so
far as these can be explained as due to differences in each person's set
of learned habits. Thus, although embracing the *general* principles of
conditioning discovered by Pavlov, behaviourist psychologists ignored
that part of his writings which referred to the possibility of there being
intrinsic biological constraints on individual action. That view was
clearly articulated by the acknowledged founder of the behaviourist
movement, J.B. Watson, in his famous remark that, given a dozen
healthy infants, he could guarantee to make of them anything he chose
– 'yes', he exclaimed passionately, 'even beggar-man and thief'[190].

Even before Pavlov's death, therefore, and to a considerable extent
afterwards, the ideas contained in his theory of nervous types formed a
very narrow vein in Western psychological thought, and scarcely
existed at all in Western psychiatry. This was not true, however, in the
Soviet Union and other parts of Eastern Europe, at least from the
1950s onwards: as already mentioned, Pavlovian theory had a
considerable influence on the way psychiatrists there thought about
mental illness. But the more substantive developments occurred in
Soviet *psychology*. Essentially in parallel with research by Western
workers like Eysenck, a group of Russian psychologists of the so-called
Moscow school set about bringing the theory of nervous types up to
date, applying it systematically to human temperament, and testing it
out using rigorous experimental techniques. The latter included not
only the conditioning procedures inherited from the Pavlovian
tradition, but also other methods, suitable for use with human subjects
and increasingly like those adopted by Western psychophysiologists,
such as measurement of sensory thresholds, study of the response to
drugs, and analysis of the EEG.

The new 'human' version of nervous type theory that emerged was,
not unexpectedly, much more complicated than the original prototype
developed by Pavlov, though the essential principles of the latter were
retained. It also continued to be couched in the same – for Western
readers – rather difficult terminology. However, an increasing
exchange of ideas between Western and Soviet psychologists gradually
began to take place, starting with the translation, in the early 1960s, of
the writings of Teplov, the pioneer of the new era in Pavlovian
psychology[67]. From then on it became increasingly evident that the two
schools of thought about the biology of temperament had many
features in common, the differences between them often being merely
one of terminology. Subsequently they moved even closer together in
the hands of Teplov's successor Nebylitsyn, who, before his untimely
death, began to cast neo-Pavlovian theory into a conceptual nervous
system model comparable in its 'physiological' format to that of its
Western counterparts[125].

The theory arrived at by Nebylitsyn was remarkably similar in general outline to those discussed in the previous chapter. On the basis of a good deal of experimental evidence using the new techniques just described he proposed that it was possible to recognise two major temperamental characteristics of 'activity level' and 'emotionality'; these appeared to coincide roughly with the dimensions of introversion-extraversion and neuroticism identified by Western workers. The physiological basis of the two sets of characteristic, he said, lies in individual variations in the excitability of two discrete but interconnected brain circuits, one involving the ascending reticular formation and the other the limbic system, or 'emotional brain'. Both, he argued, form part of negative feedback loops, involving the cortex, which regulate their activity. The similarity between this biological model and those being developed contemporaneously by Western psychologists is quite obvious, and it can be said that with its formulation two streams of thought about temperament that had started with Pavlov and then, for historical reasons, become separated from each other had finally re-converged.

Since that time other developments have occurred, continuing to strengthen the biological perspective on temperament outlined here, and again brought about by collaboration between Western psychologists and those in Eastern Europe. In Poland, for example, research having a recognisably Pavlovian flavour has been conducted since the early 1970s by Strelau and his colleagues at the University of Warsaw[170]. Strelau's special contribution has been to focus on the measurement, by self-report questionnaire, of temperamental characteristics which reflect, at a behavioural level, the nervous system properties recognised in Pavlovian theory. Evidence that they actually do so has come from studies showing that the various scales in Strelau's questionnaire correlate highly with *psychophysiological* indices of the nervous properties which each is intended to measure. Furthermore, although the items on the scales are, because of their origin, worded rather differently, the temperamental traits they cover seem to be very similar to, and have been found to correlate with, those measured by the personality inventories developed by Western psychologists[111].

In interpreting his findings Strelau has proposed a model of temperament in which two of the key concepts are those of 'reactivity' and 'stimulation control'. The former, he suggests, corresponds to what at the physiological level, and in Pavlovian terminology, would be described as 'strength of the nervous system': as such it determines an individual's general level of arousability and the intensity of his response to environmental stimulation. 'Stimulation control', on the other, acts to moderate this: depending on the person's basic level of reactivity it will impel him towards seeking out or, alternatively, avoiding strong stimulation. It is, in other words, similar to Zuckerman's notion of 'sensation seeking' which we have mentioned several times already.

Elsewhere in Eastern Europe Pavlov's theory of nervous types appears to have had less impact on the thinking of psychologists interested in the biology of personality. If anything, where it has occurred at all, its influence has been indirect, coming from the writings of Western psychologists like Eysenck, who were themselves inspired by Pavlov. Hungary is a good example. Reflecting that country's strongly Westward stance in economic affairs, psychologists there have looked in the same direction for their theoretical and empirical currency about personality, establishing a nucleus of research in the Eysenckian tradition. As indeed have some workers, outside Britain, in Western Europe.

All of this helps to bring us to the first conclusion we can draw from the ideas presented in the past two chapters. Though the process may have been away from the public eye for most of this century, knowledge has gradually accumulated about the variegated nature of temperament and its biological origins in the nervous system. Currently, this is represented in a considerable amount of experimental data and a mix of nevertheless very similar theories being pursued in different countries in the world, from the Soviet Union to the United States. If the ideas are unfamiliar to the general reader, or indeed even to some of those with a professional interest in psychology or psychiatry, it is not for lack of evidence, but for other reasons: spiritual perhaps (as Sargant said, few people like to accept that human personality, of all things, has any affinity, however slight, with the individuality of other creatures in the animal kingdom); or because the biological perspective on personality smacks, wrongly I would suggest, of a crude reductionism; or maybe it is simply the case that the literature concerned makes for a poor read, compared with Freud. Whatever the reason, and despite these objections, it is now becoming increasingly difficult to ignore what has become a sound set of theoretical principles in experimental psychology, backed up by a substantial body of empirical knowledge.

The second conclusion we can reach can be rather more specific. It seems that some of Man's basic temperamental dispositions are mediated by brain circuitry that is found quite low down in the nervous system and therefore involves structures common to other species, whose behaviour also shows comparable individual variation, albeit occurring in a simpler form. The best established of these 'dimensions' of temperament is anxiety, the actual neurophysiological basis of which is quite well understood. But others, such as impulsivity, 'sensation seeking', aggressiveness and so on are rapidly taking their place alongside anxiety as major biologically based tendencies which differentiate one person from another.

In referring to the 'conceptual nervous systems' that psychologists have constructed to try to explain these variations in temperament, we have repeatedly come across three important features which, even though the theoretical models themselves differ in the way they are stated, nevertheless recur time and time again. One is that people differ in the extent to which their nervous systems are arousable, or are sensitive to internal and external sources of stimulation. A second is that they vary in the degree to which they seek out or avoid stimulation, perhaps motivated by a need to maintain a comfortable level of arousal. And thirdly, the brain circuitry involved always contains the notion of a regulatory mechanism, operating in a negative feedback loop and implicating a process of active inhibition in the nervous system.

So far these ideas have been introduced mainly as a set of principles for understanding some of the ways in which *normal* individuals differ. In other words, the past two chapters have a formed a preamble to examining eventually how such variations in temperament can be interpreted as predispositions to some forms of mental illness. We have already briefly glimpsed the general direction that the second part of our argument will take: we saw there that there is, as we would expect, a continuity between the normal and the abnormal with respect to the kind of 'nervous type' observed in psychiatric patients with different forms of mild psychological disorder, such as anxiety and hysteria. In later chapters we shall examine the possible mechanisms whereby these different temperamental dispositions may be translated into symptomatology; after considering, in the next chapter, another facet of the theory of nervous types, namely, the question of genetic influences on individual differences in temperament.

Before moving on to that topic, however, it is necessary to take up, as our final conclusion here, an earlier point sounding a cautionary note about the view of personality offered so far. Impressive though the progress has been in understanding the biology of *temperament*, it would be misleading to argue that the theories discussed can even appproach a full account of human individuality. It is important to note that this is *not* because of our incomplete knowledge of those low level structures in the brain upon which temperamental variations almost certainly rest: that knowledge certainly *is* incomplete, but its general outline is probably correct. The inadequacy lies more in the obvious fact – recognised by Pavlov but not really satisfactorily explored by him – that what is unique about Man is his *higher* nervous system, those parts of his brain responsible for the very characteristics – thoughts and ideas – which current biological theories of personality are not well equipped to explain. The fact that contemporary 'nervous typologists' have concentrated on trying to account for fairly simple kinds of difference between people (i.e. temperament), and hence on relatively primitive brain structures, can be justified on two grounds. First, one has to start somewhere. And, secondly, there is a certain logic in moving from the bottom upwards – not only in constructing hypothetical models of the human brain, but also in studying animals in order to expose certain basic mechanisms which, as we know, demonstrate a certain evolutionary continuity right up to Man. At the same time, we also need to be constantly aware of the limitations inherent in the kinds of personality theory that have emerged out of the historical tradition emphasised over the last two chapters. As we move through the discussion these limitations will become increasingly evident in two rather convergent ways: one in addressing the *psychological* and the other when considering the *biological* aspects of disorder.

On the psychological side the problem will present itself very simply as the following question: How do we bring together relatively straightforward notions about temperament and those ideas in psychology which, in trying to account for human personality, whether normal or abnormal, have tended to put the emphasis on more complex processes, like thought and language? We can anticipate that the difficulty of doing so will not be eased by the fact that biological theories of temperament have evolved quite separately in psychology from theories having a more 'cognitive' slant. Indeed, their respective proponents have often been at loggerheads or, at best, have ignored each others point of view. To illustrate the point let us consider, as a typical example, how different psychologists might explain why people get depressed. Whatever their theoretical persuasion they would probably all agree with Pavlov's comment about the melancholic believing in nothing, hoping for nothing, and seeing only the dark side in everything. For the cognitive psychologist this would be taken as a a sign of the person having a negative mental 'set' towards the world, perhaps acquired in childhood through modelling the attitudes of a parent, or induced by the loss of a close relative. The nervous typologist, on the other hand, would tend to emphasise the individual's biological disposition to depressive mood. If he referred to learned factors in depression he would make use of the behaviourist, conditioning type of model that has been favoured by biological personality theorists. Neither view is complete in itself and both have to be taken into account when trying to understand the nature, not only of depression, but also most of the disorders that we shall be discussing here.

We shall also see comparable difficulties arising on the biological side itself, when we try to go beyond nervous type theories as they are presently formulated. As repeatedly stressed here, such theories do not refer very much to the individual's 'grey matter'. If they do, they tend to view the higher levels of the brain from the standpoint of the latters' influence on the dynamic processes that control the *state* of the nervous system; for example, the regulation of arousal in lower centres by inhibition from cortical structures. Rarely, if ever, do they pay attention to the *psychological* functions which those structures subserve. This is because such considerations do not come within the scope of the way psychophysiologists look at the nervous system: the stuff of their conceptual nervous system models is ideas like arousal and inhibition. That being so, they are not very well placed to handle data which have to do with the way brain and mind are connected. A discipline that can fulfil that role, however, is *neuropsychology*, which is specifically concerned with the problem of relating higher mental processes to the topographic organisation of the brain. As seems to be the nature of things in science, neuropsychology has evolved quite separately and in a different historical tradition from psychophysiology. On the clinical side its background has been neurology, rather than psychiatry, and the study of how different areas of the brain control various psychological functions, especially language: knowledge gained there has naturally fed back into normal psychology and enabled conceptual nervous systems to be constructed that say something about how the normal brain is organised with respect to those complex processes. On the other hand, because of its concentration on intellectual or cognitive functions, neuropsychology has not, at least until very recently, been very interested in trying to explain psychiatric disorders or answering the kinds of question about personality that are posed for psychologists working in the tradition of nervous type theory.

Fortunately this situation is now beginning to change. To take what should now be a familiar example, there has been an increasing interest over the past decade or so in the contribution to mental life made by the two hemispheres of the brain[164]. There is certainly as much myth as fact in this area of research, but some firm conclusions have been drawn already. Thus it is well established that the left hemisphere, in right-handed people at least, plays a predominant part in controlling language. The opposite hemisphere has had various functions ascribed to it, some observers having gone as far as to state that, unlike the 'rational' left side of the brain, it is the seat of the irrational, primitive and creative parts of the personality. More soberly, it does seem to have an important role in the expression and appreciation of emotion. As we shall see in later chapters, it is now beginning to look as though ideas like these might be able to provide the missing link for nervous typologists seeking more comprehensive brain models of personality.

That will become especially evident when we come to consider attempts to understand more serious forms of mental illness, such as schizophrenia. For then we shall come across a particularly promising example of how it is possible to marry psychophysiological and neuropsychological models of the conceptual nervous system in order to arrive at a better understanding of the biology of disorder.

In elaborating our final conclusions to this chapter we have jumped ahead somewhat of our present theme. However, the points raised are important ones to bear in mind for later discussion. In the meantime let us take up again the thread of ideas that form the subject matter of 'classic' nervous type theory and consider one other aspect of it, namely questions concerning the inheritance of temperament.

4

The Inheritance of Dispositions

In justifying the notion of biological differences as a basis for temperament, I have already commented on how unlikely it would be if the nervous system – the vehicle for those differences – were immune to the individual variations in structure and function that typify other parts of the organism. The same remark can be borrowed to introduce the theme of this chapter. Again, given the already well-established influence of genetic factors on many bodily characteristics, it would be extraordinary if they did not play a similar role in providing a blueprint for the nervous system. Indeed, there are several instances of brain pathology, such as various forms of severe mental handicap, where that is known to be the case. For some reason it has been less easy for many people to make the conceptual leap required to suppose that there are genetic influences, mediated via the nervous system, on *normal* psychological processes: introducing an hereditary element into explanations of behaviour is therefore almost always controversial. Debate of the question has been most public (and most acrimonious) in the case of intelligence; but equally strong views can easily be elicited if the discussion is widened to include the closely related field of personality differences. Yet to exclude reference to genetic aspects would leave our account of the biology of temperament incomplete. For virtually all of the biologically orientated writers referred to in previous chapters have either stated explicitly, or assumed implicitly, that genetic factors do play some part in determining the individual variations with which they have been concerned – and therefore the predispositions to mental disorder which, in their other guise, such variations represent. The most vigorous proponent of a genetic viewpoint has been Eysenck, though others, albeit more tentatively, have adopted a similar stance. This is true not only of Western psychologists but also of workers in Eastern Europe where, over the past twenty years, there has been a reawakening of interest in the genetical study of human temperament. So in that respect, as in theory itself, there has been a further convergence of the ideas discussed over the past two chapters. Before proceeding, however, it is necessary to insert two cautionary remarks.

The first is that only the most blinkered of hereditarians would wish to deny the importance of both genetic and environmental influences, including their interactive effect, on personality. Indeed, somewhat anticipating the conclusions to be drawn here, it is in a fairly restricted sense that the influence of genetic factors in personality will be judged important. Paralleling an earlier distinction between 'temperament' and 'personality', I shall argue that it is on the former that heredity exerts its direct effect by determining the basic style of an individual's behaviour, the content, quality and outcome of that behaviour showing wide variation that reflects the differing ways in which the underlying temperament can be expressed.

The second cautionary point is perhaps less trite, in the sense that it is more often overlooked. It is that the discovery that human variation has biological roots in the nervous system does not, in and of itself, mean that such variation is of *genetic* origin. The terms 'biological' and 'genetic' are quite distinct, though they have sometimes been confused, even by professional writers in the field. Many behaviours which we refer to the personality, and which we may be happy to trace to the nervous system, can nevertheless be due to causes other than genetic – to environmental modifications occurring pre-natally or at any time from birth onwards. The conclusions to be drawn from genetics research therefore depend crucially on how we evaluate evidence from studies using strategies that try to disentangle the effects of heredity and environment. The most commonly used strategy, and the one that has provided the bulk of evidence to be considerd here, is the so-called 'classic twin method'. This has been the subject of considerable controversy, brought into the limelight especially by those involved in the debate about whether or not intelligence is inherited. Some further comment is needed before we can consider whether twin research on temperament and personality can answer the questions to be addressed here.

The twin method relies on the existence of two types of twin: monozygotic (MZ), in which the fertilised egg divides to produce two genetically identical individuals, and dizygotic (DZ), in which two ova are separately fertilised. Since the latter are genetically no more alike than ordinary siblings, their degree of similarity on any given characteristic should be substantially less than – theoretically half – that of monozygotic twins. In principle, therefore, by comparing the relative degree of similarity (or concordance) observed in samples of the two types of twin it is possible to get some idea of the extent to which genetic factors contribute to the characteristic that is of interest, be it height, weight or some behavioural trait.

Concordance is commonly expressed in one of two ways: for dichotomous features, such as eye colour or psychiatric diagnosis, by the frequency with which twin pairs share the characteristic in question; or, for continuously variable traits, such as stature or intelligence test performance, by the degree to which the scores of pair members are correlated. In either case, for a genetic explanation to be considered concordances needs to be significantly higher in MZ than in DZ twin samples. Although, theoretically, the existence of rare embryological anomalies partially vitiates the assumptions of this comparison, in practice that is not a problem, providing reasonably large twin samples are studied, and the strategy has been used uncontroversially to investigate the genetic contribution to many human characteristics, especially morphological and other physical traits, like blood pressure. Its application to *psychological* traits, however, has generated a good deal of hostility from critics who have questioned whether the method can be validly applied to the genetical analysis of behaviour.

One criticism, which can be quickly dismissed, concerns the reliability with which zygosity, or twin type, can be determined. In fact, modern methods such as blood grouping make it possible to determine zygosity with a high degree of certainty. Even in the absence of such techniques, questionnaires designed to assess similarities on superficial features such as eye colour, hair texture and so on have been shown to be capable of classifying twin pairs very accurately. Some years ago my colleagues and I had first-hand experience of this when carrying out a large twin study – aimed incidentally at testing out some of the ideas about personality to be discussed here[28]. As part of the research we administered to our twins a specially designed questionnaire of physical similarity. When we subsequently compared the predictions about zygosity with those determined independently by blood typing, we found that the questionnaire was just as good at picking out MZ, as against DZ, twins. This, despite the fact that through an oversight we left out one of the potentially more discriminating items, to do with eye colour!

A second, and more serious criticism that has especially preoccupied opponents of the twin method in psychology concerns the assumption of 'equivalent environments'. To be really valid the method must assume that, whatever environmental influences affect the trait under study, these are the same, in strength and direction, in both MZ and DZ twins: only then can any observed differences in concordance be put down to the greater *genetic* similarity of MZ twins. The fact that MZ twins look identical, often dress alike and, it is thought, are treated more similarly by others appears, on the face of it, to give some force to this argument. Certainly, if true, it would mean that measures of concordance in MZ twins for some behavioural traits would be artificially inflated, resulting in a misleading conclusion being drawn about the importance of heredity.

However, the picture is probably less straightforward than that. For one thing, the fact that MZ twins are treated more alike does not necessarily mean that their greater similarity is 'environmental' in origin. It can be equally well argued that their very genetic relatedness tends to *elicit* more similar treatment from others: for example, two temperamentally lively monozygotic twins might well be reacted to in the same way by their parents, but the similarity in their behaviour might be entirely due their genetic make-up. Of course, there is a danger of the argument here becoming circular and difficult to resolve using standard twin comparisons. One way round trying to disentangle the genetic and environmental effects involved in the situation is to make separate comparisons between sub-sets of MZ and DZ twins, divided according to whether the parents actually *know* the zygosity of their children (surprisingly, they often do not). When this has been done it has been found that the allegedly more similar treatment received by MZ twins does, in part, reflect the fact that they start off being genetically identical[148].

Another complication for the argument that there is an environmental bias in twin comparisons – leading to inflated estimates of the genetic similarity of MZ twins – is that for some behavioural traits the effect may occur in a direction *opposite* to that expected. This was shown in one of the early classic studies of twin personality by the late James Shields who, unusually, was able to compare MZ twins reared together with others reared apart[154]. One of the traits he examined was introversion-extraversion, where he found that twins reared apart as children, and therefore not subjected to the normal degree of shared environmental influence, were actually *more* alike than those reared together. The probable explanation is that when living in close contact with each other MZ twins develop complementary roles in order to establish their own sense of identity. Of course, this does mean that psychologists' estimates of the heritability of some traits might indeed be inaccurate; especially if, as is usually the case, their observations are based on the study of twins reared and living together. But the point is that, contrary to the arguments put forward by critics of the classic twin method, the error may sometimes be in the direction of underestimation, rather than overestimation, of the importance of genetic factors.

Looking at the problem from a slightly different perspective, there is another reason why it could be said that twin comparisons may tend to underestimate the hereditary component in behaviour. This refers not to the bias introduced by factors in the *social* environment, but rather to *biological* influences occurring before birth. It has been pointed out, for example, that compared with DZ twins, the uterine environment of many MZ pairs may be more different because of a greater imbalance in their placental circulation[18]. This results in there being greater pressures towards *dissimilarity* in MZ twins than would be the case for DZ pairs, an effect which might be especially critical for the development of the nervous system.

It is clear, then, that studying twins in order to try to find out whether or not, and to what extent, there are genetic influences in behaviour cannot, as some would have us believe, be dismissed out of hand. Certainly there are inaccuracies in the method, but the errors it contains are not unidirectional in their effect, acting sometimes to inflate and sometimes to diminish the 'true' heritability of a particular characteristic. As we have just seen, even in the case of some quite gross personality traits, such as extraversion, the direction of bias may actually be opposite to the prediction made by critics of the twin method; namely that monozygotic twins are more alike because they are treated more alike. And their arguments have even less force when applied to more fundamental biological characteristics, including the central nervous properties that underlie behaviour.

The distinction just made between superficial behavioural traits and biological variations of course maps neatly on to the theoretical construction of personality and temperament introduced in the previous chapters. For the genetical analysis of personality variation has similarly proceeded at two levels, utilising two different types of measurement. One type consists of personality questionnaires and similar descriptive techniques. The other includes a variety of psychophysiological methods, some of which we have already come across when discussing how temperament can be related to the nervous system: these have also sometimes been examined from a specifically genetic viewpoint. It is on evidence of the latter kind that I shall concentrate here because it is there, in my opinion, that we find the most persuasive argument for a genetic contribution to personality; if only because the sorts of measure used, being of a biological nature, are, as it were, nearer to the individual's genes: twin comparisons on them are therefore relatively easier to interpret. Nevertheless, if we are to make plausible statements about *personality* it is also important to see whether twin studies that have relied on more conventional descriptive procedures for evaluating individual differences also point us towards a similar conclusion. Let us begin, therefore, with a brief survey of this work, before moving on to studies of a more biological nature.

Not unexpectedly, there has been a considerable amount of research, using questionnaire techniques, to try and determine the genetic contribution to superficial personality and temperamental characteristics. (Interestingly, investigators have varied in whether they have used the term 'personality' or 'temperament' when interpreting their results: broadly speaking the former seems to have been preferred by those studying adults, the latter by those studying children.) What might be termed the 'early phase' of this endeavour involved the traditional comparison of usually fairly small samples of adult MZ and DZ twins on a variety of personality inventories. The characteristics of interest covered almost every conceivable personality trait, some quite narrowly defined, others of broader scope and including several we have already encountered, such as extraversion, neuroticism, impulsivity and so on.

Several authors who reviewed these early studies agreed that despite the diversity of techniques and twin samples employed, there are some consistent trends suggesting that genetic factors do exert an influence on personality that can be detected with questionnaires[28, 182]. This seems to be especially true of those aspects of extraversion which have to do with sociability, where genetically identical monozygotic twins tend overall to be more alike in their behaviour than dizygotic twins; despite the fact that in most of the cases studied, for the reasons noted above, close contact between the twins involved probably acted to reduce their 'actual' similarity. Rather less consistent evidence of MZ twin concordance has been found for patterns of behaviour associated with impulsivity. This is a little surprising since the latter would seem, intuitively, to relate particularly closely to the biological springs of personality. A possible reason is that during the development of the individual impulsiveness is subject to strong negative social pressure, which may have the effect of suppressing natural tendencies and hence reduce the apparent similarities of twins, when studied in adulthood. In contrast, sociability is a trait that is strongly encouraged to flourish unhindered. Some of the early adult twin studies also indicated that neurotic characteristics – like placidness, self-criticism, for example – are to some extent under genetic control; though here again the picture is somewhat complicated by the fact that the actual estimates of twin similarity may be distorted by the degree of closeness between the pair members. Unfortunately (for the researcher, that is) the direction of this effect seems to be less consistent than in the case of sociability and extraversion, twins living together becoming sometimes more and sometimes less alike in neurotic traits.

More recent questionnaire research in psychogenetics is now tending to progress beyond the simple comparison of small MZ and DZ twin samples, towards a much more sophisticated analysis of personality data gathered on very large groups of subjects among whom are sometimes represented, not only twins but also other family members, such as parents, children, and other forms of kinship. This development has been brought about by the adoption of the analytic techniques of 'biometrical genetics'. The latter originated as a branch of general genetics with the aim of evaluating biological characteristics which, unlike some other inherited features, are not discrete in quality (and therefore traceable to single, major genes), but have instead the appearance of continuously variable traits and are due to the combined effects of many genes. Since most forms of human variation are of this nature, the tools of biometrical genetics were obviously of interest to those psychologists concerned with hereditary aspects of behaviour. Biometrical geneticists use fairly elaborate statistical and model-building procedures, but essentially what they do is to try, in a way not possible with the classic twin method, to disentangle the hereditary and environmental influences on a trait. They do that by looking for the best fit to observed data of models that take account of such factors as the dominance of gene action, mating patterns in the population, and so on.

Because much of the work applying biometrical genetics to personality has been carried out under the umbrella of Eysenck's theory, the results obtained with it so far relate mainly to the dimensions he has emphasised in his writings. Adherents of the approach are nothing if not enthusiastic and one of its foremost exponents, Lyndon Eaves, recently reached the following conclusion from his own research into the possible determinants of the Eysenckian dimensions of introversion-extraversion and neuroticism:

> The data on twins and other relationships, including families and adoptions, give some support to the position that personality differences, though not completely inherited, are not much influenced by the social environment . . . As far as Eysenck's personality measurements are concerned the individual is "individual". He maintains his personality "in spite of" differences in the social environment . . . . [43].

This is a strong statement and many would react violently to it, if only on the grounds that personality questionnaires are unable to capture the sheer complexity of human individuality. Even those of us persuaded of the need to take account of genetic influences in behaviour might baulk at Eaves's conclusion, principally because it misses the point about *what* it is about the personality that is inherited. If we consider as a whole all of the questionnaire data gathered over many years it is indeed difficult to challenge the view that heredity does contribute in *some* way and to *some* degree to personality variations. The problem comes when we try to go beyond that, purely on the basis of evidence obtained from personality questionnaires administered to adult subjects. After all, what we measure with such instruments is very distant from the biological roots of behaviour, distant both chronologically and in its superficiality.

One way round the first difficulty is to take a developmental perspective, looking for what may be embryonic precursors of adult personality in more basic temperamental traits to be found in children, on the assumption that it is from these that later characteristics are elaborated. There have been several attempts to describe the temperament of young children, including the neonate. Among the most notable are those carried out by Thomas, Chess and their colleagues. Their studies of children from birth onwards led them to identify three major dimensions of temperament: general intensity of reaction, adaptability or susceptibility to socialisation, and basic emotionality[178, 179]. Follow-up of infants described according to these characteristics suggest that the same temperamental differences are maintained, to a reasonable degree, at least up to the age of five years and to some extent even into adulthood.

Of course, this does not prove that the differences observed are genetic in origin. However, Mangan, who has recently reviewed a considerable amount of evidence on this point argues convincingly that heredity does lay part of the foundation for early temperament[111]. He points out, for example, that comparisons of infant twins indicate that monozygotic pairs are more alike than dizygotic pairs on several of the characteristics identified by Thomas and his colleagues. This seems to be especially true of features like approach/withdrawal behaviour, a finding that confirms some earlier work using direct observational methods, derived originally from animal ethology, to examine the same question in young babies[59]. There it was demonstrated that, when confronted by strangers, MZ twins are sometimes remarkably alike, and generally more similar than DZ twins, in their patterns of behaviour, as judged by measures of their social smiling and fear reactions. Here perhaps we are seeing an early manifestation of the greater concordance found among *adult* MZ twins on questionnaire measures of sociability. For it is reasonable to suppose that, as an adult trait, sociability partly reflects a basic dispositional tendency traceable to childhood as a style of responding to other people.

Naturally we must be cautious in projecting forward in this way from studies – even twin studies – of temperament in infants and young children to investigations of the mature personality. Marked and continuous differentiation of behaviour occurs throughout life and especially during certain phases, such as adolescence. This is represented in the fact that in twin studies of the kind discussed earlier – using questionnaires – the patterns of heritability for different personality traits do change to some extent with age. There are, therefore, really two conclusions we can draw from studies that have relied on superficial description of the individual to examine the genetic contribution to personality. One is the perhaps obvious fact that during life personality, in its fullest sense, undergoes considerable change, so that even genetically identical individuals may become less alike. The other is that despite the supreme capacity for adaptation of the human organism, each person's behaviour does contain a thread of stability, which we can identify as his or her temperamental disposition and which, even on the evidence considered so far, seems to be subject to genetic influences.

The most direct expression of those influences must lie in the biology of the individual, especially the nervous system, the activity of which is closer to the genes than gross signs of behaviour. Therefore, another and more powerful way of examining the role of heredity in personality, and one I shall spend more time on here, is to study, from a genetic viewpoint, those aspects of biological variation which are themselves known to be related to temperament and which we can measure using the kinds of psychophysiological technique referred to in previous chapters. Such work has almost always employed the classic twin method. It has also involved small or modestly sized twin samples, mainly for the practical reason that the test procedures involved are time-consuming and less convenient in use than the paper-and-pencil techniques, such as questionnaires, used elsewhere in psychogenetics. However, that disadvantage is offset by the fact that biological researchers have been able to rely on forms of measurements that are more secure than questionnaires scores, which by comparison provide relatively 'soft' data, containing many sources of error. They have therefore been able to arrive at rather less equivocal conclusions, despite their use of small twin samples. For there is now a surprisingly large amount of evidence that heredity plays an important role in determining central nervous differences which we already know, or can infer, are related to temperament[31].

Apart from obvious preferences for the kind of experimental measure studied, investigators choosing to examine the genetics of the nervous system directly have differed in the exent to which their work has had a theoretical base in the psychology of personality. Some have deliberately set out to examine the genetic assumptions of the biological theories of personality already described; while some, for historical or other reasons, have carried out their research with little or no reference to such theories, simply being interested in exploring the possible genetic underpinning of some important feature of central nervous activity. The evidence they have gathered can nevertheless often be easily assimilated into the body of knowledge about the biology of temperament.

The most direct measures of human brain activity come from the EEG, recorded as electrical signals from the scalp, and not long after Berger described these 'brain waves' in the late 1920s interest was evinced in their genetic aspects. Since then there have been many studies comparing the EEG's of samples of monozygotic and dizygotic twins. The results have been substantially in agreement: that the majority of MZ twin pairs show brain wave patterns that are sometimes quite remarkably alike, compared with the more diverse EEG's observed in DZ twins. Of the recent investigations the most comprehensive are those undertaken by Vogel and his colleagues at the University of Heidelberg[187, 188]. Their work has led them to identify a number of EEG 'types', recognised according to differences in the basic frequency and amplitude of the EEG wave-forms, and shown by them to be strongly inherited. Although not primarily interested in the biology of personality, Vogel and his co-workers were aware of work going on in that field and, as part of their research, were able to show that individuals manifesting certain of their EEG variants did differ in characteristics like extraversion.

A much more direct test of the idea that the EEG and some features of the personality share a common genetic base is to be found, however, in the work of my former colleague, Wilfred Hume, whose study formed part of our collaborative twin project referred to earlier[28]. It may be recalled from chapter 2 that we had previously shown that a certain aspect of the EEG – the frequency, amplitude and responsiveness to stimulation of the 'alpha rhythm' – is very strongly related to personality. Apparently defining a fundamental difference between people in cortical arousability, it seemed to be especially associated with anxious, introverted personality traits and 'dysthymic' forms of neurotic reaction. With this is mind, Hume set out to examine the same EEG features in groups of normal adult twins. The results were clear-cut in showing a substantial genetic influence, particularly in the case of one of the measures of alpha rhythm activity, namely its basic frequency.

The EEG studies considered so far were all concerned with the evaluation of the 'raw', background activity of the brain, taken from gross recordings of its wave forms. However, another index on which twins have been compared is the 'averaged evoked potential', so called because it relies on the use of a special technique to extract from the background EEG the typical waveform evoked in response to a specific sensory stimulus, like a tone or a light flash[41, 103]. It is described as being 'averaged' because, in practice, the same stimulus will be presented many times in order to define more clearly what is otherwise a brain response of very low amplitude and short duration – only a few hundred milliseconds. What is noticeable about the averaged evoked potential is that although its characteristic features vary according to such things as the modality and strength of the stimulus applied, its overall *shape*, under given conditions, is remarkably constant for an individual; so much so that it might almost be said to rival, in its uniqueness, some morphological traits such as finger-prints. Not unexpectedly, therefore, in MZ twins it shows very close similarity, the correlation between the wave forms of two twins occasionally having been found to be actually greater than that for the same individual tested at different times!

One application of evoked potential methodology that is particularly relevant here concerns its use in the study of 'augmenting-reducing', a phenomenon which by now will be familiar to the reader as one feature of EEG differences with which temperament is quite closely associated. It will be recalled that the individual's tendency to 'augment' or 'reduce' sensory stimulation is measured by examining the way the amplitude of the EEG changes as the intensity of the stimulus increases. This is normally done not from the raw EEG, but from evoked potential measurements taken after presenting sets of stimuli of varying strength. As in other corners of research on the biology of personality, augmenting-reducing has also been looked at in twins and here there is some quite good evidence that the fundamental style of central nervous responding which it seems to represent is partly under genetic control[16].

Let us turn now, briefly, to a slightly different strategy for trying to uncover the genetic basis of temperament. This involves comparing twins for their reaction to drugs that affect the central nervous system. One method of doing so is to study differences in the 'sedation threshold', described in chapter 2. There we saw that when tested with that technique, anxious individuals were found to have a very strong tolerance for barbiturate drugs, reflecting their very high central nervous arousability. It is therefore pertinent to ask whether, and to what extent, such differences are genetically determined. An experiment we carried out some years ago, using the sedation threshold, but this time applied to twins, suggested that drug response variations are indeed under genetic control, to a very significant degree[28]. And there is other evidence pointing to the same conclusion. For example, a colleague of Vogel, whose work on the EEG was mentioned earlier, did a very elegant experiment in which he examined the influence of alcohol on the the EEG's of monozygotic and dizygotic twins, looking also at the time-course of the drug's effect[135]. He found that the EEG changes occurring in MZ twin pairs were much more alike than those observed in DZ pairs. Especially important, however, he was able to show that the result was not due to peripheral factors, such as the rate of absorption or elimination of alcohol from the body. (This was demonstrated by the fact that the *blood alcohol* curves of MZ twins were no more similar than those of DZ twins.) Instead, individual variations in response to the drug – and their genetic determination – represented true differences in the *central* effects of alcohol on the nervous system.

Even the evidence considered so far is sufficient to demonstrate that some features of the the biology of temperament are under substantial genetic control. There is, however, a still larger body of twin research that has relied on forms of psychophysiological measurement other than the EEG, such as the recording of heart rate, muscle tension, galvanic skin response and so on. Although these procedures indicate less directly what is going on in the brain they have, as we have already seen, formed an important part of the psychophysiologist's armoury of techniques for evaluating activity in the central nervous system. They have also provided a good deal of the evidence for concepts like 'arousal' that have figured so prominently in the conceptual nervous system explanations of temperament and personality devised by psychophysiologists. Studies, specifically of twins, using these techniques are numerous and began many years ago: concern with the possible genetic influences on the galvanic skin response, for example, dates back at least 60 years. Here let me quote just one experiment which illustrates the evidence particularly well and which also happens to bring together very neatly several of the themes that have so far run through this book.

The study or, more correctly, set of studies in question was carried out some years ago by Lader[96]. The original purpose of Lader's research was to examine the psychophysiological status of psychiatric patients suffering from anxiety states. To this end he compared a group of such patients with normal subjects on several psychophysiological measures; though his main focus of interest, and the one we shall concentrate on here, was the galvanic skin response. The experimental arrangement used by Lader involved measuring the change in the size of the individual's galvanic skin response with frequent repetition, at irregular intervals, of a series of identical tones. This 'habituation' procedure is well established in psychology and is of considerable theoretical importance, since it represents a way of examining a crucial feature of the behaviour of all organisms; namely, that when presented with a novel stimulus (in this case the first tone) they show a strong orienting response but then, with further experience of the stimulus, adapt it to and eventually fail to react.

Lader's prediction, which was fully borne out, was that neurotic patients with chronic anxiety would not only show a large initial response to the tone stimulus, indicative of their higher arousability, but would go on responding to the tones long after normal subjects had ceased reacting to them. (Incidentally, this has some interesting implications, considered in the next chapter, for understanding how anxiety symptoms arise and why they persist.) Having established this basic association between neurotic anxiety and habituation – which of course fits in nicely with other evidence described here – Lader then went on to use the same method to examine several other related questions. He demonstrated, for example, that his measure was sensitive to the effects of sedative and tranquillising drugs which, as we would expect, markedly accelerated the rate of habituation. He also discovered, by studying a group of normal twins (both MZ and DZ), that the characteristic is influenced to a significant degree by genetic factors. Lader's experiments are therefore exemplary in laying out the chain of association for which we are arguing here, a chain which starts with the manifest features of disorder, runs through certain character- istics of the normal temperament, and then, via representation in the nervous system, connects eventually with the genetic make-up of the individual.

The conclusion just reached finds further support in parallel research being carried out in Eastern Europe where, having been proscribed for many years, interest in the genetics of behaviour is now being revived. Furthermore, it is possible to find many points of similarity between the observations made by Western psychologists and those made by researchers, mainly in the Soviet Union, who have looked at the same questions from the standpoint of Pavlovian theory[31]. Thus several twin studies of the EEG have been reported, demonstrating genetic influences on central nervous properties like strength, which, as we saw in the previous chapter, can be readily translated into Western concepts about the brain. One particular feature of the Soviet research which stands out is that compared with similar work in the West, there seems to have been a greater tendency to take a developmental perspective on the link between the genetics of the brain and psychological variation; that is, to recognise more explicitly that the inheritance of 'nervous properties' merely provides a blueprint of *disposition* and is itself subject to many environmental influences, both pre- and post-natally. This is exemplified in one observation that genetic factors may be more important in determining *right*, as compared with *left*, hemisphere functioning of the brain: the suggested interpretation is that the left hemisphere, being more associated with language, has greater potential plasticity and is therefore more readily modified by environmental forces.

This stance on psychogenetics research helps to recall a point introduced right at the beginning of this chapter; namely that we would also be arguing for heredity having an important, but nevertheless narrowly definable, influence on personality. In the heredity/environment debate about behaviour those who take an extreme genetics position, while paying lip-service to the idea that both hereditary and environmental influences are important – indeed considering the point so obvious as not to require further emphasis – in practice rarely get down to the actual business of determining in detail how, and in which of its aspects, environment interacts with the genetic effects that are their main focus of attention. The impression is often given (recall the earlier quotation from Eaves) that the individual is somehow a victim of his endowment, if unaffected at least unmodified by the slings, arrows and other missiles he encounters during life. The extreme environmentalist is, of course, equally obtuse, trying to argue the unlikely case that, like one of J. B. Watson's healthy infants, people can be moulded into whatever society wishes, despite differences so manifest, even at birth, that it scarcely requires a rigorous scientific experiment to demonstrate them. Disappointingly for those who like a good fight, the conclusion here has to be less exciting.

From the evidence described it seems certain that on entering the world the infant does so with a nervous system which, like its other physical characteristics, is unique; unique and yet describable in terms of a finite number of what Pavlovian psychologists like to call 'nervous properties'. Even before birth these will have been modified by intra-uterine events and they will continue to be modified throughout life. But certain core features will remain, manifesting themselves in the variegated pattern of reactions which we label temperament and which we can best observe (and measure) in the individual's pattern of physiological responding. Beyond this, for the psychogeneticist, the trail begins to peter out slightly, because it is not always easy to trace the continuity from the genetic endowment of the nervous system to those complex characteristics which we ascribe to the personality. However, *some* continuity can be discerned, as witness the evidence about sociability referred to earlier: there is surely a link between the individual variations we observe in physiological reactivity and the differences in approach/withdrawal behaviour that can be observed in infants and which probably help to lay the foundations of that trait as an adult characteristic.

Not unexpectedly, such connections are more clearly articulated when the behaviour in question is very exaggerated and if, like Lader for example, we use forms of psychiatric disorder as our reference point then the continuity between gene, nervous system and tempera- ment becomes quite manifest. Turned round, and looked at from another perspective, we may also see how types of temperament can be represented as predipositions to various kinds of mental illness and how the latter are genetically determined to the extent that the individual's inherited make-up provides him with a nervous system which, in states of abnormality, helps to steer his behaviour in one direction or another. How this occurs and the variety it takes will occupy us over the next two chapters.

However, before turning to those questions it is necessary to make one final comment. In discussing the genetic aspects of predisposition in this chapter I have stayed close to my plan of considering first that evidence pertaining to an understanding of less serious forms of mental disorder. But there is another thread of evidence, relevant to the general topic, that should be mentioned briefly and which will be discussed more fully later. It concerns the role of heredity in more severe, psychotic types of psychological illness. Until recently, to discuss that separately would in any case have formed a natural division in our account, since most research on the problem – and there has been a great deal – has been carried out largely independently of the ideas that have guided much of the work discussed in this chapter: it has been conducted more in the tradition of medical, or psychiatric, genetics than as part of the work by *psychogeneticists* on normal individual variation. The reason for this has been a prevailing view of disorders like schizophrenia as organic brain disease which, like some neurological conditions, might be explained genetically in a similar way. However, opinion is now changing rapidly. A shift of emphasis in psychiatric genetics towards trying to disentangle the role of inheritance in *predisposition*, coupled with the application by psychologists of 'dimensional' ideas to the psychotic states, has begun to blur some earlier distinctions between the less severe and the more severe disorders. Conceptually, therefore, it is no longer possible to regard the latter as so very different from other psychiatric illnesses. Nevertheless, some of the evidence and arguments relating to their genetic aspects *are* slightly different and it will be easier to elucidate these when we come to consider the psychotic disorders as a whole.

5

Phobias, Compulsions and Melancholy

The previous three chapters of this book have concentrated on questions about the *predisposition* to psychiatric disorder. We have seen how properties of the nervous system, in part genetically determined, constitute a biological basis for personality and how, pursuing our earlier analogy with the systemic physical diseases, we can construe individuals as varying according to certain temperamental characteristics which do not in themselves constitute abnormality but which, if occurring in extreme form, might make them more susceptible to forms of illness that their type of nervous system helps to dictate. The next two chapters will pursue the thrust of that argument to its next logical step and examine some of the mechanisms through which predisposition may be translated into illness. The emphasis so far has been on predispositions to milder, non-psychotic forms of illnesses. In this and the following chapter the same theme will be continued, considering in turn the possible aetiology of those disorders which, in most current psychiatric classifications, are considered to fall outside the domain of psychosis. Actually, as we shall eventually see, the exact boundaries between the psychotic and the non-psychotic are not as sharp as is sometimes supposed. Indeed, to give some flavour of the debate about this issue, and in order to define the intended scope of the discussion that follows, it is worth starting by considering some of the criteria that are often used to distinguish the psychotic from other forms of disorder.

One criterion is severity: the psychotic person is often considered more seriously disturbed, as judged by the degree of impairment of function shown both in mental activity and in his or her social interaction with others. However, severity is not by itself a sufficient basis on which to label someone psychotic. Many patients considered by psychiatrists to be suffering from non-psychotic illnesses, such as grossly neurotic or psychopathic individuals, may actually be more incapacitated than some mildly psychotic people.

Another feature sometimes used to distinguish the psychotically disturbed is that such individuals have lost touch with reality, a characterisation summed up in the unempathic suggestion that 'the neurotic is the kind of person who builds castles in the air, whereas the psychotic is someone who lives in them'! However, as one schizophrenic pointed out in a recent letter to the press, this is indeed a crude observation, failing to recognise, as it does, the subtle boundaries that exist between the sense of inner self and the appreciation of external reality. Nor does empirical evidence bear out the claim that all people labelled psychotic have a distorted view of reality: as we shall see later, when we come to discuss schizophrenia, they are sometimes actually more perceptive than normal people in judging what is 'real' in a situation.

A third, and related, criterion sometimes used to distinguish the psychotic is that he shows loss of insight into his own aberration of mind; that, unlike the neurotic for example, he fails to appreciate that there is anything wrong with him. Again this is not universally true. Many psychotics, except during periods of acute illness, are often only too painfully aware that they are different, set apart, from others. Furthermore, few psychopaths would consider themselves abnormal: yet they are not judged psychotic, either legally or according to conventional psychiatric criteria.

Fourthly, the term 'psychotic' is often used to denote a pattern of disturbance which, from the outside, looks bizarre and incomprehensible, discontinuous with or outside the realm of normal behaviour and experience. Here again such an evaluation may reflect as much upon the observer's own psychological insightfulness as upon that of the person being judged. For example, when pressed, many quite normal people will admit to experiences having a psychotic quality about them. Or, viewed from a different stance, the irrational beliefs and behaviours of some neurotics, such as those with severe obsessional preoccupations, can seem just as puzzling to other people as the apparently weird symptoms of the psychotic.

Of course, if these *several* criteria are all met and the person shows certain recognisable symptoms then it is possible to consider him, without too much doubt, as suffering from, say, schizophrenia or a manic-depressive illness: which is why psychiatry has rightly found it useful to distinguish between psychotic and non-psychotic forms of mental disorder. But it is only the existence of these extreme examples that lends validity to the distinction. In practice, there are many cases in whom it may not be at all easy to differentiate mild psychosis from severe neurosis or chronic aberration of the personality. The blurred nature of such boundaries is recognised in some quarters, especially in the United States (though scarcely at all in Western Europe), by acknowledging the existence of so-called 'borderline syndromes'. The term has been used to describe individuals who seem to show a genuine mixture of neurotic and psychotic symptomatology. Later a whole chapter (chapter 9) will be devoted to these borderline patients, who have been left to the very end of our discussions about disorder because, as we shall eventually see, in order understand their particular forms of aberration we first need to appreciate some of the ideas that have grown up around more clearly defined types of neurotic and psychotic illness.

To some extent, then, the aspects of disorder to be considered at this point in the book are arbitrarily chosen. Even the division of subject matter across this and the following chapter is not entirely clear-cut, though it does have a certain historical and theoretical justification. This chapter will examine forms of reaction that are associated with deep-felt emotion, especially anxiety. Traditionally, these 'dysthymic' conditions have been regarded as having certain features in common, an observation supported by the evidence, already reviewed, about the kinds of temperament that predispose to them. The next chapter will be concerned with antisocial behaviour and various forms of hysterical reaction: although rather more heterogeneous than the dysthymic conditions, these disorders have often been lumped together to form a rough and ready category which, for the moment, will suit our purposes here.

Probably the most straightforward illustration of how temperament and disorder are connected occurs in the case of illnesses associated with manifest anxiety. As we saw in earlier chapters, there is good evidence that some people show, as an intrinsic feature of their biological make-up, a tendency towards heightened reactivity in certain parts of the brain which control the expression and feeling of fear or anxiety. In its least complicated pathological form this may simply display itself as the neurotic disorder of 'anxiety state'. Here the person shows, and reports, what is sometimes called 'free-floating' anxiety, a pervasive sense of fearfulness accompanied by the familiar signs of increased emotional arousal such as racing pulse, sweating and so on. EEG recordings taken from such an individual during an attack will generally have a distinctive flat profile, due to the disappearance of the 'alpha' waves that normally signify a relaxed state of mind. As the term 'free-floating' implies, these states are unconnected with any obvious situational factor and are simply experienced as inexplicable waves of panic, usually exacerbated by the person's awareness of the unpleasant physiological changes that are going on inside.

While serving to remind us of the sometimes easy transition between normal temperamental reaction and disorder, the occurrence of such pathological anxiety in its pure form is rare. Almost always the unpleasant emotion gets attached to, or is selectively triggered by, some external or internal cue: the person becomes irrationally afraid of some object or situation. It is the behavioural and psychological reactions associated with these 'phobic states' which form much of the symptomatology of most anxiety neurotics. Of course, in their milder and more circumscribed form, phobias are relatively common: many people are afraid of spiders, or apprehensive about flying or travelling in lifts. It is when the problem gets out of hand or, more likely, the anxiety becomes attached to *many* situations – as in the agoraphobic or social phobic – that the person is driven to seek psychiatric help.

Experimental psychologists investigating the possible mechanisms of phobic reactions have frequently turned to explanations based on the conditioned reflex theories of behaviourism. Historically, this approach became firmly planted early on in J. B. Watson's famous study of the unfortunate Little Albert, in whom it was claimed a conditioned fear of a rat had been established by associating the sight of the said rodent with fear, induced by loud noise. The experiment also helped to explain why phobics often become afraid, not just of one thing, but of many: Little Albert was also said to have attached his fear to other furry objects. This was accounted for according to the principle of 'generalisation', whereby a response conditioned to one stimulus usually spreads to others of a similar kind.

In the intervening years since that study was carried out behaviouristic explanations of phobias have become considerably modified, in order to try to account for their more detailed features. One obvious question they (or indeed any other forms of explanation) raise is: Why do some people develop phobias and not others? Part of the answer, of course, is that some individuals – those of anxious temperament – are more likely to respond to the conditions that produce phobic reactions. It should be said that this has not always been uncontroversial. As noted in a previous chapter, Watson himself and many later behaviourist psychologists who followed his lead were generally hostile to the idea of intrinsic, biological differences between people: indeed, for some psychologists the very rationale for behaviourism was that it could actually explain whatever differences there were as environmental in origin, due to learned patterns of conditioned reactions. It was left to writers like Eysenck to re-introduce, from Pavlovian theory, the notion of individual variations in personality which, through their association with nervous system differences, account for the fact that some people are, in certain situations at least, more conditionable than others. How this idea applies, specifically, to learned *anxiety* reactions has been further clarified by Gray, who argues that some individuals – those we have referred to here as 'dysthymic' – are inherently more sensitive to 'signals of punishment' in the environment and hence more likely to become phobic of them[71].

Even if we take into account these individual differences in susceptibility to anxiety reactions, there are some other puzzling features about phobias that need to be explained. Why is it, for example, that certain kinds of phobia are very common, while others are quite rare? Few people have an irrational fear of electric light sockets (even if they have nearly been electrocuted!); yet a great many of us get more than slightly uneasy in the close vicinity of spiders or snakes. This selective nature of the sources of anxiety is brought out especially clearly in surveys of clinical populations, where agoraphobia is very commonly encountered – as, to a slightly lesser degree, is social phobia. On the other hand, irrational fears of animals like dogs or cats are quite rare.

An explanation that is often given makes use of the notion of 'biological preparedness', the idea that all organisms, including Man, are somehow primed to react more strongly, and therefore form conditioned responses more easily, to certain *kinds* of environmental stimuli[152]. It is interesting to note, for example, that studies trying to repeat Watson's 'Little Albert' experiment generally failed when attempts were made to condition children to become afraid of harmless objects like wooden ducks, opera glasses and curtains! Little Albert's nervous system, it seems, was already partly predisposed to respond vigorously to the sight of the rat, the conditioning procedure simply acting to stamp it in more strongly. More recent laboratory experiments with adult subjects, carried out by a group of Scandinavian psychologists, Öhman and his colleagues, have confirmed this[86, 127]. They used the galvanic skin response as the sign of conditioning of anxiety, pairing an electrical shock with pictures of several different kinds of object. They found that the physiological response was greater and persisted longer if the conditioned stimulus was a picture of a snake than when pictures of neutral objects (human faces or houses) were presented to the subject. Interestingly, this was especially true of subjects whose galvanic skin reactions were in any case very strong, indicating that they were naturally very arousable. The result provides another example of how the individual's type of nervous system is important in determining whether he or she develops a phobia of a particular object or situation.

If we combine these two ideas – biological preparedness and a predisposed, highly reactive nervous system – we can see how certain aspects of phobic reactions may not actually be learned at all. They may simply arise in the first place because some very anxiety-prone people are more likely to show strong emotional responses to stimuli which in a real, perhaps evolutionary, sense *are* fear-producing, the behaviour that they lead to being later elaborated through learning. The same point has been made by Marks who, in his authoritative review of the whole topic of phobias, comments as follows:

> Many principles behind the learning of fear have been mapped
> out from sound experimental evidence over the past 50 years –
> these are now freely accepted, but innate factors have been
> neglected and the subject is in disfavour.... Of course,
> acceptance that there are innate elements in fear responses does
> not imply that they are immutable since environmental factors
> can modify the expression of inborn elements[112].

A variety of evidence supports the view that some phobias, at least,
originate as innately or maturationally determined responses that are
'released', in certain prone individuals, at particular times in the
person's life. For one thing, phobic patients cannot always recall a
discrete traumatic event from which to date the beginning of their
phobia: they have not generally been conditioned, like Little Albert, to
react in the way they do. This may be especially true of agoraphobics,
whose symptoms may appear following some rather non-specific life
event, such as a change of job or a general upset, like a bereavement.
The consequent increase in anxiety then appears to trigger the phobic
reaction.

Even in the case of very specific phobias of common objects, such as
spiders, the origins of the anxiety may be lost in the mists of childhood
and may not be traceable to actual traumatic experience of the feared
stimulus. Here maturation of the nervous system may be more
important than an actual learning experience in determining when a
phobia begins. Gray, for example, in his book *The Psychology of Fear and
Stress*, draws our attention to the fact that the development of different
kinds of fear in children takes a very definite chronological course,
anxiety about animals (or even the dark) being quite rare in young
infants and appearing – apparently spontaneously – at a later stage of
childhood[69]. A very particular example of this innate nature of fear is
illustrated in the well-known experiments on the 'visual cliff'
phenomenon, the tendency for many species, from chicks to human
infants, to show an apparently inborn wariness of heights; from which
later adult phobias, occurring in especially fearful individuals, might
partly originate[64]. A similar conclusion could be reached about social
phobias. Fear of strangers emerges quite suddenly in infants and, as we
saw in the previous chapter, varies considerably in degree according to
genetic endowment. This combination of maturational and inherited
factors is probably important in laying the groundwork for the
response of some phobic neurotics to social situations.

If it is true that many fears are innate, does this mean that the human
nervous system is in some way 'hard wired' to react to certain very
specific stimuli, like snakes, which signal threat and which, as a result of

evolution, have been left residually represented in Man and are more likely to be triggered into action in some people than in others? Undoubtedly this is a possibility: the work of animal ethologists has indeed shown that in some lower species alarm reactions are set off by very narrowly defined stimulus configurations, like the wing shape of a bird of prey. However, a much more likely explanation is that Man, in common with other creatures, has an innate tendency to react defensively to more *general* features of the environment which might be potentially harmful. In fact, any novel stimulus will cause him to show an 'orienting response' which, as discussed briefly in the previous chapter, can be measured physiologically and is very strong in anxious individuals. But certain qualities of the environment are especially likely to elicit such reactions. These include factors like the size, proximity and intensity of the stimulus, all of which may indicate a possible threat to the integrity of the organism.

Another, less easily definable factor that also needs to be considered here is the 'surprisingness' of the stimulus. In chapter 2, it may be recalled, reference was made to the writings of Berlyne on this topic, including his idea that there is a fine balance, which varies in different people, between curiosity about the novel and aversion to the strange. According to Berlyne, which of these two reactions occurs may depend on the perceptual quality of the stimulus – its complexity, incongruity, bizarreness and unexpected departure from the familiar. Certainly, everyday experience seems to confirm this, as the following story illustrates.

Some years ago I had occasion to take a group of students on a professional visit to a residential home for the severely mentally handicapped. At one point during the tour the group turned a corner and suddenly came face to face with one of the residents who suffered from profound, untreated hydrocephalus, typically characterised by enormous enlargement of the upper part of his head. Even to your writer, inured to such things, this unfortunate sight was quite shocking, the more so because, as is usual in the condition, the person's face was otherwise perfectly formed. The whole impression was one of total incongruity, so much so that two of the students looked visibly shaken, one of them shortly afterwards asking if she could detach herself from the group because she felt that she was going to faint. It is easy to see how a phobia might arise out of such an experience.

Even assuming that many phobias spring from a combination of naturally based fear and temperamental disposition, it is still necessary to explain how and why they become elaborated and especially why they persist, often for many years. The phobia is after all an *irrational* response to something which is not, in most cases, actually biologically harmful and normally we would expect the person to adapt once he realised that the source of his anxiety is not really threatening. And of course this does happen in most people, who from childhood onwards learn to ignore or cope with otherwise mildly frightening situations. But the process seems to be delayed or arrested in the very fearful.

Part of the explanation is contained in the anecdote related a moment ago. Although the nature of my swooning student's anxiety was quite physiological, it rapidly motivated her to escape from the dreadful sight that had caused it. In other words, the *feeling* of anxiety in the presence of the feared object is only one aspect of the phobic reaction. The other important element is the *behaviour* it brings on, first of trying to escape and then later, because of anticipatory anxiety, of trying to avoid re-entering the same situation. Even if the person does encounter the source of his fear again, he may not stay long enough to let the anxiety subside. We can understand the physiological nature of this latter process by referring to the idea of 'habituation' referred to in the previous chapter. We saw there that anxious individuals, especially anxious neurotics, adapt extremely slowly to arousing stimuli. This means that under the real-life conditions responsible for their phobic symptoms they will continue to remain at a high level of anxiety much longer than the normal individual. In fact there is some reason to believe that they may become even *more* aroused because their slow habituation, coupled with their awareness of it, may be self-reinforcing, pushing them into a vicious circle of increasing anxiety that motivates them to avoid even more the feared situation.

An important factor here, and one which behaviouristic explanations find difficult to handle, is that many of the events that help to maintain phobic behaviour involve complex mental processes that are generally out of the reach of theories based on the conditioned reflex. To put it simply, even away from the situation that he fears, the phobic person can think about, imagine, and rehearse his own behaviour in it. This – according to the old adage that things are always worse in prospect than they are in reality – almost always exacerbates the anxiety and strengthens the tendency to try and avoid whatever it is that brings it on. The childhood origins of some adult phobias can also be explained in a similar way. Fears of the dark and things associated with it – ghosts, monsters and so on – rely on vivid imagining which, in an especially sensitive child, may be elaborated and lay down memories that are re-awakened in later life. Such a child may also 'learn' its phobia in the first place by merely imitating, or modelling, the fearful behaviour of an adult displaying his or her own anxiety about thunderstorms or revulsion from edible snails. And how many fears of spiders have been reinforced by cosy bedtime readings of Little Miss Muffet?

The point I am making is that it would be wrong to suppose that even the very anxious are somehow passive victims of overactivity in their 'emotional brains', an impression sometimes given by psychologists who, writing about phobias, have tended to stay closer than we would prefer to traditional behaviourist interpretations. In this respect I have to disagree with Gray who, commenting on the precise similarity of the brain mechanisms responsible for anxiety in both rats and men, states that this '...at once rules out of court any attempt to explain human anxiety in terms that are specific to man (by recourse, say to the vagaries of the Oedipus complex), let alone specific to the pressures of modern life'[71]. It is surely the unique self-consciousness of Man, paralleled in the evolution of his higher nervous system, that provides an important clue to understanding how temperamental characteristics associated with anxiety – undoubtedly traceable to variations quite low down in the nervous system – become elaborated during life. It is true that the phobic states, of all of the psychiatric disorders, provide the most straightforward example of how direct a link can sometimes exist between known brain physiology and behaviour: indeed that is why we chose to start here by considering them first and why behaviouristic psychology has been most successful at explaining them, compared with other forms of mental illness. But the psychic structure of the temperamentally anxious is no less complex for that reason, and the phobias from which they may suffer undoubtedly involve, to a considerable degree, what psychologists nowadays – admittedly somewhat fashionably – describe as 'cognitive processes', referrable in the nervous system to the upper reaches of the brain. This does not mean – and here Gray is probably quite right – that ideas like the Oedipus complex are helpful in trying to understand the origins of human anxiety. On the other hand, it does draw our proper attention to the qualitative differences that exist in the mechanisms that mediate anxiety in Man and lower animals.

The above remarks apply with particular force when we come to try to explain another form of 'dysthymic' disorder, namely obsessive-compulsive neurosis, where there has been a much more overt division of opinion about the role of so-called 'cognitive' factors in aetiology[5]. Obsessional neurosis is a relatively rare and extremely intractable condition in which the individual is plagued by irrational, repetitive thoughts and feels compelled to indulge in ritualistic behaviours, such as frequent hand-washing, checking or counting. People who develop such symptoms are very similar in temperament to those who are prediposed to other dysthymic illnesses, in the sense that they show the same physiological signs of heightened arousability: for example, like anxiety neurotics, they too manifest increased reactivity and slow rates of habituation when tested with measures such as the galvanic skin response. They are also similar in basic personality structure, generally being introverted and highly neurotic on tests like the Eysenck questionnaires. These facts, together with an apparently superficial similarity in the form of the symptoms, has led to one view that obsessional disorder arises in much the same way as phobic reactions. The argument here is that performance of an obsessional ritual helps, temporarily at least, to relieve anxiety, which powerfully stamps in the habit – in much the same way that avoidance of others reinforces the cloistered behaviour of the socially phobic.

Although plausible up to a point the parallel is not quite complete, however, because obsessional neurosis differs from the straightforward phobia in some important, and interesting, respects. One way in which it differs is that the anxiety of the obsessional is much more 'symbolic' in quality, usually taking the form of guilt that focuses on certain areas of preoccupation, like cleanliness, tidiness, sexuality and fear of harming others. The compulsive behaviour is therefore very often triggered off by internal events – thoughts, ideas or imagined consequences. This means that the circle of cause and effect which we saw was important in maintaining the phobic's symptoms is likely to be that much more vicious for the obsessional: for he, to an even greater extent, carries his neurotic concerns constantly around in his head and is continually forced into dialogue with them.

Even if, as is frequently the case, the obsessional neurotic's preoccupations are projected on to some external stimulus, this usually takes a particular form, a fact which further helps to explain why his symptoms are so persistent. Take, for example, the compulsive handwasher. The environmental stimuli that evoke the ritual – dirt, germs and so on – are widespread and likely to be constantly encountered. Furthermore, they are 'invisible' – actually so in the case of germs, relatively so in the case of dirt, which is never entirely absent from the environment. Consequently, unlike, say, the spider phobic, the obsessional can never completely avoid the source of his anxiety or test out its reality; nor can he ever be sure that the ritual has achieved its end, of getting rid of the source of his ruminations. He is therefore kept in a high state of arousal and driven to continue repeating the ritual 'in order to make sure', often to the point where his everyday life is totally disrupted.

A case encountered some years ago is typical and helps to illustrate the point very well. The patient had a fear of dirt that took the form of an obsession about soiled clothes which he was compelled to take frequently to launderettes. However, he was totally convinced that a particular washing-machine could only be used once since thereafter it would, he thought, be contaminated with the dirt from his previous batch of clothes. (Odd though it may seem he was not at all concerned that other people might have used the machine in the meantime!)

Driven by his obsession he took to using a different washing-machine each time and, having quickly exhausted those, to seek fresh launderettes. Eventually, when referred for treatment, he was covering an ever expanding area of the South of England in pursuit of a virgin Bendix, with crippling consequences for his work and other parts of his daily routine.

Another difference between obsessional neuroses and ordinary phobias is that although in the former anxiety is clearly just as powerful a driving force for the symptoms, it is probably not the only source of emotional arousal present. This was certainly the conclusion reached from a study that looked at the changes in mood which surround the performance of handwashing rituals in obsessional patients[189]. There it was found that the rituals were just as likely to be preceded by increases in depression and hostility as by increased anxiety, very prolonged rituals being associated with a *generally* very bad mood state. It was also observed that patients often actually became *more* anxious after completing the handwashing, the worry about not being able to resist doing it adding further to the disturbed mental condition.

Experimental studies like that just quoted are not the only ones to emphasise the importance of emotions other than anxiety in obsessional neuroses or to suggest that hostility – particularly suppressed anger – is a crucial feature in their aetiology. Psychoanalytic writers have always argued that this is true and if, from the rather different perspective of this book, we are to seek part of the basis for obsessionality in the emotional aspects of the temperament then we might do worse than see where their point of view leads us. Put very briefly, what it suggests is that there are some, very emotionally reactive, individuals who are brought up in family environments that happen to place undue emphasis on cleanliness, sexual repression and control of anger, and who are therefore more likely to develop anxious guilt that comes to motivate pathological obsessional behaviour. A not insigificant factor here – and indeed one that is often not, but should be, taken account of when considering the 'environmental' influences in most forms of psychiatric disorder – concerns the genetic endowment shared by parent and child. In the case of obsessionality this means that the strict, meticulous, overconscientious father or mother may already have transmitted to their offspring the very temperamental qualities that sensitise the child to the rearing practices which they, as parents, are likely to adopt.

Temperamental features associated with emotionality, albeit having a more complex biological base than in the case of anxiety *per se*, therefore go some way towards explaining why certain people develop obsessive-compulsive neurosis. But this is probably not the whole story and indeed some psychologists have taken a quite different approach to the question, placing a great deal of emphasis on the cognitive aspects of obsessionality to which I drew special attention earlier. Even here various viewpoints have been adopted, though they have in common the general idea that obsessional personalities, and therefore people predisposed to obsessional neurosis, have a characteristic cognitive *style*, or way of attending to, perceiving and analysing events in the environment.

One example of this approach is the suggestion that obsessional individuals have a narrowly focused attentional style and, as a result, develop a convergent, rigidly bound mode of conceptual thinking. The idea has sometimes been investigated under the umbrella of research that originated in attempts to understand forms of thinking in schizophrenia. As we shall see in a later chapter, it has been found that schizophrenics vary with respect to a supposed cognitive dimension of 'overinclusive-overexclusive' thinking, a pathological version of the more familiar notion of divergent-convergent thinking. Thus, some schizophrenic patients show very loosened, divergent, or overinclusive thinking styles, possibly related to other cognitive disorders they manifest, including dysfunctions of their attentive mechanisms. At least one study that examined this characteristic in obsessional neurotic patients suggested that they were just the opposite[139]. The experiment involved a fairly typical test procedure in which the subject has to choose, from a number of response words, those that are definitive of a given stimulus word. Obsessional neurotics were found to underline significantly fewer of the essential items, a result which was taken as evidence that such patients have more narrowly defined concepts and therefore less flexibility in their thinking than normal people. By inference it could also be concluded that obsessionals have, too, a more narrowly focused mode of *attending* to stimuli; which could explain why they are characteristically preoccupied with minute detail and why, as neurotics, their symptoms so often take on a similar quality.

It should be mentioned, incidentally, that the view of obsessionality just referred to is not as distant as it may seem from those discussed earlier, which emphasised the more emotional aspects of the compulsive neuroses. Thus, it is known that there is an inextricable link between those mechanisms that have to do with the general arousal of the brain and those processes, in the higher nervous system, which control the breadth and narrowness of attention: generally speaking, the more emotionally aroused the organism is, the more focused its attention becomes. If we join these ideas together we can therefore see how, at a physiological level, part of the obsessional's problem may lie in his having a *combination* of very high emotional reactivity and a tendency to focus on the detail of events, both internal and in the external environment. Translated into the terminology of cognitive psychology, this means that he is likely to develop thought structures that are highly circumscribed and which, if the person is exposed to very particular kinds of child rearing that attach guilt to his ideas, become potentially pathological in form and content.

A slightly different viewpoint on how the psychological 'style' of obsessionals might relate to the brain has recently been suggested by work looking at differences between people in the way the functions of the two cerebral hemispheres are organised, a newly emerging neuropsychological approach to psychiatric disorders briefly mentioned at the end of chapter 3. As with more traditional applications of cognitive psychology to psychiatry, like that mentioned above, hemisphere research has, too, been mainly concerned with schizophrenia, but other forms of disorder have now also begun to come under scrutiny. Thus, it has been suggested that personality characteristics, for example those that predispose to obsessional neurosis, may reflect differences in cognitive style which are, in turn, associated with the relative dominance of one or other hemisphere. One way of investigating this question is to examine differences in the extent to which each hemisphere is activated when subjects are required to process the various types of stimulus material for which the two sides of the brain are specialised. The degree to which a particular hemisphere is activated can be determined by noting which way the eyes move when the stimulus is presented: this is usually in a contralateral direction, the eyes moving to the left when the right hemisphere is aroused and vice versa. A recent experiment using these methods found that subjects rated as obsessional in personality tended to show more rightward eye movements (left hemisphere activation)[160]. Although not too surprising when verbal stimuli were involved (the left hemisphere does normally process that kind of material), it also proved to be true, in the case of obsessional personalities, for spatial and emotional stimuli that would usually be expected to preferentially arouse the *right* hemisphere. It was concluded from the study that very obsessional people show overdominance of the left hemisphere which, through its strong association with the control of language, could account for their intellectualised, repressive stance on the world. The comparison group in this experiment, incidentally, consisted of individuals rated as having hysterical personalities. I will comment briefly on the significance of that finding when considering hysteria in the next chapter.

It will not have gone unnoticed that several references have just been made to schizophrenia and to the fact that research on that condition has often inspired some of the ideas about obsessional neurosis: that is especially true of the work mentioned on overinclusive and overexclusive forms of thinking. The connection is not coincidental, for it has often been observed by clinicians that the two disorders show a remarkable similarity. Thus, the symptoms of the obsessive-compulsive neurotic can sometimes be extraordinarily bizarre, being based on beliefs that are almost delusional in quality, even bordering on the mad: the launderette gentleman is a case in point. It is therefore interesting that although many schizophrenics seem quite the opposite of obsessionals in cognitive style, that is not always true. In certain forms of paranoid psychosis the patient is characterised, like the obsessional neurotic, by an extremely narrow style of attention and thinking as a result of which he develops a highly systematised and circumscribed delusional system for which he selectively seeks out – and inevitably finds – evidence to support. One could almost say that the paranoid psychotic is 'obsessed' with his chosen set of beliefs. Why then do obsessional neurotics themselves not become psychotic in this extreme psychiatric sense? The answer is that sometimes they do – in perhaps up to about ten per cent of cases – a fact that again underlines the slim borderline between the mild and the severe disorders. What is more puzzling, is why so *few* obsessional neurotics proceed into frank insanity. One possible reason – and this is a view held, for example, by some psychoanalytic writers – is that for many such patients developing obsessional routines and belief structures allows them to order their world, acting as a kind of psychological defence which, unless some other factor intervenes, helps them to ward off the complete disintegration of personality found in schizophrenia.

Now let us turn, in the last part of this chapter, to the third form of disorder that is most often associated with the 'dysthymic' temperament, namely neurotic or reactive depression. In using the latter terms, I have already introduced a note of controversy and it is perhaps worth starting by considering some of the more general issues that surround the topic of depression, bearing in mind that some of the points raised will be taken up again in later chapters.

Although, unlike some other mental illnesses, the symptoms of at least mild depression are beyond dispute – and familiar to most – there is some disagreement about classification and theoretical perspective, especially when the whole range of 'affective disorders' is considered. In psychiatric terminology affective disorder refers to a condition in which the main symptoms are a severe alteration in mood, specifically an extreme lowering or elevation of mood. One clearly distinguishable form is manic-depressive illness, sometimes described as 'bipolar'. Here the person suffers swings in mood from extreme elation to deep despair, though in some cases showing only one phase of that cycle. The condition is considered to have a strong biological basis and to be recognisably psychotic in quality and severity: it is therefore outside the purview of this chapter.

There has been somewhat less agreement about how to evaluate different varieties of primary depression. Some authors prefer to make a distinction between 'neurotic' and 'psychotic' forms, hence emphasising not just a difference in severity but also their separateness as psychiatric illnesses. Other writers have focused more on the causes of depression as a criterion, distinguishing between 'reactive' and 'endogenous' types, the former being considered due mainly to environmental stress and the latter due principally to biological (including genetic) factors. Here the question of severity of the illness is often dealt with by suggesting that there is really a continuum of depression: the more serious the depressive symptoms the more likely it is that they reflect an intrinsic change in brain functioning, rather than being caused solely by a reaction to environmental circumstances.

Neither of the dichotomies just referred to is entirely satisfactory though each, in its own way, draws attention to certain distinctions that can be made when comparing extreme examples of the different forms depression can take. Thus, it is possible to identify a type of depression in which the behaviour and alteration in mood seem to be qualitatively different from normal. The patient shows wretchedness and despair, profound slowing of speech and movement, and possibly delusions, especially of guilt or hypochondriasis. In such cases the symptoms go beyond those of ordinary, even persistent, sadness and even if there is a triggering event that causes them the reaction is disproportionate to its psychological importance. Against this can be set a milder, and more common, variety of depression where there is an alteration in mood that looks more like a quantitative extension of normal sadness and which is perfectly understandable as a response to some preceding stress, such as a bereavement or other change in personal and social circumstances. It is this 'reactive' or 'neurotic' form of depression with which we shall be concerned here.

Although most authorities assume that some physiological changes accompany even mild depressive mood – the widespread use of drugs to treat it is evidence of this – contemporary accounts of neurotic depression pay relatively little attention to its biological aspects, especially in the sense in which we shall judge them to be important here; namely as temperamental characteristics that make some people more prone to the disorder than others. The emphasis in most recent research on mild depression has, instead, been rather different. On the one hand, it has had a *social* perspective, being concerned with such questions as the influence of life events in precipitating depressive reactions; while, on the other, it has been interested in the possible mechanisms whereby, in the individual, the *psychological* features of depression are induced and maintained. Both of these approaches have sometimes addressed the question of variations in susceptibility to depression, social psychiatry by focusing on factors in the person's early life, other research by proposing characteristic styles by which way people evaluate events in their lives. Rarely, if ever, has either of those two ways of looking at the problem tried to incorporate ideas about the biology of temperament and here we shall suggest why it is necessary, and how it might be possible, to do so.

Let us begin with two 'psychological' views of reactive depression from which a great deal of contemporary research on the problem has stemmed. The first of these arose from the suggestion by the American psychologist Seligman that depression can be regarded as a state of 'learned helplessness'[153]. Seligman originally developed this view from observations made on animals subjected to uncontrollable punishment. In a typical experiment the animal is first exposed to inescapable electrical shock and then later placed in a situation where avoidance of the shock is actually possible. As a result of the earlier experience the animal regularly becomes passive and apparently less able to learn that it can now escape punishment: it has, in other words, learned that it has no control over environmental events. According to Seligman, in human depression a similar feeling of helplessness occurs, induced by previous experiences, like failure or loss of a loved one, which have the same quality of being beyond the control of the individual.

A great deal of research guided by this model has attempted, with some success, to produce experimental 'depression' in human subjects in the laboratory and Seligman's views do seem to have a certain merit in accounting for some forms of real-life depression. The main problem is to explain why some people do *not* get depressed after punishing experiences (either inside or outside the laboratory), while other people do: indeed they may get very depressed. In order to answer that question Seligman, recognising an important difference between animals and humans, argued that individuals exposed to the same 'learned helplessness' experience will differ in how they evaluate it: in particular, they will differ in where they attribute the *cause* of the experience[1]. Individuals who are likely to become depressed are said to be those who assign the cause to themselves, in the form of personal inadequacies of a rather permanent kind. They also tend to be people who generalise the experience to other, similar situations.

Seligman's emphasis on the personality or cognitive style of the individual as a prediposing factor in depression is very like that adopted by Beck, whose writings have formed the other major focal point for a good deal of contemporary research on the psychology of depressive reactions[4]. Beck, starting from a more clinical standpoint than Seligman, reached the conclusion that whether or not people get (and remain) depressed depends very much on the characteristic way in which they perceive events around them. The more depressively prone, he says, are those who have what he refers to as a 'negative set' on the world: they have a poor regard for themselves (i.e. low self-esteem), they cast a melancholic eye over everything, and they view the future pessimistically.

Although painting a convincing picture of the depressive personality, neither Seligman nor Beck satisfactorily explain how such people get the way they are. One possibility – and this is the opinion of sociologists and social psychiatrists who have considered the question – is that the person's life history has a great deal to do with it. A good example of this view is to be found in the work of Brown and his colleagues[15]. After an extensive study of the past histories of depressed individuals and of the life events surrounding their illnesses, they identified as an important vulnerability factor the loss of a close relative – especially the mother – in childhood or adolescence. Explicitly relating their findings to Seligman's learned helplessness theory, they suggested that such loss is a particularly catastrophic example of the kind of trauma which could lead to a permanent perception that events are uncontrollable – or, in Beck's terminology, make a person have a generally pessimistic attitude towards the world. However, a difficulty with this interpretation, and one that bedevils most sociological work of its kind, is that it fails to explain those cases where such loss does *not* occur. Nor, more critically perhaps, does it account for the fact that in our society separation from the parent, especially by divorce, is very common; yet the incidence of clinical depression is still, relatively speaking, quite low. In other words, most people cope adequately as adults with their experience of early loss.

While not wishing to minimise the obvious importance of childhood experiences in the causation of depression, it is clearly also necessary to introduce some other factor if we are to explain fully why some people get depressed and others do not. This, I would suggest, has to do with the individual's 'nervous type'. The proposal is not new. Pavlov, in an accurate anticipation of Beck's description of the depressive personality, also wrote, it may be recalled, of the melancholic's mournful outlook on life: '...in everything he sees only the dark side, and from everything he expects only grievances.' Of course, for Pavlov, unlike Beck, this stemmed from the depressive's *biological* make-up, a conclusion which can now be supported by a considerable amount of evidence, from psychophysiological and personality studies, that people who develop neurotic depression are indeed, from the very beginning, of a particular type of dysthymic temperament.

Where does this get us in trying to trace the chain of events linking temperamental disposition to clinical depression in adult life? A good place to start is by considering the close association that exists between *anxiety* and depression, a connection which Gray, whose work I have referred to several times already, has discussed in detail[71]. Gray, it may be recalled, has argued that differences in the trait of anxiety are due to variations among individuals in their sensitivity to punishment, assumed to exist as a biological characteristic from birth. In view of the fact that the anxiety prone are also more likely to develop depression, it is easy to see how a catastrophic event in childhood, such as parental loss, could cause an especially sensitive individual to generalise the experience and so develop the pessimistic personality style emphasised by Beck and others. This would explain why early adversities, otherwise experienced by many, sow the seeds of depression in only a few – those who are *temperamentally* vulnerable.

Gray's analysis also goes some way towards explaining the mechanisms of the depressive reaction itself. Again the link with anxiety is important. In common with many other writers Gray has suggested that depression is really an end-state, arrived at following a period of chronically sustained anxiety, a point well-recognised in both clinical and introspective accounts: recall C. S. Lewis's report of the grief reaction as anxiety, or even fear bordering on panic, leading later into the dull apathy of despair[102]. Translated into physiological terms this process, according to Gray, may literally involve a depletion of neurochemicals that normally mediate arousal in the brain and which, in some very anxious people, are easily exhausted when the stress to which they are exposed is very sustained. Even in normal mood swings it may be noticed subjectively as a feeling of 'emotional draining' following a period of intense effort.

The changes just referred to are, of course, relatively transitory, clinical depression having a more longstanding quality. They also explain only one aspect of depression – the shift in *mood* – whereas the psychological state of the depressed person is more complicated. He or she not only *feels* bad, but also thinks sad thoughts, ruminates over unpleasant memories, and so on. It is this latter, cognitive, element, first emphasised by Beck, that is currently receiving a great deal of attention in research, not only on the mechanisms of, but also on possible ways of treating, neurotic depression[197]. What emerges from the research is that mood and ideation in depression are very closely interconnected. For example, depressed individuals – whether the mood is induced experimentally or studied as a naturally occurring change in clinical patients – tend, more frequently than normal, to perceive and remember items that have a 'bad' connotation. Similarly, requiring them to concentrate on negative thoughts or recall gloomy memories will significantly worsen their mood: people can literally think themselves into being depressed.

A crucial point here is which of the two effects – emotion or ideation

– is primary in producing depression. Does the person become depressed because of his lowered mood – and therefore, we might assume, because of his disturbed biochemistry – or because he is thinking negative thoughts? The answer is important because it could have implications for the way we treat the depressed patient; that is, whether we do so by manipulating his thinking or by attacking the neurochemistry of his mood, say with drugs. The dilemma was nicely summed up a few years ago by a colleague of mine who asked psychology undergraduates taking their final examinations to comment on the following quotation from Lewis Carroll;

'Can you stop crying by considering?' said Alice.
'That's how it's done', said the White Queen.

But is it? The evidence suggests that neither mood nor ideation actually has precedence in causing depression, but that each feeds constantly upon the other. At least this is the conclusion reached by one psychologist, Teasdale, who has specifically addressed the issue[176]. Basing his argument on 'semantic network' theories of the way events are established in long-term memory, Teasdale has proposed that the gloomy thoughts, ideas and recollections that plague the depressive are made more accessible to consciousness by the low mood, which in turn is worsened by their presence in the mind, thus leading to a vicious cycle of cause and effect. Teasdale's suggestion is perhaps an obvious one, but it makes use of a view of the illness process which is very important and which we constantly come across in trying to understand how, once set in motion, mental disorder can often take on a life of its own, the person being driven further and further away from normality by a mutually destructive interaction between processes – both physiological and psychological – that otherwise may merely denote a dispositional or personality style. We encountered the same feature earlier when discussing anxiety and obsessional neurosis and will find other examples later in the book.

To conclude this chapter, let us briefly consider together, rather than separately, the three types of disorder that have been discussed. All of them appear to spring from a common temperamental source and it may be asked: How, then, can they be distinguished, since, as described here, each seems to show some unique clinical features? The answer is that, in practice, they often cannot. The very close association between anxiety and neurotic depression has already been noted. Likewise individuals suffering from those two disorders – or, as is more usual, a mixture of both – may also display mildly obsessional personality traits. And, as we have seen, obsessive-compulsive neurotics are usually anxious and depressed. Nevertheless, distinctions *can* be made between them: otherwise psychiatric diagnosis would be an entirely unproductive exercise. Why is it, then, that dysthymic personalities, if and when they become ill, can develop one of several different types of disorder?

One reason presumably is that the life events to which they are exposed, from infancy onwards, will vary, shaping the expression of basic temperamental dispositions and establishing the precise form which vulnerability to later mental disorder will take. For example, a dysthymic individual who experiences serious loss, of say a parent, during childhood may well become specifically sensitised to events that help to revive the depressive reaction which accompanied the original trauma. On the other hand, had the parent lived, or stayed with the child, different traits of vulnerability – or styles of responding to stress – may have been established, in the form of acquired obsessional preoccupations or fear-ridden reaction patterns. Or, of course, in a particularly sympathetic family environment the person may actually be protected from, or even learn to utilise positively, temperamental characteristics that could otherwise make him more susceptible to psychological breakdown.

Another explanation we need to consider – and it is one that is quite compatible with the above suggestion – arises from the incomplete nature of current biological conceptions of personality. It has been emphasised several times that these are still very crude and that they typically refer to quite low-level brain structures which, even then, are not fully understood. It is very probable – indeed virtually certain – that individuals differ with respect to other features of brain organisation, especially in the higher nervous system: recall the example given earlier of the differential involvement of the cerebral hemispheres in personality. Since it is these higher brain structures that form the biological vehicle for much of what we normally regard as personality, there is clearly considerable scope for differentiation and elaboration of relatively simple underlying temperamental characteristics – a point, of course, made early on by Pavlov. How, in detail, the psychology of the individual maps on to the concomitant neurophysiology remains largely to be discovered; as, by the same token, do the precise mechanisms whereby normality becomes abnormality. On the other hand, to end on an optimisitic note, there is already, as we have seen, sufficient known about the relationship between temperament and disorder to be confident that the ideas presented in this chapter are at least along the right lines and that there is a real sense in which the several disorders described here can be said to have a common origin.

6

Fugues, Rogues and Histrionics

All of the disorders discussed in the previous chapter have a common disposition in dysthymic temperament and, although differing somewhat in symptomatology, are alike in that they all seem to proceed from a high susceptibility to personal anxiety or guilt, causing the individual considerable pain and suffering. There is, however, another group of disorders where that criterion often does not seem to apply and about which it has been said that it is not the individual who suffers most, but those around him. As we saw in chapter 2, there are also some good empirical reasons, based on psychophysiological and other evidence, for thinking that such disorders stem from temperamental characteristics that are very different from those which predispose to the dysthymic states. The conditions in question form a rather heterogeneous category, covering cases to which psychiatrists may apply various labels, including 'hysteria', 'psychopathy', 'personality disorder', 'character disorder', and even, in some parts of the world, 'borderline state', a designation which in itself occupies a whole chapter of this book. Mirroring the varied clinical manifestation of these forms of abnormality, and partly because of their psychological complexity, it is sometimes less easy than in the case of the anxiety-based illnesses to find a common thread connecting temperament and disorder. Indeed, it is in this chapter that we shall begin to encounter more explicitly than hitherto the possible overlap between the mild and serious mental aberrations and will be brought up against questions which can only be properly answered after discussing the psychotic states in detail. Bearing these remarks in mind, let us start by considering what at first glance might seem to be a well-defined disorder, namely hysteria.

In fact, as Kendell pointed out in a recent review of its clinical usage, 'hysteria' has come to take on *multiple* meanings, ranging from a diagnosis with fairly precise features to a description of patients who merely irritate their psychiatrists[89]. Its most clear-cut form is conversion hysteria. Here the individual develops what can best be described as a pseudo-neurological symptom in the form of a sensory or motor loss. For example, the patient may complain of blindness, deafness or loss of voice, or of paralysis or muscular weakness in a limb.

Alternatively, the hysterical reaction may take the more diffuse form of what might be called the 'Agatha Christie syndrome': the person suffers from partial or complete amnesia, wandering away from home in a state of fugue and losing awareness of his or her real identity.

A common psychological explanation of these conversion hysterias is that they occur through mental dissociation which removes the individual from some source of distress, solve a conflict to which it gives rise, or blot out its unpleasantness. Where a more localised symptom occurs it may be interpreted as having additional symbolic significance, representing a channelling of anxiety into a bodily form which again allows the patient to escape or avoid a particularly stressful situation: the hysterically blind patient, for example, no longer has to 'face up to' whatever it is that upsets him. Classically, such individuals have been said to show *belle indifférence*: having successfully translated their anxiety into an acceptable physical symptom, they may now display a bland unconcern for the problem which triggered the reaction.

Surrounding, as it were, the clearly recognisable syndrome just described there is then a rather ill-defined group of conditions in which it is sometimes assumed a similar conversion mechanism is at work, but this time producing bodily symptoms of a more 'psychosomatic' kind. Thus, some doctors would regard as a form of conversion hysteria symptoms like pain and vomiting that have no apparent organic basis but which appear, instead, to be a physical expression of emotional turmoil. The most florid examples are where the patient, usually female, complains of multiple bodily symptoms which are overdramatised and which result in repeated demands for medical treatment.

Related to, and in a sense underpinning descriptions of hysteria in this broader sense is a usage of the term to refer to some patients who seem to have a chronic disorder of the personality that frequently brings them into contact with the psychiatric services for a variety of reasons, such as marital problems, suicide bids or drug abuse. These 'hysterical personalities' typically show traits like manipulativeness, egocentricity, attention-seeking behaviour – including sexual provocativeness – and emotions which, while labile and exaggerated, seem unconvincingly shallow to the perceptive observer. Another characteristic traditionally ascribed to them is heightened suggestibility, which is often considered to be an important component in yet another form of hysteria that has been recognised, namely mass hysteria. This is an epidemic phenomenon in which a set of psychosomatic symptoms or abnormal behaviours spreads through a group of individuals, usually girls or young women, closeted together in an institution such as a school or hospital.

Of the different manifestations of hysteria the most clearly recognisable is conversion hysteria of the first type described above, in which the symptoms take on a neurological character and although, as we have just seen, there has been an attempt to widen the concept of 'conversion' to include other types of reaction in which bodily symptoms occur, this is probably unhelpful when we come to try to understand the possible mechanisms involved in the classic form of the neurosis. Unlike pain and other psychosomatic symptoms that have sometimes been included under the heading of 'conversion hysteria', pseudo-neurological reactions – hysterical blindness, deafness and so on – all have one important feature in common. They all refer to a *loss* of function and always serve to block out some source of stimulation. Herein lies a clue to how, from a neurophysiological viewpoint, they might occur.

In the earlier chapters of this book several references were made to the fact that a crucial feature of brain function is *inhibition*, which enables the nervous system to regulate its level and pattern of response to stimulation. We also saw that inhibition has often been considered to be an important biological characteristic in which people of different temperament might vary. Pavlov certainly considered this to be so; which is why his idea of 'protective' inhibition has sometimes been used to explain the fact that some individuals show a paradoxical diminution in brain response when stimuli are very strong – as seen, for example, in experimental studies of 'augmenting-reducing', referred to previously. According to Pavlov the symptoms of conversion hysteria represent a similar phenomenon, occurring in individuals of hysterical 'nervous type' whose brains were considered by him to be more susceptible to inhibitory effects. How does this idea fit in with contemporary neurophysiological evidence?

Some connection can certainly be seen with research that started originally as investigations of the way the nervous system selectively attends to stimuli in the environment. It is known that this occurs through a process of active inhibition, the brain having the capacity to deliberately block out or attenutate its response to stimuli to which it does not wish to attend. A pioneer demonstrating these effects in animals was Hernández-Peón whose work is particularly relevant here because he and his colleagues went on to apply to the study of conversion hysteria certain ideas arising out of their basic research on attention[82]. What they did was to investigate the EEG responses of a girl suffering from a classic conversion symptom, so-called 'glove and sleeve' anaesthesia of the left arm. The method they used was to measure brain evoked potentials elicited by sets of electrical stimuli applied on some occasions to the left and on other occasions to the right arm of the patient. Comparisons were then made between the size of the EEG responses occurring on the appropriate (contralateral) side of the head; that is, over the left hemisphere for stimuli applied to the right hand, and vice versa. It turned out that when the patient's unaffected (right) hand was stimulated clear-cut evoked potentials could be recorded on the left side of the brain. On the other hand, no definite response could be found in the corresponding area of the right hemisphere when the 'paralysed' *left* arm was stimulated. The conclusion reached was that hysterical anaesthesia – and indeed other similar forms of conversion reaction – might involve an active and highly selective inhibition of nerve transmission somewhere along the sensory pathways that mediate the symptom: the patient's brain, in other words, may literally be cutting off from consciousness information coming along certain channels.

It has to be said that it has not proved all that easy to replicate the result just described, perhaps partly because the experiment is technically quite difficult to carry out. In any case, even if the effect observed could be genuinely ascribed, as suggested, to a very specific influence of inhibition in the nervous system, it could only account for the mechanisms underlying the conversion *symptom*. In other words, it would not give any real insight into the possible neurological basis of the complex – and probably unconscious – psychological motivation that underlies conversion hysteria. However, some other evidence about the condition does allow us to chase conversion hysteria a little further into the nervous system.

It is now well established – indeed it has been known for more than a century – that conversion symptoms are significantly more likely to occur on the *left* side of the body[167]. This curious fact has recently been interpreted from the viewpoint of theories about the nervous system, to which I have already alluded, that personality differences may to some extent reflect variations in the organisation of function across the two hemispheres. We saw some evidence for this in the previous chapter, when discussing obsessional neurosis. According to the experiment described there, individuals of obsessional personality show a pattern of arousal across the brain suggesting that the left, so-called 'intellectual' hemisphere is more likely to be activated, even under conditions which normally excite the right hemisphere. The comparison group in that study consisted of people rated as having hysterical personalities, whose pattern of brain response proved to be quite the reverse: in their case it was the *right* hemisphere which was more regularly activated by the task conditions used by the experimenters. This was interpreted as a sign that, unlike obsessionals, people of hysterical make-up have more access to and are more affected by the frequently unconscious, emotional contents of the psyche, in the control and representation of which the right hemisphere has sometimes been thought to be especially involved. If that were true then it might explain why, following the usual principle that brain and body are connected in a crossover fashion, the conversion mechanism, when it occurs, is more likely to produce its inhibitory effects on the side opposite to the hemisphere that is the seat of the emotion causing the symptom.

However, we do have to be slightly careful here, for two reasons. First, it is all too easy to ascribe to what has sometimes been called the 'silent' right hemisphere romantic-sounding properties that correspond to psychoanalytic notions about the unconscious and to conclude, therefore, that some people are literally more in touch with and influenced by that side of the brain than others. There is probably *something* in the idea, since the evidence does suggest that, despite not being able to 'speak', the right hemisphere does contribute substantially and of its own accord to mental life. And there is every reason to believe, as we shall discuss more fully in a later chapter, that psychological differences between people do depend to some extent on the way the functions of the hemispheres – both left and right – are organised. It is merely that we should not be lured into a too simplified idea of how personality and this aspect of brain organisation are related.

There is a second, and quite different, reason for urging caution about the possible significance of results pointing to a connection between conversion hysteria and the brain hemispheres. It arises from a question which in any case deserves attention in its own right; namely whether it is indeed true, as the drift of our discussion so far would suggest, that people who develop conversion reactions are always more likely, even in their normal state, to be of hysterical *personality*. It would be satisfyingly neat, and would suit our arguments here very well, if that were so. The evidence, however, is somewhat equivocal[121]. This is the case whether one relies on questionnaire scores, like those obtained from Eysenck's personality scales, or on clinical evaluations made by psychiatrists. Although it is true that many conversion hysterics – perhaps up to a half – do show hysterical traits in their basic personality, some clearly do not. In fact, as I myself witnessed in some early studies of conversion hysteria, a few patients suffering from quite classic pseudo-neurological symptoms of blindness, deafness, paralysis and so on may have predisposing personalities of a manifestly dysthymic nature[22]. Why is this?

I would suggest that it is because, compared with almost all of the other disorders discussed in this book, conversion reactions are much more determined by the immediate social, cultural and other environmental events that help to precipitate them, and slightly less dependent on the individual's premorbid personality. To illustrate this point let us consider a typical situation in which conversion symptoms are more than usually likely to occur. They are particularly common as a reaction to acute and very severe stress, such as that experienced, for example, by military personnel under the very traumatic conditions of battle: indeed, what was first labelled during the First World War as 'shell shock' was, in many cases, almost certainly a form of conversion neurosis suffered by soldiers no longer able to cope with being 'eye deep in Hell'. It is not surprising that men of any kind should react in a similar way, given the right circumstances. And we can see why if we consider the nature of the stress to which the soldier in battle is exposed. This, more than is usually the case, has the quality of a quite primitive physical assault upon the nervous system, an extreme of stimulation which, as we have seen (and as Pavlov himself emphasised), will eventually induce in even the strongest nervous type a 'protective' response, probably brought about by some inhibitory mechanism of the kind that could be responsible for the conversion symptom.

There is, incidentally, another reason why in the battle environment conversion reactions are not confined merely to individuals of hysterical temperament. It concerns the motivation of and situational constraints on the behaviour of the front-line soldier. Disciplined not to show lack of moral fibre but faced with the stress of battle, he may find it more acceptable to his conscious self to convert his fear into a 'respectable' bodily symptom than to display it openly and face his own and others' accusation of cowardice. Furthermore, it may actually be the more conscientious and conformist individuals – that is, those with dysthymic personality traits – who are likely to be plagued by a need to suppress their anxiety.

Piecing together these various ideas, then, we can see why it is that the nature of the stress and the psychological and situational factors surrounding it may at times be just as powerful a determinant of conversion reactions as the temperamental make-up of the individual in whom they occur. Of course the example of battle neurosis just quoted is still, fortunately, quite rare and the circumstances fairly extreme. Although cases found in civilian populations may sometimes be precipitated by broadly similar events – experiencing or witnessing accidents, for instance – the situation in other respects may be different: among other considerations the civilian faces fewer moralistic contraints on how he or she 'chooses' to respond to stress. This probably means that the prediposing personality is that much more important as a causal factor in conversion neuroses found among the general population.

Study of the connection between temperamental 'type' and conversion hysteria is made more difficult by the fact, referred to earlier, that the boundaries of the syndrome have often been widened to include other forms of 'hysterical' reaction in which the classically observed *loss* of function does not occur: on the contrary, the patient's symptoms are more often those of exaggerated psychosomatic reactions, such as pain or other physical discomfort. Here the underlying personality looms larger and it might almost be said that in these cases the individual's neurosis is more a chronic *disorder* of the personality than a discrete reaction to stress, as in the true conversion hysteric. The prominent features of such people are the tendency to externalise distress by producing imaginary bodily symptoms, continuing to complain of genuine, but usually minor, physical illness long after its real effects have disappeared, and adopting the sick role in order to gain sympathy or manipulate others. Many of these behaviours are driven by what has been called 'secondary gain' motivation, a phenomenon well-known to insurance brokers as compensation neurosis, in which the symptom disappears once the claim for damages is settled!

Certain of the characteristics just described may, incidentally, also be found in some cases of conversion reaction proper, especially those occurring in civilian populations, a fact which serves to underline an earlier point: that the boundaries between various manifestations of hysteria are not as sharp as, for illustrative purposes, I have had to draw them here. For there is no doubt that some patients with conversion symptoms do share a core of temperamental traits with other individuals whose hysterical aberration takes the more diffuse form of chronic personality disorder. It is merely that it is in the latter where we see the traits in question most clearly articulated.

Moving on from conversion hysteria in its narrow sense, the next questions we need to ask concern the explanation of those more florid abnormalities of behaviour associated with hysterical personality disorder. Can we, for example, account for them in a manner that is comparable to, or somehow parallel with, our explanations offered for the dysthymic states; that is, by finding a link between temperamental disposition and consequent behaviour? As we saw in the previous chapter, behaviourist psychology has been able to go some, if not all, of the way towards explaining phobias and other anxiety-based conditions by calling upon principles of learning and combining these with notions about the biology of temperament. How far can a similar approach help to account for hysterical disorders? In order to find the answer to these questions we need to go back to some of the ideas discussed in chapter 2, where we saw that biological differences in susceptibility to anxiety constitute only one of the dimensions of temperament that can be used to describe people. Two other, closely related, sets of characteristics are those associated with impulsivity and 'sensation seeking' on which, not unexpectedly, hysterical personalities tend to rate highly. These qualities can be said to explain several features of the hysteric's behaviour.

Consider the implications of being driven, as is the high sensation seeker, by a need for constant stimulation. Such a person will be inclined towards restleness, changeability, intolerance of boredom and the flamboyant behaviour that not only draws attention to the self but, in doing so, also offers fresh sources of excitement: in pathological form the exaggeration of minor bodily symptoms, or the creation of new ones, will scrve a similar purpose. Extreme sensation seeking can also explain what at first glance may seem a slightly puzzling aspect of the hysteric's personality, namely the tendency towards 'neuroticism', but in the absence of anxiety as we normally undersand it. Thus, hysterics are certainly neurotic, in the sense that they show great emotional lability, and they frequently rate themselves as such on questionnaires: they also often suffer from depression. But their 'anxiety' is often perceived by others as superficial and shallow, verbally expressed but largely unfelt. These features of hysteria can probably be explained as due to the consequences of having a nervous system that is chronically in a low state of arousal, which the constant seeking of sensation serves to try to put right. Such a state would be as subjectively unpleasant as the opposite, chronically high arousal experienced by the dysthymic and almost certainly contributes to the apparent neurotic make-up of the hysteric, especially the tendency towards 'depression' (though *ennui* might be a better term) when new sources of excitement are lacking.

The hysteric is also frequently referred to as having an immaturity of personality and it is indeed true that the traits just described are reminiscent of those seen in childhood. It therefore has to be asked how and why they persist, in some cases, into adulthood and are occasionally maintained so strongly that they lead to the formation of clinically neurotic symptoms of the kind seen in hysterical disorder. One reason is that the individuals in question are almost certainly of such extreme nervous type – in the direction of high sensation seeking – that normal environmental pressures do little to modify expression of the underlying biological predisposition. Added to this is the fact that the behaviour is often actively reinforced, both in childhood and into adulthood. Many of the traits seen in hysterical personalities are by no means unattractive. Such people are frequently spontaneous, vivacious, sociable creatures, responsive to others and able to elicit very positive reactions from those around them; and, as commonly noticed, they are often individuals of above average physical charm. Repeated positive reinforcement for behaviours which in childhood are considered delightful may establish an adult personality structure that is immature but which continues to be successful in allowing the individual to manipulate others, both inside and outside the psychiatric clinic.

Another characteristic that seems to go along with the personality traits just described is that of heightened suggestibility; which probably helps to explain why another form of hysteria referred to previously, epidemic or 'mass' hysteria, tends to affect the more hysterical members of the group in which it occurs. This was certainly found to be true in an epidemic of fainting that occurred some years ago in an English girls' school, where the pupils were later asked to complete a personality questionnaire[122]. It turned out that the girls who succumbed to the fainting attacks were more extraverted and more neurotic than average; showing, in other words, precisely the combination of traits commonly associated with hysterical personality. Of course, there are many other factors, related to group dynamics, that contribute to mass hysteria. We saw earlier that it tends to be especially prevalent in tightly knit communities. Relative isolation and the cohesiveness that may exist among certain members of such groups can provide a fertile breeding ground for contagious effects. The triggering event is often an esteemed member of the group developing what may actually be a genuine physical illness (or it can itself be 'hysterical'), the symptoms then spreading, through suggestion, to other individuals whose behaviour is easily influenced by that person. However, certain kinds of hysterical personality do seem to be more vulnerable in this regard, once the process has been set in motion.

As the astute reader will have gathered, if he (or she) did not realise already, the terms 'hysteria' and 'hysterical personality' have been more frequently associated with the female of the species! This may simply reflect diagnostic usage; for, employed in its most degraded form, the description 'hysterical' is more often applied by psychiatrists, most of whom are male, to their difficult female patients. Or it may indicate a genuine sex difference in the incidence of at least some manifestations of the condition; as indeed has been claimed for mass hysteria and for hysterical disorders characterised by chronic psycho-somatic symptoms overlaid with persistent complaining behaviour[198]. Even so, the question still remains as to whether this represents a genuine difference in biological predisposition or arises from other causes. It has been argued, for example, that cultural and social factors account for the greater observed frequency of hysterical reactions among women who, from an early age, are taught the passive, dependent role which provides a fertile soil for the development of traits like manipulativeness that form the hallmark of the hysterical personality[101]. However, if true, that would suggest that at a *biological* level a similar predisposition should also be represented among males, in their case merely finding a different behavioural and psychological expression.

Several considerations would support that conclusion. First, there is the fact that some male disorders of personality *are* referred to as 'hysterical': that is true even if we set aside conversion hysteria which, as we have seen, is something of a special case. Secondly, the traits associated with hysterical personality – impulsiveness, sociability, emotional lability and so on – are, for all intents and purposes, equally represented among males and females. The main difference is that in males such individuals are more often described as 'psychopathic' and the underlying temperamental characteristics more frequently observed as criminal propensities, which are fairly rare in women. This would indicate that the biological traits responsible for female hysteria are also present in males, but that in the latter they become manifest as more deliberate antisocial behaviour. Some support for that conclusion, incidentally, has recently come from evidence that there is a familial association between the occurrence of hysteria in women and of psychopathy in men[55].

Despite the evident overlap between hysteria and psychopathy, the latter does present some special problems. The description 'psychopathic' is an extraordinarily vague one and in its widest sense can be used to refer to any kind of antisocial behaviour, arising from whatever cause. Furthermore, psychopathy frequently, if not inevitably, involves breaking the statutory laws of society. Its definition therefore interwines psychiatric and legal criteria, a fact illustrated in the agonising that occurs over such questions as criminal responsibility and the admissibility of psychiatric evidence in court trials of individuals who may or may not be considered mentally unsound. A recent case in point is that of the so-called Yorkshire Ripper, who was found guilty of a series of horrific murders of women in the North of England. Although it was subsquently recognised that he had all along been suffering from paranoid schizophrenia (being driven to kill his victims by delusional religious beliefs), he was at the time of his trial judged to be a psychopath, and therefore fully responsible for his actions. The case is slightly unusual because it now seems that the original decision was swayed by an awareness of the public outrage that would almost certainly have followed had the court accepted a plea of insanity from a man who had terrorised the local populace for many months and who, despite the macabre nature of his acts, had apparently been cunning enough to evade capture. But it does illustrate the genuine bewilderment felt by the public at large – and the knots of illogicality that ravel legal decision-making – when faced with behaviour so bizarre as to evoke the instinctive response that the person committing it must be mad, yet simultaneously stirred by sentiments of retribution. The example just quoted is only one among many others (the annals of criminology are awash with such cases), in some of which the line between the psychotic and the psychopathic is even more difficult to draw.

It is perhaps worth noting at this point that the association between psychotic and antisocial behaviour is not confined to those more dramatic (and horrendous) instances of murder or other brutal crime where the courts are forced consciously to deliberate about the mental state of the accused and are persuaded sometimes to adopt the term 'psychopath' in order to justify letting the law take its proper course. It is also true that in many cases of more minor law-breaking mental illness and criminality are often confused. For example, a recent survey of inmates being kept on remand in an English women's prison demonstrated that nearly a third were suffering from serious psychiatric disorder – and had been at the time of their arrest; yet this had not been recognised by the courts disposing of them[177].

Evidence pointing in the same direction has come from a quite different quarter; namely, studies of personality guided by the kinds of theory on which we have drawn heavily in this book. I am referring here to the fact, already mentioned briefly in a previous chapter, that part of the normal personality structure is now known to consist of traits which in their extreme form are found in clinically psychotic individuals. The most fully developed version of this idea is to be found in Eysenck's demonstration that there is a major dimension of personality which, appropriately, he has labelled 'psychoticism'. Now, interestingly, the defining features of psychoticism are characteristics like social deviance, aggressiveness, lack of empathy for others, antisocial behaviour and so on. Not surprisingly, many psychopaths and other criminal or psychologically deviant individuals score highly on measures of psychoticism; so much so that it has sometimes been said that Eysenck has given the wrong name to the dimension – it would, so the argument goes, be better described as a dimension of *psychopathy*. The comment, however, misses the point: which is that the traits identified by Eysenck as defining his new dimension are *also* to be found occasionally in the psychotic as well. In other words, the results of work on basic temperamental dispositions exactly mirror the observations made in legal and psychiatric circles that some forms of psychopathy and some forms of psychosis are genuinely not easy to distinguish from each other.

It should be mentioned here that the above remarks raise some quite complicated issues which it is inappropriate to try and disentangle at this stage of the discussion. That will be attempted in later chapters. In the meantime it is worth making a very general point, first in order to clear away any misunderstanding to which our comments so far about psychopathy may have given rise and, secondly, in order to define the scope of our discussion in the remainder of this chapter. Although it certainly seems to be true that some expressions of antisocial behaviour rest on temperamental traits that can be considered genuinely 'psychotic', this does not mean that most clinically diagnosed psychotic patients, such as schizophrenics, are thereby necessarily more likely to be aggressive criminals: on the contrary, just the opposite is frequently the case. Nor, by the same token, does it follow that all individuals who are labelled 'psychopaths' are really psychotic. Indeed, as we shall see in a moment, it is possible to derive an explanation for some forms of psychopathic behaviour from ideas very similar to those already introduced to account for hysterical disorders.

Taking up that theme, it is clear that certain types of antisocial behaviour in men can be traced to the same traits of impulsivity and sensation seeking which drive women towards hysterical disorder. How, then, do we to explain the fact that among males it takes the different form of aggressiveness, law-breaking and so on? This largely depends on which of the two well-worn stances one takes on feminist arguments. The difference could be due to the fact that there is a greater tolerance, even encouragement, of assertive and aggressive behaviour in boys. Or it might reflect sex differences of biological origin, due to the allegedly stronger tendency for the male of the species to be 'naturally' more aggressive. Either way, seen in pathological form – whether as hysterical or as psychopathic disorder – the outward expression of this type of temperament is definitely different, even though the underlying traits seem common to both.

Although extreme impulsiveness and sensation seeking probably account – as a male equivalent to hysterical personality disorder – for some types of criminality, this is certainly not true in all cases. Indeed there is a further distinction to be made here in trying to explain psychopathic behaviour, a distinction that has not been brought out very clearly, if at all, in discussions of female hysteria. For reasons given earlier, the latter is frequently associated with high degrees of emotional lability, neuroticism, depression and other signs of instability which, we argued, probably stem from the unpleasant psychological and physiological state to which chronic lack of stimulation may give rise. These qualities are also characteristic of those male psychopathic individuals who share the same temperament. But there is a quite different combination of traits to be found in some psychopaths. These appear to reflect not a frantically neurotic search after stimulation, but rather an excessive *lack of anxiety*. In other words, some psychopaths seem to be people who are diametrically opposite in temperament to those fear-ridden persons discussed at length in the previous chapter.

It is these abnormally unanxious individuals who are considered by some writers to form a recognisably distinct group of *primary* psychopaths, quite different from psychopaths who are driven, secondarily as it were, to antisocial behaviour by their unstable personalities[33]. These primary psychopaths tend to show a distinctive profile of personality characteristics. While often sociable and outgoing, they are frequently not at all impulsive. Nor do they manifest neurotic traits: on the contrary, their marked lack of 'nervousness' is more often emphasised. Indeed, it is the latter that helps one to understand many of the intrinsic qualities of the primary psychopath: his unreliability; his lack of remorse, shame or guilt; his insincerity; his shallow interpersonal relationships; his tendency to respond to the here and now; and his failure to learn from experience.

A basic lack of anxiety in primary psychopaths can also be inferred from the results of experimental studies – of which there have been a great many – demonstrating that they show all of the expected signs of low physiological arousability, defective fear conditioning and so on[81]. In other words, they do indeed appear to occupy the opposite end of that dimension of 'anxiety' which we saw could account for part of the behaviour of the dysthymic neurotic. It will be recalled that the latter are thought to be the way they are because they are extremely sensitive to punishment, leading to them having strongly oversocialised, conscience-stricken personalities. In contrast, the primary psychopath's absence of conscience can be put down to his pathological *insensitivity* to punishment, observable even under laboratory conditions.

The most rounded explanation of how such experimental findings, and the theory that lies behind them, are related to the real-life behaviour of the psychopath has been offered by Trasler in a perceptive analysis of the psychology of social deviance. Trasler comments that the primary psychopath is the 'type case' of deviance, to be regarded as such because he strongly resists the normal process of social conditioning through which conscience and other internalised controls over behaviour develop. Central to Trasler's argument is the suggestion that this aspect of social conditioning is a matter of learning what behaviourist psychologists call 'passive avoidance responses'; that is, acquiring the ability to suppress or inhibit actions that are associated with punishment. What is important about the process is the extent to which it generalises to other elements outside the immediate situation in which punishment, and therefore anxiety, are experienced; in other words, how far the individual learns to respond to secondary cues which come to signal possible threat. In the human these secondary cues are usually mediated at a verbal or symbolic level and Trasler sees here a powerful mechanism whereby controls over potentially punishable or socially proscribed acts become internalised. Failure or weakness in the development of such *internal* controls will result, he argues, in behaviour being guided merely or more frequently by *external*, or situationally specific, controls. A relative predominance of the latter over the former could help to explain many features of primary psychopathy; or as he puts it:

> The notion of the balance of intrinsic and external controls – the extent to which the individual's behaviour is controlled by immediate environmental contingencies, as contrasted with processes that are distinct from and temporarily prior to the immediate situation – articulates several quite different observations by students of psychopathy. . . . . The opportunism, the callous 'maximization of personal advantage' and the extravagant overreaction of the primary psychopath; his carelessness of obligations and innocence of feelings of guilt and anticipatory anxiety, are readily subsumed within a model that emphasises the imbalance between situational and intrinsic controls over motivated behaviour[180].

Of course, as Trasler readily acknowledges, there are several reasons why an individual may show an apparent 'psychopathic' lack of social conscience. For example, he may simply have received inadequate parental guidance as a child. And this may take more than one form. In some instances he may have been brought up in what, superficially, appears to be a 'good' home, but indulged, not allowed to experience the punishment, frustration, and necessity to withold gratification that form the basis of later socialised behaviour. Alternatively, he may have been reared in a manifestly deprived environment, or even one that borders on a criminal subculture the rules of which he *has* successfully internalised; but those rules may be inappropriate to the wider social context in which he is forced to live. Many writers, especially those of a narrow sociological persuasion, would consider that the 'deprived environment' hypothesis provides the more comprehensive explanation of antisocial behaviour and that may indeed be true of a great deal of criminality. But environmental causes alone can certainly not account for it all. Otherwise it would be difficult to explain why occasionally certain quite grossly deviant individuals – recognisable as primary psychopaths and sharply distinguishable even from other members of the same family – emerge from an upbringing that is patently neither socially deprived nor psychologically neglectful. In these cases the more important element seems to be a temperamental disposition to resist the normal pressures towards socialisation.

Although the account given here of the behaviour of the hysterical and psychopathic disorders offers, I believe, a reasonably convincing explanation of those forms of aberration, it clearly does not go as far as we would like in trying to capture their more subtle psychological qualities. In making that remark I am, in a sense, echoing the caution of the previous chapter about the explanatory power of our current biological theories of temperament. Referring, as they do, to relatively low level brain structures and giving rise, as they often have, to predominantly behaviouristic explanations of disorder, such theories are necessarily limited in what they can tell us about the psychology of the kinds of disorder considered over the last few pages; just as that was true of the dysthymic states discussed earlier. To conclude our account here, therefore, it is worth reflecting briefly on some features of hysterical and psychopathic behaviour that remain difficult to explain. Let us do so by again taking as our example the case of the primary psychopath.

As we have just seen from Trasler's analysis, it is possible to trace a plausible thread from experimental evidence about the biological disposition of primary psychopaths (i.e. their low anxiety), through their consequent inability to learn fear motivated responses, up to their failure to acquire a social conscience. What is lacking, however, is a proper understanding of how the 'internalisation' of social rules to which he refers actually comes about. Trasler quite rightly emphasises the involvement of symbolic, or verbal, processes. Since these are mediated through the higher nervous system and since, as we have seen, present nervous typological theories are ill-equipped to deal with such events, there is an inevitable gap in our understanding of how the blueprint provided by the temperament of the psychopath gets translated into the psychological structure that forms his personality. The difficulty is similar to that encountered when trying to move from the purely temperamental aspects of the dysthymic disorders to an appreciation of those features of them which are uniquely human.

The problem just referred to is highlighted in the case of psychopathy by considering the kind of experimental evidence upon which Trasler, through no fault of his own (for that is where the emphasis in research has been) was forced to rely in formulating an explanation of the psychopath's lack of socialisation. The evidence in question has come mainly from studies that have tried to set up laboratory situations in which the psychopath's unresponsiveness to punishment can be investigated. Very frequently, following a long tradition in experimental psychology, the conditions employed have involved eliciting anxiety responses to stimuli of an entirely non-social kind, usually the threat of mild electric shock. And, usefully, it has been shown that psychopaths are indeed chronically retarded in their ability to learn responses which require them to anticipate anxiety consequent upon such punishment. But what about other kinds of punishment that are closer to those encountered in real life? There is some evidence – from looking at what happens to the psychopath's behaviour when the threat he faces is, say, loss of a financial reward – that he is perfectly capable of learning an appropriate response to avoid punishment[50]. In other words, notwithstanding the fact that the psychopath has a basic insensitivity to punishment, the way this disposition comes to be elaborated so as to guide his real-life behaviour clearly depends on psychological processes – in this case concerned with the perceived social significance of money – that are quite distant from those mechanisms which in a purely biological sense may account for his temperament.

There is other evidence, too, suggesting that the psychopath is quite able – and willing – to act in ways which, on the face of it, seem to contradict his temperamental disposition. For example, a typical trait found in psychopathy is said to be an inability to delay gratification of pleasure. Yet it is known that the psychopath is actually no different from anyone else in being able, on occasions, to withold getting immediate satisfaction[196]. The point is that he will do so when it suits his own purpose and it is this capacity of the psychopath to internalise *his own set of rules* that constitutes one of his most intriguing qualities. For the psychopath is all things to all men, supremely flexible in his behaviour, able to change as the situation demands, a chameleon altering his emotional colouring to suit the needs of those around him – though always through motives that serve himself best. Such is the adaptability of the psychopath that some writers have been driven to comment that the traits he possesses have immense social, even biological, utility, when occurring in subclinical form[138]. And it is indeed true that provided he – and his female equivalent, the hysterical personality – keep on the right side of the law, they are usually highly successful in many walks of life. Here, more than anywhere else in the study of psychopathology, do we find the division between normality and abnormality very difficult to draw.

Finally, looking back over the last two chapters it is clear that none of the disorders discussed can be properly accounted for unless we take some account of the temperamental dispositions from which each emerges. Of course, as we have just seen in the case of psychopathy, there are many missing links in our attempt to trace the chain of events connecting temperament to disorder. These mainly occur at points where we are forced to abandon behaviouristic views of Man in favour of explanations that focus more on mental mechanisms and, simultaneously with that, on the higher nervous system. Bridging the gaps (where this has seemed possible) has not been made easier by the fact that, even in normal psychology, let alone psychopathology, the points of contact between different explanations are not all that obvious: the languages in which they are formulated are often quite distinct from one another and adherents of the various viewpoints frequently make little reference to those adopted by others. Despite these obstructions the discussion so far has perhaps served to illustrate the essential correctness of the model of mental disorder outlined in chapter 1: that, like the physical systemic diseases, psychological illnesses do seem to proceed from, and involve an elaboration of, biological dispositions that are recognisable in normal individuals as temperamental differences. In pursuing that idea so far we have concentrated on *mild* forms of disorder. In the next chapter we shall begin the somewhat more intricate task of examining the serious, psychotic diseases from a similar point of view.

7

A View of Madness

So far this book has followed the arrangement of first examining the biological characteristics underlying the major forms of non-psychotic illness, then going on to look at how the predispositions which these represent issue in different types of disorder. In the next two chapters we shall proceed the other way round. There are good reasons for adopting this different strategy in the case of the psychotic disorders. Although a *biological* approach to the latter is widely supported, a *dimensional* perspective on them – the idea that they have some continuity with normal behaviour – is more controversial: indeed it would be rejected by a large part of the psychiatric establishment. Those 'antipsychiatrists', like Laing and Szasz, who do accept the principle of dimensionality for the psychoses – in the sense that for them the whole notion of 'psychological disease' is anathema – at the same time ignore biological factors in aetiology. A view of the psychoses which combines *both* dimensional *and* biological aspects – similar, in other words, to that taken of other disorders already considered – therefore requires special arguments. These can best be constructed by proceeding in the way outlined: by discussing disorder first and then going on to examine where, in normal behaviour, the dispositions to illness lie.

The fact that we need to adopt this form of presentation is itself a sign of the dispute that exists about the origins of psychotic behaviour, reflected in the bitter conflicts between psychiatrists and antipsychiatrists, between disease and anti-disease theorists. This in turn stems from the very nature of the psychoses themselves. Depending on one's focus, they can intuitively appear to be quite set apart from normal experience or merely look like an unusually extreme derivative of it; an apparent sign of gross brain dysfunction or simply a psychological reaction of excessive proportion. In keeping with the approach adopted to other disorders, the perspective to be taken here does, I believe, encompass all of these features, without doing violence to the conception of mental illness as disease, outlined in chapter 1. At the same time it must be recognised that the psychotic states *are* peculiar in many ways and that for some readers it may not be immediately obvious how the bizarre qualities of disorders like schizophrenia can derive from underlying characteristics that are essentially continuous, in some respects, with normal biology and psychology. Hence the intention, in this chapter, to try to impart something of the flavour of the clinical syndromes and of the ideas that have grown up from experimental evidence about them, before returning, in the next chapter, to questions relating to disposition and normal personality.

The discussion will be principally concerned with schizophrenia, a disorder − or set of disorders − which, among the psychoses, has received most attention from clinicians, theoreticians and experimentalists, and which, significant for our argument here, has formed the main platform of debate about the disease issue in psychiatry. However, the term 'psychotic' has been used as a descriptor for other forms of severe disorder that we came across briefly in chapter 5. At the risk of repeating part of that account it may be helpful to start by looking at the way psychiatrists classify psychoses in general. This is important because it will help to provide a background against which to examine issues that we shall eventually need to confront; such as the relatedness or distinctiveness of different forms of psychosis, and the possibility or otherwise of their having a common predisposition.

Excluding organic psychoses, due either to some traceable pathophysiology in the brain itself or to some physical bodily change − for example hormonal imbalance − that indirectly upsets the central nervous system, we are left with a group of illnesses which involve a quite severe disruption of behaviour and psychological experience but appear to have no obvious structural basis. To these disorders psychiatrists have usually attached the somewhat euphemistic label 'functional', a term that has been variously intepreted: that there is some pathophysiology, probably microscopic, yet to be discovered; that neurophysiology and neurochemistry are irrelevant to the understanding of such disorders; or that biological disturbance does occur but cannot by itself entirely explain the psychotic behaviour. Either way, further subdivision of these 'functional psychoses' relies, as elsewhere in psychiatry, on gathering together groups of signs and symptoms that seem frequently to cluster together. Although arbitrary and overlapping to a considerable degree, these groups nevertheless form the syndromes on which a necessary working classification of the psychoses is based.

We have already briefly come across one subcategory of serious disorder, namely the affective psychoses, further subdivisible into psychotic (or endogenous) depression and manic-depressive psychosis − or, as some psychiatrists would prefer to call them, 'unipolar' and 'bipolar' forms of affective illness. From a descriptive point of view there are two reasons why these affective illnesses are considered psychotic and therefore distinguishable from *neurotic* disorders of mood. First, the emotional shift associated with the former is simply more severe, often to the point where it appears to be qualitatively distinguishable from a normal change in mood. And, secondly, they are accompanied by other symptoms that are distinctly unusual, including gross changes in motor activity and in the form and content of thought and speech. The profoundly depressed person will move and talk very slowly and may express ideas that are delusional in nature. These delusions may be hypochondriacal – for example that the body is riddled with cancer or being eaten away by worms – or they may be pervaded by feelings of guilt that go beyond the bounds of rationality, perhaps extending to the belief that the individual is responsible for all of world's social and political ills. The manic person shows the opposite features. He is restless, quick and impulsive to act, and his rapid talk expresses frequently changing trains of thought that are sometimes difficult to follow. In this case delusional ideas will reflect the manic individual's supreme optimism and grandiose beliefs about himself, beliefs that may lead him to undertaken wildly improbable schemes that are far beyond his capacity or financial resources and which, if thwarted by others, may cause him to become irritated and paranoid.

Psychotic states in which the affective element predominates are relatively easy to define. However, schizophrenia – by far the most common form of functional psychosis – has proved more difficult. A major problem is deciding on the exact boundaries of the condition, a fact reflected in the variety of ways in which psychiatrists of different schools of thought use the term 'schizophrenic' in their clinical practice. This was clearly brought out some years ago in the results of the now widely quoted US/UK Diagnostic Project, in which a comparison was made of the frequency with which a group of New York psychiatrists, and a group of pschiatrists in London, diagnosed schizophrenia. The Americans tended to do so about twice as often as their British counteparts[36].

The narrower view of schizophrenia that has prevailed in Britain, and in most of the rest of Western Europe, is undoubtedly due to the strong emphasis placed there on what the psychiatric writer Kurt Schneider called 'symptoms of the first rank'. These are certain sorts of very unusual experience reported by some psychotic individuals. They include auditory hallucinations of a particular kind – for example, a voice giving a running commentary on the person's behaviour – and bizarre delusions, such as the feeling of being controlled by an alien force. Many psychiatrists will insist that the diagnosis of schizophrenia cannot be made unless at least one of these first-rank symptoms is present. However, some doctors, taking a broader view of the condition, would diagnose schizophrenia in cases where, even in the absence of such symptoms, other signs of abnormality are present, such as grossly incoherent or illogical speech, marked loosening of the association of ideas, and strange, inappropriate emotional reactions. And finally, extending the concept of schizophrenia even further, there are some clinicians, trained in the psychoanalytic tradition – which, of course, is especially strong in the United States – who would base their diagnosis on an evaluation of the patient's psychic structure, in terms of the person's sense of personal identity and the extent to which the boundaries of the self-concept have disintegrated. Aware of these differences in usage, psychiatry has in recent years tried to arrive at some agreed criteria for defining schizophrenia, partly by carrying out co-operative research studies on an international scale. An example was the US/UK Diagnostic Project mentioned a moment ago. A follow-up to that exercise was the International Pilot Study of Schizophrenia, or IPSS, a project that is worth considering in a little detail here because the results obtained from it illustrate very well both the success and the failure of psychiatrists to agree on what they mean by schizophrenia[200].

The study in question was designed to test the usefulness of employing a standard interview procedure, the Present State Examination (PSE), and basing diagnosis on a common set of defining criteria. The latter had been established in earlier research by the originators of the PSE, using a computer programme to identify clusters of symptoms that seemed reliably to describe a syndrome of schizophrenia. (It is worth noting at this point that, the PSE being of British origin, the system was heavily weighted towards first-rank symptoms of the kind described earlier.) The IPSS itself involved collaboration between nine psychiatric centres across the world – from the USSR to the USA – comparisons being made between the clinicians' 'local' diagnoses of their patients and those arrived at by the computer on the basis of PSE ratings of the same individuals. It turned out that agreement between the two methods was very good in the case of certain patients; namely those suffering from what was clearly recognisable, both by the computer and by psychiatrists, as a 'nuclear' form of schizophrenia, characterised by first-rank symptoms, such as hallucinations. This suggested, in other words, that clinicians throughout the world can reliably identify *one* kind of disorder that should be called schizophrenic.

Taken as a whole, however, the results of the study revealed quite considerable disagreement when it came to assessing the whole range of patients who might conceivably to regarded as suffering from schizophrenia. For example, a very large number – nearly 50 per cent – of patients who were not judged by the computer as meeting the criteria for the nuclear syndrome were nevertheless considered by their local psychiatrists to be schizophrenic. In some cases the discrepancy was quite marked. One example was the American centre – in this instance Washington – where the broader concept of schizophrenia previously encountered in New York again prevailed. Another was Moscow, where the term 'schizophrenia' is also used to cover a wide range of psychotic disorder, of varying severity.

The findings of the IPSS therefore have a double-edged significance. On the one hand, it is clear that if the boundaries of schizophrenia are drawn tightly enough and the criteria used to define it are very narrow then it is possible to identify a disorder whose features most people can agree on: these seem to consist, as we have noted, of certain, very peculiar symptoms, which even the layman would recognise as 'mad'. On the other hand, exercises like the IPSS are deceptively self-fulfilling, for they still fail to answer the question of what should properly be called schizophrenic. It is, after all, impossible to ignore the fact that two major world centres of psychiatry use the term in a different way from that specified by a computer programme, the rules of which have been built in beforehand! Furthermore, the PSE structured interview used in the study represents only one of a number of attempts to arrive at an objective set of features for describing schizophrenia. None has been entirely successful; or, as one review of the many attempts that have been made, gloomily concluded, 'they are all, in a sense, arbitrary'[51].

The reason for this, we shall argue here, is partly because of certain unique features that are intrinsic to the psychotic nervous system and partly because schizophrenia conforms to the model of disease outlined in chapter 1, showing a genuine continuity of behaviour, blending into a spectrum of illness which may manifest itself in varying degrees of disorder; thus making it virtually impossible to delineate an all-or-none category – except, of course, at the very extreme where some degree of discontinuity does become apparent. Any attempt to convey the quality of schizophrenia, on the basis of its clinical features, is therefore bound to be something of a compromise between the very narrow description of its most severe form and a characterisation that is so broad as to obscure some of its essential features.

Looked at from a diagnostic standpoint, probably the most informative description of schizophrenia is that contained in the latest revision of the psychiatric glossary (DSM-III) compiled by the American Psychiatric Association[40]. Even this, shown below, has been considered by some psychiatrists to be too restricted: indeed, it demonstrates an interesting recent shift in the 'official' American view towards the narrower conception of schizophrenia preferred in Western Europe. But it does, better than most, bring out the range of

clinical features that, in some measure, can be found in patients who
are diagnosed as schizophrenic. It also mirrors quite well the variety of
psychological dysfunctions which research workers in many disciplines, and for most of this century, have been trying to explain.

DSM-III Diagnostic Criteria for Schizophrenic Disorder

A   At least one of the following during a phase of the illness:

1 bizarre delusions (content is patently absurd and has *no*
   possible basis in fact), such as delusions of being controlled,
   thought broadcasting, thought insertion, or thought withdrawal
2 somatic, grandiose, religious, nihilstic, or other delusions
   without persecutory or jealous content
3 delusions with persecutory or jealous content, if accompanied
   by hallucinations of any type
4 auditory hallucinations in which either a voice keeps a running
   commentary on the individual's behaviour or thoughts, or two
   or more voices converse with each other
5 auditory hallucinations on several occasions with content of
   more than one or two words, having no apparent relation to
   depression or elation
6 incoherence, marked loosening of associations, markedly
   illogical thinking, or marked poverty of content of speech if
   associated with at least one of the following:
   (a) blunted, flat, or inappropriate affect
   (b) delusions or hallucinations
   (c) catatonic or other grossly disorganised behaviour

B   Deterioration from a previous level of functioning in such
areas as work, social relations, and self-care.

C   Duration: Continuous signs of the illness for at least six
months at some time during the person's life, with some signs of
the illness at present. The six-month period must include an
active phase during which there were symptoms from A, with or
without a prodromal or residual phase.

The working description of schizophrenia shown here relies on
several different kinds of criterion, including well-recognised symptoms (hallucinations, delusional ideas, incoherent thinking and so on),
signs of change in the person's day-to-day functioning, and details of
his or her history of illness. The untidy nature of schizophrenia is
also revealed, since only one of a very disparate set of core symptoms –

and that symptom need not be of a 'first-rank' type – is necessary for the individual to be diagnosed as schizophrenic. Nevertheless, each of the symptoms in question does represent a distinctively psychotic aberration of mental activity.

Having examined the clinical features by which the psychiatrist recognises schizophrenia, let us now look, from the viewpoint of the psychological processes responsible for them, at where the disorders of function lie. Actually, in varying degrees *every* aspect of mental life and behaviour can be threatened, encompassing all of the things which in normal psychology we susbsume under such headings as personality, emotion, intellectual activity and social relations. To appreciate this fact there is no substitute for reading not the case-histories quoted by professional psychiatrists, but the autobiographical accounts written by schizophrenics themselves. There are now hundreds of these, stretching back many centuries: Peterson, in a fascinating book entitled *A Mad Peoples' History of Madness*, has collated just a few, which at one and the same time reveal the changing preoccupations of the psychotic mind throughout the ages, as well as the common thread of mental aberration that seems to run through all schizophrenic experiences[133].

In a somewhat different context, the Scottish psychiatrist James Chapman some twenty years ago made an important contribution to our understanding of the psychology of schizophrenia, in a classic paper in which he described in detail the reported introspections of some of his own patients[20]. One important point which Chapman makes, and which will be referred to several times here, concerns the distinction that has be drawn, in understanding schizophrenia, between those primary features of psychological experience that form the psychotic state itself and those aspects which constitute the individual's secondary reaction, or adaptation, to it. As many of Chapman's patients reported, among the primary experiences one of the most basic is an alteration in simple sensation and perception. The most obvious example is the 'hearing of voices' suffered by some schizophrenics; but changes may also occur in other modalities, including disturbances in the visually perceived world. Referring to the latter, one of Chapman's patients described his own experience as follows: 'I was sitting listening to another person and suddenly the other person became smaller and then larger and then he seemed to get smaller again. . . . . There is a brightness and clarity of outline of things around me.'

Such changes as these are closely connected to disturbances in the attentive process, many schizophrencs reporting that the sensory apparatus is 'flooded' with stimulation, a phenomenon which, at a higher level of mental functioning, translates into an experience of too many *ideas* coming into the mind at once, leaving the person unable to organise a consecutive train of thought. Occasionally, however, the opposite may happen and the person describes having *no* thoughts, as though the head were an empty vessel.

Not surprisingly language, the vehicle of thought, is often disorganised, speech being incoherent and the ideas expressed illogical and tangential to the theme of conversation. But this may not always be the case. Sometimes the structural form of the person's language may be normal, but the content bizarre, the person lucidly expounding a well-thought out and coherently organised set of beliefs, usually of a persecutory nature. These delusional ideas, while logically watertight, are based on an initially false premise, often derived from a misperception of some external event that is wrongly intepreted as personally significant. Here we see an example of a primary experience giving rise, secondarily, to a disruption of thinking that comes about because the schizophrenic, in this case, is trying to formulate for himself a rational explanation of his peculiar sense data. Once set in motion such beliefs are frequently maintained by an unusual degree of selective perception which causes the individual to seek, and inevitably find, confirmation of his ideas, pushing him further and further into madness. A famous historic example is the case of Daniel Schreber, a turn of the century high-ranking German advocate whose account of his own 'nervous illness' illustrates how the most bizarre beliefs, stemming originally from his attempt to find reasons for extraordinary body-image and other sensory distortions, can be sustained with a perfect sense of logic and apparent rationality[107].

An important sign of the schizophrenic's disturbance lies of course in his emotional reactions, which may range over extremes of anxiety, elation, anger and, paradoxically, indifference. Often it is difficult to tell how far these alterations in affective response are primary, or secondary to changes in other psychological functions, such as attention or perception. Sometimes they certainly appear to be reactions to the fact that the outside world seems physically distorted, causing anxiety or – as was the case with one of Chapman's patients – a sense of elation. On other occasions they seem to occur as irrational and sudden changes in mood, inexplicable both to the person and to an observer. Often, however, it is almost impossible to disentangle the emotional from the cognitive in schizophrenia: they are so interwined. Indeed, it was the 'splitting' or separation from each other of these two important areas of psychological functioning – the dissociation of the affective and the intellectual part of mental life – which Eugen Bleuler considered to be the central characteristic of schizophrenia and which caused him first to coin that name to describe the disorder.

Individually, all of the psychological processes that are deranged in schizophrenia have, at one time or another, come under research scrutiny, giving rise to a vast experimental literature on the disease and a matching number of explanations. The problem has been to find a unifying theme that can encompass all facets of schizophrenia: the primary disorders of perception and attention; the secondary reactions of delusional thinking and coping strategies of social withdrawal; a clinical manifestation which, despite a common thread of similarity, is as varied as the sufferer's individuality; and, last but not least, an inherent variability or unpredictability of function that has made consistent findings about schizophrenia often difficult to obtain.

Some – indeed currently the most popular – form of research on schizophrenia has, in essence, tried to side-step many of these issues by going straight to the question of 'cause', usually conceptualised as some discrete underlying abnormality of brain function, either structural or neurochemical, and having little or no reference point in normal psychology or normal neurophysiology. According to that view, the psychological and interpersonal disabilities of schizophrenia can, in effect, be merely regarded as epiphenomena, events which 'trail behind' the organic aetiology, certainly of some interest to the novelist – even, in the case of their social consequences, of vital therapeutic concern – but of little relevance for the medical researcher.

The position to be adopted here is, of course, quite different. We shall argue that the problem of understanding schizophrenia reduces to a similar set of questions to those asked about other, less severe, disorders. This means that the kinds of thing we need to enquire about are whether there are particular psychological and biological traits, represented as a 'type of nervous system' to be found generally in the population and predisposing certain individuals to schizophrenia; what, given that this may be true, are the nature and origins of such characteristics; and whether, comparably with milder forms of mental aberration, we can suggest some way in which disposition gets transformed into illness. Most of these topics will be taken up in the next chapter. First it is necessary to see whether, for schizophrenia itself, it is possible to arrive at a 'conceptual nervous system', a view of how the psychotic brain, when ill, might work and whether in that exaggerated form it might nevertheless be seen to contain certain inherent features that could, plausibly, describe ways in which some normal brains function.

Needless to say, it would be impossible to give a complete answer to the last question. All we can do is to draw out some of the more important themes in the experimental literature on schizophrenia in order to show how, when they are taken in conjunction with the ideas to be presented in the following chapter, a continuity view of psychotic behaviour becomes not just feasible but the most probable explanation of currently available evidence. The kind of facts with which we shall be concerned are very similar, in form, to those quoted in our discussions of less serious disorder. That is to say, they include evidence about the psychophysiology and neuropsychology of the psychotic patient, as well as data from studies of thinking, attention, perception and other traditional concerns of experimental psychology. The models formulated to explain these findings mirror the quality and variety of the empirical data, some being quite narrowly focussed micro-theories designed to account for limited features of schizophrenia; while others have been more ambitious in scope. They have also varied in the extent to which they have made direct reference to the nervous system, some explicitly doing so, others being couched in the language of the 'black-box' theories beloved by experimental psychologists. Even to the expert eye trying to survey all of these studies together their results sometimes look like a jumble of pieces from a mammoth jigsaw – and many of the bits, we can be sure, are missing. It will therefore be helpful here if, initially, we proceed in an historical fashion, since this will make it easier to show how the view of schizophrenia to be offered here represents an attempt to synthesise a set of accumulated ideas, some of which have emerged, disappeared, and re-emerged in different guises over many years of research effort.

Attempts to establish an 'experimental psychopathology' of schizophrenia properly began at the end of the last century when a number of workers, mostly clinicians on the continent of Europe, applied to the measurement of abnormal states some of the techniques of the newly emerging discipline of experimental psychology. A notable example was Kraepelin, the father of modern psychiatric classification and the first person to use the term 'dementia praecox' to describe the disorder which Eugen Bleuler was later to rename 'schizophrenia'. Another was Charles Féré, a French physician who, as the discoverer of the galvanic skin response, provided psychophysiologists with an experimental tool which, as we have seen, continues to be widely used in research on mental disorder: schizophrenia is no exception. And Jung, better known now as the founder of analytical psychology, in his early career, while an enthusiastic apprentice to Bleuler at the Burghölzli Hospital in Zurich, made pioneering contributions towards our understanding of schizophrenic thinking by administering word association and reaction time tests to his psychotic patients.

Later work in the same tradition, conducted now mainly by experimental or clinical psychologists, continued through the first half of this century. As a result, a considerable amount of information was gathered about the behaviour of schizophrenics on many types of laboratory task, designed to tap particular features of their psychological dysfunction: for example, primary sensor and perceptual experiences reported by schizophrenics, such as visual distortions, were found to be easily captured as disturbances in the constancy effects that normally help the individual to maintain a stable view of the world. Particular interest was paid, however, to what was considered by many to be the central deficit in schizophrenia, or at least as having the widest connotation for understanding the rest of the disorder; namely the disturbance of *attention*, or, to put it in more contemporary psychological jargon, 'information processing'.

Studies of attention in schizophrenia were conducted from several different points of view, but by the 1960s they came increasingly under the influence of the theory of attention put forward in normal psychology by Broadbent[10]. His suggestion that the processing of information flowing into the nervous system is critically dependent upon the operation of a central filtering mechanism was quickly applied to the study of attentional *disorder* and even found confirmation in the subjective reports of some schizophrenics, one of whom wrote at the time: 'So the mind must have a filter. . . sorting out stimuli and allowing only those which are relevant to the situation into consciousness. . . What happened to me was a breakdown in the filter. . .'[109]

A great deal of empirical research, using this filter model as a guideline, helped to demonstrate that schizophrenics do indeed have difficulties on tasks which capitalise on the need to screen out distracting stimuli or divide their attention – for example when being required to process information listened to with one ear, while ignoring that presented to the other ear[115].

Contemporaneously with that work on attention, the same filter theory was adopted as an explanation for another, closely related, schizophrenic characteristic – the disorder of the thought processes. Of particular interest here was that aspect of thinking seen clinically as cognitive 'slippage', tangential thought, the inability of schizophrenics to follow a coherent theme, and their apparent difficulty in maintaining a tight boundary for their abstract concepts. Historically, such phenomena were regarded as evidence for the schizophrenic's 'overinclusiveness', an idea which in its opposite form – 'overexclusiveness' – we have already seen has been used as one explanation for obsessional thinking. The term itself goes back to the 1930s, but the idea behind it became especially popular with the advent of filter theories of attention which, it was considered, might also explain overinclusive thinking; on the grounds that the latter represents at a higher mental level – the ordering of *ideas* – a similar disability in information processing[132].

It will be evident that 'defective filter' accounts of information processing were attempting to explain the phenomenon of sensory and ideational 'flooding', the experience reported by many schizophrenics,

especially in the early stages of illness, of being constantly over-
whelmed by internal and external stimulation. A somewhat different
approach, being pursued in parallel, was concerned more with the
active features of attention, the aim here being to explain why
schizophrenics, in their deliberate monitoring of the environment,
show pecularities in the way they selectively process information.
Again the ideas utilised were adopted from normal psychology – in this
case the psychology of individual differences in 'cognitive style'. The
main proponent of this viewpoint, Silverman, argued on the basis of a
good deal of experimental evidence that schizophrenics do seem to
have a distinctive style of cognitive processing; as judged, for example,
by the way they scan the environment (reflected in the pattern of their
eye movements) and the degree to which they 'articulate' stimuli, that is
bring clearly into the focus of attention certain features of the visually
scanned field[159].

As a separate tradition in schizophrenia research, there also evolved
during the same period a school of thought that rested more on data of
a psychophysiological kind. It sought explanations of schizophrenia in
terms of ideas like 'arousal' and was therefore explicitly committed to
the problem of trying to devise a conceptual nervous system model for
the disorder, couched in physiological language. Hundreds of
experiments, inspired by this approach, put beyond reasonable doubt
the fact that schizophrenics do show a wide range of physiological
peculiarities, whether judged by the EEG, or from bodily signs of
emotional reactivity, such as galvanic skin response, heart rate,
pupillary reactions, and muscle tension[163]. The problem, to which I
will return, was to find a consistency among them, when taken as a
whole. The same can be said to be true of the other types of research
considered earlier, all of which occasionally demonstrated quite gross
abnormalities in schizophrenia, but unpredictably, offering a tantalis-
ing though frustratingly incomplete glimpse of the psychotic nervous
system.

The different lines of enquiry into schizophrenia summarised above
(it actually represented a massive research effort) reached a noticeable
turning-point in the mid-1960s; which happened to coincide with the
publication of an important paper by Venables, himself one of the
foremost contributors to the field[184]. As well as reviewing in detail the
many psychological and psychophysiological experiments that had
been undertaken up to that time on schizophrenia, Venables tried to
find a unifying theme which could describe the great variety of
abnormalities that could be observed in the disorder. He came up with
the term 'input dysfunction' which, imprecise though it is, seemed to
capture, for those experimentalists familiar with the clinical symptoms
of schizophrenia, the impression it imparts of the psychotic state as one

of chaotic interaction between the person and his environment, manifest in swings of physiological arousal, fluctuating attention, disordered mood, distorted perceptions of reality, and patterns of thought and language that disrupt social communication.

In the same paper Venables also drew attention to an extremely important fact that has bedevilled attempts to understand schizophrenia and which at this point we need to bring into the forefront of our discussion. I am referring to the extraordinary variability that is almost always observed in the behaviour of schizophrenics, on whatever measure the experimentalist chooses to study. Given such variability, it has often been the case that results reported by one investigator cannot be replicated by another, despite the use of the same experimental procedure; or, more significantly (since the latter is an experience not unknown in psychological research!), the group of schizophrenics included in a particular study shows a massive degree of statistical variance, some individuals being very low and some very high on the measure under scrutiny. There are at least three, not entirely unrelated, ways in which this phenomenon can be explained. In order to appreciate these – and, at the same time, see how more sophisticated conceptual system models might be evolved – we need to move on now to more recent research on schizophrenia, which has nevertheless carried on the same tradition as that already outlined.

One explanation offered for the variability referred to is that it demonstrates the existence of different *types* of schizophrenia. A great deal of schizophrenia research has been, and to some extent still is, guided by this interpretation, attempts being made to try and establish subgroups of patients who might differ in some important respect on measures of arousal, thinking, attentional style, or whatever is of interest to the investigator. Here Venables himself, with his colleague Gruzelier, made an important contribution, based on some elegant experiments using the galvanic skin response to study the same phenomena of orienting to novel stimuli and habituation that we came across in our earlier discussions of neurotic anxiety. The reason for Venables's choice of experimental technique was that the orienting reaction provides a microcosm for attention, offering a precise physiological model of it. Not unexpectedly, in view of the evidence that has been obtained using cruder measures of attention, Venables and his colleagues found that schizophrenics also show abnormalities in simple orientation to a novel stimulus and in the extent to which they adapt if the stimulus is presented repeatedly. Particularly significant, however, was the fact that some schizophrenics reacted *excessively* to the stimulus and thereafter failed to adapt to it; whereas other patients were quite *unresponsive*, even when the stimulus was new to them. Subsequent enquiry demonstrated that the physiological status of the patients corresponded to some extent with their clinical symptoms, schizophrenics who were classified as 'responders' being rated as more anxious, manic and hostile, and regarded as perhaps belonging to a different subgroup of schizophrenia from the very unreactive individuals[77].

Offering an explanation for these findings, Venables suggested that they provide evidence for an involvement in schizophrenia of the limbic system, a part of the brain which we have already seen probably accounts for some important features of other forms of psychological abnormality. Emphasising its role in schizophrenia, Venables pointed to the fact that, during attention, different parts of the limbic system act in a reciprocal fashion to 'gate-in' and 'gate-out' stimuli and that, at a psychological level, this might correspond to a variation in 'openness' or 'closedness' to the environment[185]. According to this view, therefore, in some schizophrenic individuals the mechanism might be permanently switched to an 'open' mode, allowing many stimuli into the nervous system and giving rise to psychotic symptoms of a more paranoid, emotionally reactive kind. In other cases the opposite may be true, the person being psychologically and physiologically shut-off from his surroundings, the signs of psychosis being those of social withdrawal and emotional blunting.

Another explanation of the variability observed in schizophrenia – and one which does not negate that just considered – would, however, place more emphasis on the *time-course* of the illness. Like many illnesses schizophrenia has a progressive nature and may vary in its manifestation at different periods in the individual's life: it is also to some extent self-limiting. The most evident sign of this is the transition, in some cases, from acute to chronic states. Part of the variability observed can therefore probably be put down to the fact that the schizophrenic's nervous system gradually adapts to the upheavals associated with the acute phase of illness, a change mirrored in an altered clinical symptomatology. To give an example, the phenomenon of sensory 'flooding' in schizophrenia which the early attention theories were intended to explain – and which can be said to correspond to Venables' idea of 'openness' – is mainly characteristic of acute psychotic reactions. In chronic states the opposite seems, if anything, to be true, the schizophrenic's mode of attention shifting more to what Venables characterised as 'gating-out' of stimuli.

It is interesting to note here, incidentally, the very similar conclusion reached by Silverman, mentioned earlier in connection with his work on schizophrenic attention from the viewpoint of theories about cognitive style. He particularly emphasised the fact that differing stages of psychotic illness are accompanied by alterations in the way the schizophrenic monitors his environment. Silverman suggested, for example, that states of chronic withdrawal represent an excessive narrowing of attention, occurring as a defensive manoeuvre against threatening or otherwise intense stimulation. Relating this idea more directly to the brain, he further argued that a possible physiological mechanism might be that responsible for the 'augmenting-reducing' effect which we have already encountered several times before in various contexts. Silverman's suggestion was later taken up by several investigators, some of whom have demonstrated that schizophrenics do indeed show rather deviant modes of responding when judged with techniques, like augmenting-reducing, where the strength of the sensory stimulus is progressively varied[97].

A third perspective on variability, and one which I believe offers a particularly important clue to our understanding of schizophrenia, is that it is itself an *intrinsic* feature of the psychotic nervous system. In other words, I would suggest that the reason schizophrenics are like they are is partly because their nervous systems are inherently unstable or unregulated, unable *consistently* to respond in the integrated fashion that is necessary for normal functioning; whether this is evaluated as physiological lability, or looked at from the point of view of the schizophrenic's ability to mobilise resources during attention, or judged by the manner in which thought is organised. Let me explain how I came to this conclusion.

In order to do so it is necessary to go back to some ideas, first introduced in chapter 2, about how conceptual nervous system theorists have visualised the way in which the brain works in different individuals, and the kinds of property that describe those variations. A difference in arousability, it will be recalled, is certainly one such property. But we also emphasised the fact that most attempts to construct a conceptual nervous system contain the notion of *homeostasis*, the idea that regulating mechanisms in the brain help to constrain it, keeping arousal within certain bounds as well as maintaining an orderly configuration of activity. This homeostatic property has normally been construed as a negative feedback loop between different parts of the brain, and to involve active inhibitory processes. It may also be recalled that application of such models to personality (and to disorders like anxiety) has generally made use of the idea that different people have different 'setting-points' for the homeostat, thus allowing for individual variations in arousal without serious disruption of the brain's activity – since, in cases of very high arousability, there will normally be a matching degree of inhibitory control.

The conclusion I reached some years ago was that a crucial feature of the psychotic brain may be a loosening, or relative failure, of its homeostatic regulation, possibly due to a weakening of inhibitory mechanisms, which causes the nervous system to 'overshoot' the acceptable levels of arousal necessary for its normal functioning[22, 29]. The evidence on which this idea was based came originally from a series of investigations of the psychophysiological responses of schizophrenic patients. Two significant facts emerged from those experiments.

The first, confirming other research, was that the schizophrenics we studied showed considerable variability in their physiological responsiveness. This was true, not only when different subjects were compared but also, more importantly, when the *same* schizophrenic patient was examined on different occasions: indeed, in some instances, the fluctuation was so great – and here I am referring to the individual's level of skin conductance – that it covered the whole range generally found across samples of normal subjects. The finding of differences *between* schizophrenics of course echoes Venables's observations, referred to earlier; but what is also interesting is that the 'typology' he describes – of excessive responders and extreme non-responders – is admitted to be a not entirely stable one, individual schizophrenics often shifting from one pole of galvanic skin reactivity to the other when tested at different times. In other words, it does seem to be true that schizophrenics show an unusual degree of physiological lability, suggesting that their nervous systems are subject to less regulating control than normal.

The second, and more intriguing, result of our own experiments has been the observation that schizophrenics – and, incidentally, the blood relatives of schizophrenics – also manifest a very curious *profile* of response when different aspects of their psychophysiology are examined simultaneously. Here the experiments have involved looking at an individual's sensitivity to sensory stimulation and comparing it at different levels of general arousal, again measured from galvanic skin activity. Sensory sensitivity was measured in these studies in one of two ways: either by determining how well the subject could discriminate pairs of flashes presented in quick succession or by examining the degree of 'augmenting' or 'reducing' in the EEG when the intensity of a single flash is varied. Now, generally, the sensory response is related to background arousal in a predictable, and intuitively sensible, way: for example, when the person shows evidence of being in a state of low arousal his reaction to an external stimulus will be rather weak. However, we have found that in the schizophrenic brain the opposite is true: there, when physiological arousal is very low, the sensitivity to environmental stimuli seems to be much *increased*. This phenomenon, which, in both humans and in the monkey, we have shown can also be produced by the psychedelic drug, LSD, seems to be a uniquely 'psychotic' configuration of brain response[23].

How do these findings relate to the question of variability and the idea that the schizophrenic brain might lack homeostasis? We can get some clue by looking particularly at our studies using the augmenting-reducing technique to evaluate stimulus sensitivity. It seems very likely that underlying augmenting-reducing is some sort of regulatory mechanism which modifies the brain's response to external stimulation and that this, in turn, is intimately connected, through feedback loops, to general arousal systems. Normally these circuits would be expected to work smoothly together, making it possible for the nervous system to maintain an appropriate strength of sensory response for its prevailing level of arousal. What appears to happen in the schizophrenic brain is a kind of 'uncoupling' effect; or, put another way, a weakening of its regulatory properties. If this were true then it would almost certainly cause the brain to veer to extremes of activity, not just in one system (say, general arousal), but also as reflected in the mutual disconnection of *different* systems. Incidentally, it is of interest – and perhaps not coincidental – that the particular systems that seem to be involved here are precisely those which might be responsible for some of the more significant psychological processes underlying schizophrenic behaviour; namely, disordered responsiveness to environmental stimuli and dysfunction of emotional arousal.

It is possible in principle, then, to give some account of the schizophrenic's brain (and associated psychology) in terms that are not dissimilar to those used elsewhere in personality theory to describe other kinds of brain and to formulate a conceptual nervous system which refers to the same properties of arousability, inhibition, and homeostasis. If the schizophrenic nervous system is peculiar it is in the last respect – that of regulation – which, though a simple principle of difference, could have far-reaching consequences for the way the brain organises its resources when carrying out important functions, like attention, perception, and thinking, all of which depend upon a fine balance being maintained between excitatory and inhibitory influences. To take an example, focusing attention on a stimulus involves not only excitation in apppropriate neural pathways, but also active suppression of activity in others. Serious irregularity in this process, perhaps due to weakening of its inhibitory component, could lead to the kind of disordered attention found in schizophrenia. It is indeed this kind of fault which Venables pointed to when proposing his idea of 'gating', referred to earlier. He, as we saw, referred it neurophysiologically to the brain's limbic system, a neural circuit that has frequently been considered to be a principal site of schizophrenic pathology by those who have adopted a more traditional 'organic lesion' view of the disorder. However, it is clearly not necessary to take such a stance in order the sustain the idea that the limbic system is implicated – in a more functional sense – in schizophrenia; since that part of the brain does have important excitatory and inhibitory properties and is a crucial staging-post for the integration of emotional and cognitive events. The quality of these properties is such that it is perfectly feasible – and this is our argument here – to conceive of a *continuum* of variability in them; thus allowing for degrees of functional irregularity, present to some extent even in some normal nervous systems, but exaggeratedly so in the schizophrenic's.

Even so, referring schizophrenia solely to a low-level brain circuit such as the limbic system is not, as with the other disorders we have discussed, entirely satisfactory. Indeed, in the case of schizophrenia we are brought up more forcibly than ever against questions which current conceptual nervous system theories are not designed to answer. Many of the most striking features of schizophrenia consist of disordered language, distorted thought, delusional belief, a fragmented self-concept and other abnormalities of consciousness that necessarily involve the higher nervous system. Such phenomena might of course be dismissed as mere consequences of irregularities lower down in the brain; but that begs some important questions about the nature of schizophrenia and most serious observers of the disorder have considered that they require explanation in their own right. As we have seen, psychologists' attempts to do so have usually been based on various models of 'information processing'. Although these theories have not been strong in explanatory power they do, nevertheless, seem to be pointing in the right direction.

The conclusions recently reached by Frith on this point are instructive here[60]. Returning to the old filter theory explanations of schizophrenia, he has offered a reinterpretation of some of the earlier data, in the light of contemporary evidence about the way attentive processes direct conscious awareness. Although accepting that the idea of a 'weak filter' in schizophrenia is basically correct, Frith notes that the original models were vague about the stage in information processing at which the breakdown occurs. He himself argues that it lies at a very early point of *preconscious* processing, the schizophrenic having an unusual capacity to become aware of the many stimuli to which we all potentially have access but which in most of us lie just below the level of consciousness. This hyper-awareness, he proposes, can account for important features of schizophrenia, such as delusions and hallucinations, both of which he sees as due to misinterpretation, at an early stage of processing, of stimuli spilling into consciousnesss. Similarly, according to Frith, it is possible to explain why many schizophrenics become excessively aware of their own motor movements, losing the ability to carry out acts automatically.

Some insight into how these disorders of consciousness relate to the brain is now beginning to come from another set of research findings which, while not specifically mentioned by Frith, are very relevant to his observations about schizophrenia. I am referring to what has now become something of a boom industry in research on schizophrenia; namely the study of it in relation to the differential functioning of the two cerebral hemispheres. As we saw in previous chapters, several psychiatric disorders are now beginning to be looked at from this point of view, but the most intensive research effort has certainly been directed towards schizophrenia. The background to the approach in normal psychology consists of observations that the left hemisphere has a dominant role in language, is analytic in its mode of perceptual processing, and is more concerned with rational, logical, or linear styles of thinking, compared with the right hemisphere's greater visuospatial capacity, tendency to process the world globally or holistically, and supposedly more emotional, intuitive way of operating. The greater generalisation that the two halves of the brain contribute two streams of awareness to consciousness has made schizophrenia a natural focus of interest, even leading some writers to suppose that here at last is a biological substrate for that 'splitting' of affect and cognition that led Bleuler to describe the disorder as he did[155]. Contained within what has now become a mixture of fact and speculation there is nevertheless considerable evidence that, in addition to their many other peculiarities, schizophrenics do show deviations of hemisphere function[75].

Consideration of the hemisphere perspective on the brain introduces a new 'dimension' into the discussion of schizophrenia, in more than one respect. It does so literally because it forces us to take account of aspects of brain function that reflect its *horizontal* organisation, as distinct from the *vertically* organised properties that have preoccupied those psychologists who have constructed conceptual nervous systems of the kind mainly discussed so far in this book. Thus, most designs for the nervous system in relation to personality and mental disorder, where they have referred to anatomically identifiable structures or neural circuits, have always done so according to a perceived hierarchy of functional organisation, which involves a mutual interaction between upper and lower parts of the brain. This is no less true where such models have been extended to schizophrenia; as, for example, in my earlier suggestion about brain regulation, which was originally conceptualised as being organised in an up-down fashion. Recently, however, serious attention has been paid to the possibility that the physiological processes like arousal, which form the constructs of these theories may have a lateralised aspect, observable horizontally in the nervous system. As it happens, recognition of this fact has come about mainly through research on schizophrenia.

This is clearly brought out, for example, in studies that were directly descended from research, already described here, on the psychophysiology of schizophrenia. The observation that schizophrenics show extreme modes of galvanic skin responding – excessive overreactivity or its diametric opposite – is now further complicated by the finding that they also manifest greater differences than normal when recordings made from the right and left hands are compared[76]. Which means that particular individuals can appear to be 'responders' on one side of the body and 'non-responders' on the other! A similar asymmetry can be observed in the EEG, using the augmenting-reducing technique[35]. Here the tendency of the amplitude of the evoked response to change with increasing stimulus intensity has been found to differ in degree in schizophrenics according to the side of the head from which it is recorded; while this, in turn, varies in different individuals. There is also some evidence that the pattern of lateralisation – whether in galvanic skin responding or EEG – corresponds, to some extent, to patients' clinical symptomatology, more emotionally reactive, paranoid individuals showing evidence of greater 'activation' of the left hemisphere. However, as with earlier comparisons on similar types of measure, but made without reference to lateralised effects, it is doubtful whether such relationships indicate a stable connection between psychotic 'type' and the brain. Instead, they are probably yet another sign of the instability of the nervous system in schizophrenia, this time observable *across* the brain.

Another, and very exciting, reason why hemisphere research adds a new dimension to discussions of schizophrenia arises from a rather different set of experimental studies. These have been carried out more in the tradition of neuropsychology, than of psychophysiology. Of the two disciplines neuropsychology has been more explicitly concerned with trying to map psychological functions, especially those involving higher mental processes, like language, on to the *topography* of the brain. This form of enquiry has, inevitably, taken into consideration the possible division of labour – and, by the same token, the possible cooperation – between the two sides of the brain. Considerable impetus was given to such research by the now famous studies of so-called 'split-brain' patients in whom, for therapeutic reasons (the treatment of intractable epilepsy), the hemispheres were surgically separated by cutting through the corpus callosum, the bundle of fibres that normally join the two halves of the brain together[161]. Although the theory that some functional mental illnesses may be due to disturbed hemispheric activity is by no means new – it goes back well into the last century – it was nevetheless those split-brain studies that were most directly responsible for reviving experimental investigation of the idea, using neuropsychological research techniques. The approach seemed particularly appropriate for exploring the psychotic states because the neuropsychological perspective on the

brain which the work offered provided a more direct point of contact –
than, say, psychophysiology – between brain and mind, and hence
between brain and the disordered consciousness in which the clinical
symptoms of illnesses like schizophrenia can be said to originate. The
result has been an explosion of research attempting to see whether the
organisation of psychological functions across the hemispheres is
somehow different in schizophrenia and, if so, to suggest why this
might be.

Unlike split-brain research, it is not of course possible in the intact
human subject to examine the hemispheres entirely independently of
each other. Study of the problem in relation to schizophrenia therefore
has to rely, as in normal psychology, on drawing inferences from data
obtained in experiments using special testing techniques which try to
'probe' the two halves of the brain separately, always bearing in mind
that they are actually connected, both anatomically and functionally.
The most commonly used of these methods – the 'divided visual field'
technique – capitalises on the fact that one half of each retina
projects to the same (opposite) hemisphere; so that a visual stimulus
presented, say, to the left visual field will go first to the right
hemisphere. Similarly, in the case of the auditory modality, a sound
presented to one ear to will go most directly to the opposite side of the
brain.

In applying these methods to schizophrenia, particular attention has
been paid to the possibility of an abnormality in the processing of
verbal stimuli, for the obvious reason that language difficulties are a
prominent feature of the disorder. Although the results are by no
means unequivocal, they do on the whole support the conclusion that
schizophrenics have particular problems processing verbal information presented to the left, normally language dominant, hemisphere[34].
A typical effect is that the schizophrenic is slower or less accurate in
responding to, say, nonsense syllables presented to the right visual field
(left hemisphere) compared with the left visual field (right hemisphere) – a pattern of performance opposite to that normally observed.

One interpretation that might be, and indeed has been, put on such
evidence is that schizophrenia is due to a specific defect, possibly of
organic origin, in the language hemisphere[53]. However, there are
several arguments against this. One is that no consistent structural
defect has ever been established in schizophrenia, despite the
availability, now, of very sophisticated techniques for examining the
brain; nor does schizophrenia, as a total picture, very much resemble
that seen in people where a lesion in the language centres of the brain *is*
demonstrable. Another argument is that the asymmetry of performance observed in schizophrenics on divided visual field, or similar tasks,
is not necessarily stable: on the contrary it may flucutate with the

mental state and clinical symptomatology of the person during psychotic illness[194]. We ourselves recently came across a particularly dramatic example of this in a patient, clearly schizophrenic, who was tested many times on a nonsense syllable task of the kind described above. On the first occasion of testing the patient showed the typical left hemisphere inferiority found in schizophrenia. Eventually, however, the direction of this asymmetry shifted until it corresponded to the more usual left hemisphere *superiority*.

We have to remember here that the kinds of task used in hemisphere research constitute a very artificial situation. The brain does not normally just receive its information from one side of the world. If we *force* it to – as we do in, say, divided visual field tests – and the side we stimulate first does rather badly, this does not necessarily mean that side has a defect, in a structural sense. Even though each hemisphere may be *specialised* for certain functions, in real life when the brain carries out a task *both* hemispheres are always involved – in a cooperative exercise, as it were. This is true even of linguistic processing – probably the most 'lateralised' of functions – since the right hemisphere has, in varying degrees, been considered to have some language capacity and, in any case, certainly contributes contextual and other detail to the thought processes which language expresses.

It is this idea of cooperation, of the way information from both halves of the brain is integrated, that is now emerging as the most plausible guideline for trying to understand the unusual form of hemisphere organisation that does seem to exist in schizophrenia. An early statement of this viewpoint came from Beaumont and Dimond, who carried out one of the first divided visual field experiments on schizophrenics[3]. In the task they used, a different stimulus was presented simultaneously to each hemisphere, the subject being required to say whether they were the same or different. Schizophrenics were found to perform badly on this test, a result which the authors took as evidence that in such individuals there may be poor communication between the two hemispheres. In other words, they proposed that the two halves of the brain are relatively disconnected in schizophrenia, in somewhat the same way as, in a more complete sense, they are in the surgically split-brain patient. Beaumont and Dimond considered that there might be a certain degree of support for their hypothesis in some evidence, from post-mortem studies, that the corpus callosum of schizophrenics is thicker than average[7].

An alternative interpretation to that just considered would state the opposite: that, far from the two hemispheres in schizophrenia being disconnected, there is actually *too much* communication between them, a greater flow of information than is desirable, leading to disruption of the brain's ability, as a total unit, to perform effectively. An important set of findings which would be consistent with that conclusion was reported by Green and his colleagues[73]. They examined the ability of schizophrenics to recall stories presented over headphones to both ears simultaneously or to one ear only. Schizophrenics were found to perform better when only one ear was stimulated, suggesting that full engagement of both hemispheres during the task caused interference with verbal processing.

Several writers have speculated on the possible neuroanatomical and neurophysiological basis for the apparent failure, in schizophrenia, of interhemispheric integration or communication. Randall, arguing partly on the basis of evidence, referred to earlier, about corpus callosal width in schizophrenia, and also taking account of some of the psychological data, has proposed that the schizophrenic brain may contain an abnormal number of active fibres connecting equivalent areas in the two hemispheres[136]. If that were the case, then it would mean that activity occurring at sites, say, in the language centre of the left hemisphere, might bring into play, to an unusual degree, associative processes occurring in the appropriate homotopic points in the right hemisphere. Such exaggerated 'connectivity' between the two halves of the brain could, under some conditions, seriously disrupt thought and language.

A not dissimilar theory, though expressed more in terms of the functional properties of the brain, has been put forward by Wexler[193]. He bases his ideas on the fairly well-accepted principle that the integration of information from the two hemispheres depends upon a constant interplay of excitatory and inhibitory influences, occurring across the corpus callosum. During performance of a verbal task, for example, it is probable that the left hemisphere actively inhibits the right to some degree. Wexler suggests that in schizophrenia there may be a weakening of interhemispheric inhibition, a state which would have effects on verbal processing formally similar to those proposed by Randall.

A third proposal, by Galin, is couched in the same language as Wexler's but reaches the opposite conclusion[61]. He argues that in the schizophrenic brain there is a tendency for inter-hemispheric inhibition actually to *increase*. This, he suggests, would cause the two halves of the brain to become, to some extent, functionally isolated from one another, each hemisphere taking on a life of its own. If true, then it might explain why in schizophrenia there seems to a duality of consciousness – a sense not of dual personality as that term is usually employed, but of separating of the stream of ideas, its division into sometimes contradictory elements of thought and impulse, amounting on occasions to a feeling of alien influence. The following example illustrates the point very appropriately. The man in question, having had a schizophrenic breakdown some years ago, has continued to suffer from many of its primary symptoms, including auditory hallucinations. He described his own state to me as like having two selves, a rational self – and what he considered to be his normal self – that deals with the real world and another, foreign, self which, through the voices he hears, tries to influence his behaviour. What is particularly interesting about his account is that he actually located the two parts to his personality on opposite sides of his head!

The case just described also illustrates, incidentally, an application of some of the ideas being discussed here to the understanding of one of the most dramatic signs of psychotic illness, namely auditory hallucinations. Earlier mention was made of the work of Green on deficiences among schizophrenics in binaural processing of auditory information. He and his colleagues, who also embrace the interhemispheric integration hypothesis, have speculated on how it might help to explain auditory hallucinations. Basing their views partly on evidence that schizophrenics whisper subvocally when hallucinating, they have suggested that the voices heard may originate in the right hemisphere and represent ideas or thoughts, normally below the level of awareness, which spill over into consciousness and which find expression through the left hemisphere's control of speech[72]. The suggestion offers an interesting extension into hemisphere research of Frith's argument that it is to the preattentive stage of information processing that many of the disorders of consciousness occurring in schizophrenia can be traced.

Let me now try to draw together some of the main ideas that have emerged out of the discussion here. One consistent theme, both in the psychophysiological literature and in hemisphere research is that there seems to be a certain *irregularity*, or lack of homeostasis, in the schizophrenic brain. This is manifest at several levels and in more than one direction in the nervous system. It occurs as an apparent 'uncoupling' of some quite basic processes, like arousal and the sensitivity to sensory events, an effect, it seems, repeated across the brain. Reflected in higher mental activity, the same instability finds expression in the disordered, and fluctating, performance of functions that rely on cooperation between the two hemispheres and an integration of information passing to and fro across the corpus callosum.

A second, and related, theme has been that the irregularity referred to reflects an imbalance in excitatory and inhibitory processes in the schizophrenic brain. This idea has been explicitly stated, or implicitly contained, in several accounts of schizophrenia offered by psychophysiologists and has also been used to explain specific features of the disorder, especially in attention research. And, as we have just seen, it has also been suggested as a serious explanation for the unusual form of interhemispheric communication that seems to characterise schizophrenia. At present, it is unclear whether this imbalance should be specifically construed as a weakening of inhibitory controls in the nervous system or as a tendency for *both* excitatory *and* inhibitory influences to veer towards extremes of activity. Intuitively the latter seems most likely and better able to capture the overall quality of schizophrenia: it would also encompass more of the experimental evidence about the disorder.

The third idea we have come across is that there must be an intimate connection between those dynamic processes, like arousal and inhibition, that have formed the stuff of psychophysiological models of the nervous system and those mental events which neuropsychologists have tried to locate in the structure of the brain. The question raised here is, of course, as much a general one as a problem for schizophrenia research, a point to which I shall return at the end of the book. However, there are some immediate implications for understanding schizophrenia that need to be considered here.

It could be argued that the constructs to which psychophysiologists refer define a range of possible – and in schizophrenia very deviant – *states* for the individual nervous system: changes in arousal, altered thresholds for perception, the directional shift in resources that occur during attention, and so on. If these states are very fluctuant, then their configuration at any one time would much affect the way the brain utilises those psychological functions that can, to some extent, be located in its physical structure. In other words, it is possible that the arrangement of the schizophrenic brain, at its highest level, is not particularly unusual: it merely happens to be the victim of irregular dynamic processes. To take a straightforward example, the disturbance of thought and language which occurs in schizophrenia – and which finds a parallel in altered hemispheric function – might merely reflect a temporary upset, due to increased arousal associated with psychotic breakdown.

However, this interpretation is too simplistic, if only because it fails to take account of the time-scale along which the development of the brain occurs. Thus, it is certainly the case that the laying down, in childhood, of structurally represented psychological functions, such as language, will itself be influenced by the same dynamic processes that, in the adult, steer their use. The corpus callosum, for example, takes some years to mature and it is upon this that the specialisation of the two hemispheres partly depends. If, in certain brains, the interplay between excitation and inhibition is inherently deviant (especially if this occurs both vertically and horizontally in the nervous system, and includes its upper and lower parts), then an unusual structural

arrangement of the two hemispheres might be permanently established. One possible outcome is that the hemispheres might become
relatively less specialised, less distinct in the division of function on
which, paradoxically, the unity of the self depends. From this might
flow the disorders of consciousness and consequent symptomatology
which we see, in the adult, as schizophrenia and which are likely to
occur when the system as a whole is pushed, for one reason or another,
into states that are even more deviant than usual.

The ideas developed so far have a number of other implications
for our understanding of schizophrenia and we shall return to these
later. However, it is appropriate to stop at this point and consider some
other arguments which both help to buttress those already presented
and are important in their own right. They refer to the suggestion that
schizophrenia as a pathological state may spring out of forms of brain
organisation that also underlie some types of normal behaviour,
personality, and psychological experience. It is this search for the
'psychotic temperament' that will occupy us in the next chapter.

8

The Psychotic Temperament

At the beginning of the previous chapter reference was made to the fact that arguing for a strong biological basis to the psychotic illnesses is not difficult. I would suggest that our subsequent discussion there confirmed that conclusion convincingly enough for all but the most rabidly antipsychiatric. It was noted, however, that, in some quarters at least, the notion of a continuity between psychotic and normal behaviour is more controversial. In this chapter we shall examine the idea within the same general context as the earlier discussion of less severe forms of mental illness. The main thesis will be that underlying the psychotic disorders, as in the less severe forms, there are certain dimensional characteristics which account for some normal psychological variations, including personality, and that these, in turn, define predispositions to develop illnesses like schizophrenia; that, translated into Pavlovian terminology, there are constitutionally determined 'psychotic' nervous types, just as there are types of nervous system that are 'neurotic' in their organisation. Before considering the arguments in detail it is perhaps necessary to clarify one point, which refers back to an earlier observation made about the psychoses, namely that compared with the neuroses they *are* qualitatively more distinct from the normal, a feature that has made a dimensional perspective on them harder to accept. This difficulty is reflected in popular usage of the terms 'neurotic' and 'psychotic'. It is common, and seems quite acceptable, to refer to someone as 'neurotic' even though he or she does not show the psychiatric signs of actual neurosis. It is much rarer for a normal person to be called 'psychotic', even less so 'schizophrenic', except in the wrong, journalistic sense in which those words are sometimes employed. This apparent problem for a dimensional view of psychosis disappears, however, if we adopt the interpretation of the disease concept outlined in chapter 1 and bear clearly in mind the distinction made there between symptoms and traits, between illness and predisposition to illness. The fact that the transition from one to the other often involves a discontinuity of function, occurring in varying degrees, allows us to recognise that the psychoses may contain dimensional features, while preserving the idea that they are diseases in the true sense.

That it is possible to construe the predisposition to psychosis in this fashion is supported by several kinds of evidence. However, two main lines of enquiry stand out which, although occasionally overlapping, and now rapidly converging, are historically separable from each other. One has its roots in the study of normal personality and can be seen as a direct development of theories like that of Eysenck, towards the view that 'psychotic' modes of behaviour can be observed in otherwise normal people; and that these are understandable, at a biological level, as variations in those same central nervous mechanisms which may be implicated in psychosis itself. What is involved here, in other words, is a mapping across from the clinically abnormal state to the normal personality, in an attempt to isolate common nervous typological characteristics that can be taken as defining the predisposition to psychotic illness. The second line of research has firmer origins in the study of psychosis itself, especially schizophrenia, and in efforts that have been made to identify individuals who are considered, for one reason or another, to be at risk for schizophrenic breakdown. Here again, because of the prevailing biological emphasis of research on the aetiology of the psychoses, a good deal of attention has been focused, particularly recently, on the central nervous characteristics of such individuals. Common to both approaches is an interest in genetic aspects of the questions that each has sought to answer: in the first case for the reasons made plain in chapter 4; in the second case because an inherited liability to schizophrenia has proved to be one of the most reliable ways of defining risk for the disorder. It is therefore appropriate to start by looking briefly at the genetics of schizophrenia.

Starting with several twin studies carried out earlier this century, there has long been an interest in the extent to which genetic factors play a part in schizophrenia, though failure to demonstrate a clear mode of inheritance, together with the rise of exclusively sociopsychological explanations of the disorder during the 1960s, caused this emphasis to be temporarily eclipsed. Recently, however, coincident with the swing back towards a more biological perspective on schizophrenia, interest in its genetic aspects has revived, accompanied by a newer, methodologically more sophisticated, series of studies, together with a re-evaluation of earlier evidence[66]. Despite the difficulty of arriving at a universally agreed definition of schizophrenia, the conclusion that can be reached, while more guarded than previously, certainly points to a significant influence of heredity on the *predisposition* to develop psychotic disorder. Several kinds of data support that view.

First, there is the fact that the risk for any given individual varies in an orderly manner according to his or her degree of relatedness to a known schizophrenic. Bearing in mind that the lifetime risk in the general population is about 1 per cent, this figure increases to roughly 3 per cent for second degree relatives (grandchildren, nephews and so on), to 10 per cent for siblings, and to as high as 45 per cent for the child of two parents who are themselves diagnosed schizophrenic. Secondly, more recent twin studies have continued to confirm that MZ twins are more often concordant for schizophrenia than DZ twins. Admittedly the actual figures quoted by different investigators have varied, sometimes quite widely. But, averaged out over a number of studies, it is still the case that where one twin is schizophrenic there is a 45 per cent chance of the other member becoming so, if the pair is monozygotic: the corresponding figure for dizygotic pairs is about 15 per cent. The concordance rates for MZ twins now quoted are well below some earlier estimates, which sometimes reached as high as 90 per cent, and leave considerable room for an influence of non-genetic factors in schizophrenia. At the same time, the *relative* concordance rates consistently observed in the two types of twin – about three times greater for MZ than for DZ pairs – add weight to the importance of heredity in the aetiology of the disorder.

Neither of the two research strategies referred to so far – pedigree studies and twin studies – entirely overcomes the objection that varying degrees of shared environmental influence could account for the observed data. We have already seen that this is a criticism sometimes made of the 'classic' twin method and, although occasionally over-stated, it is an argument that perhaps carries slightly more force in the field of psychiatric genetics where the index of twin concordance – diagnosis – is a relatively 'soft' one which attempts to summarise in a rather crude fashion a complicated set of characteristics that reflect not only the individual's genetic make-up, but also his accumulated life experiences. Fortunately, other kinds of evidence are available from studies that have tried to disentangle some of these effects. Thus there has been a series of investigations examining the outcome – in terms of the tendency to develop schizophrenia – for individuals adopted away from their natural parents in early life and brought up in other families. The pioneer study of this type was carried out by Heston in the United States[83]. He compared the later incidence of schizophrenic breakdown in two groups of fostered children: some whose natural mothers were schizophrenic and some whose mothers had no record of psychiatric hospitalisation. At follow-up it was found that none of the latter developed schizophrenia, whereas nearly 17 per cent of the children of the children whose biological mother was schizophrenic, but who were reared away from her, also developed the illness. Heston also made two other observations, the relevance of which will become plain later. One was that the schizophrenics' children also showed a higher incidence of other forms of abnormality, especially psycho-

pathy and personality disorder. The second was that in cases where no
psychopathology was found the individuals concerned had frequently
tended to pursue more artistic and other creative professions.

A considerable amount of confirmatory evidence from adoption
research has accumulated since Heston's original report. The centre-
piece of that work has been a series of collaborative studies carried out
in Denmark, a country which forms an ideal setting for such research
because of its small size, the relative immobility of its residents, and the
existence of a unique system for recording population statistics,
including psychiatric admissions. Capitalising on these advantages it
has been possible to carry out larger scale investigations than hitherto
and to pursue variations on the basic strategy used by Heston. One
such variation is that utilised by Kety and his colleagues[93]. Instead of
focusing on the psychiatric status of the *adoptees* they looked back at the
frequency with which schizophrenia had occurred in the biological, as
compared with the adopting, *families* of such individuals. In accord-
ance with a genetic hypothesis, it was observed that schizophrenia was
to be found most frequently in the biological parents of adoptees who
themselves later became schizophrenic. Incidences were much lower
among the natural parents of those adoptees who did *not* develop
schizophrenia and among both sets of fostering parents, whether or
not the adopted child became schizophrenic.

There are, of course, a number of inherent biases in research of the
kind just described. It cannot be assumed, for example, that adoption
agencies, in choosing families in which to place children for fostering,
do so on an entirely random basis: on the contrary, they are very
selective in the criteria they use. The age at adoption, the reasons for it
in the first place, and the degree of continuing contact with the natural
parents may also be important factors that confound attempts using
this strategy to try to disentangle genetic and environmental effects.
Nevertheless, considering the results of adoption studies alongside
those from other research, especially twin comparisons, it is impossible
to escape the conclusion that genetic factors are important in
schizophrenia. That this should be so is unsurprising given the
evidence and arguments, presented here in chapter 4, for the influence
of heredity on individual variations in general: it would be remarkable
if schizophrenia were an exception.

The question is: What form does this inheritance take? The most
convincing suggestion is that offered by Gottesman and Shields who,
after a thorough and balanced review of all of the studies carried out to
date, propose a theory that is now emerging as the most likely
intepretation of the genetic evidence about schizophrenia[66]. They
come down in favour of what they call a 'multifactorial-polygenic-
threshold' model. The essential feature of the model is that the

underlying inherited liability to schizophrenia is continuous in nature, the genes for it being widely dispersed, to varying degrees, in the general population. Breakdown into clinical schizophrenia would then be seen as occurring only once an individual has passed beyond a certain threshold of response, determined by a combination of genetic loading and accumulated life experience. As Gottesman and Shields point out, genetic models of this type have been successfully applied to several forms of systemic physical disease, including of diabetes: their application of it to schizophrenia is therefore not particularly unusual or idiosyncratic. Indeed, the polygenic model has the considerable advantage that it allows us to preserve the idea of schizophrenia as a disease, without doing violence to the argument that certain features of it are biologically continuous with normality.

The 'dimensional' perspective on schizophrenia to which the genetic evidence leads us therefore neatly fits the general viewpoint on the psychotic states introduced at the beginning of this chapter. If, as now seems likely, the predisposition to schizophrenia *is* inherited in a graded fashion, then it should find a counterpart in the behaviour of normal individuals, forming part of observed human variation. Earlier reference was made to two kinds of research that bear directly on that idea: one, by personality theorists, explicitly based on the assumption that it is possible to observe psychotic traits among normal people; the other – so-called 'high-risk research' – which is implicitly similar in aim, in the sense that it tries to describe the characteristics of individuals who, though not schizophrenic, are considered, for one reason or another, to be liable to the disorder. Historically these two lines of research sprang from rather different roots, developing independently of each other, and only recently showing signs of coming together with a common purpose. Here I shall deliberately conjoin them, on the grounds that the questions each is trying to answer are, in effect, identical. Because of its proximity to the discussion of the genetics of schizophrenia let us look first at high-risk research.

It has been recognised for many years that attempts to understand schizophrenia are bedevilled by the fact that once the person has broken down it is difficult, if not impossible, to disentangle the secondary effects of the illness from its antecedent causes. Commenting on this problem in 1968 Mednick and McNeil wrote as follows:

> Schizophrenics excite a good deal of behavioural research. The goal of much of this research is to produce information concerning the aetiology of schizophrenia. It may be difficult, however, to isolate aetiological factors through studies carried out with individuals who have lived through the process of becoming and being schizophrenic. The behaviour of these

individuals may be markedly altered in response to correlates of the illness, such as educational, economic and social failure, prehospital, hospital, and posthospital drug regimens, bachelorhood, long-term institutionalisation, chronic illness, and sheer misery[117].

At the time of writing, Mednick himself was already six years into a collaborative study which must be considered the first true longitudinal follow-up study of a group of children thought to be at high-risk for schizophrenia: we shall return to it in a moment. By 1974 the editor of *Schizophrenia Bulletin*, introducing a review of the topic by Garmezy, was able to do so under the heading 'The study of children at risk – a research strategy whose time has come'[62, 63]. Garmezy himself, in his two-part survey, summarised some twenty projects which were already in progress at that time. Since then use of the high-risk strategy has captured the interest of many investigators in schizophrenia research.

In principle, the search for predisposing factors in schizophrenia, as in any illness, can encompass several methodologies including, for example, the examination in retrospect of the earlier characteristics of currently ill individuals. But the most powerful method, if the one most difficult to see through to completion, involves selecting a group of people, preferably in childhood, and following them up to the point where, if illness is to occur, it can be observed. Among its many advantages this procedure allows a free choice of potential measures of predisposition and the possibility of later assessing their ability to predict later breakdown. The classic example in schizophrenia research is the study initiated in 1962 by Mednick and Schulsinger[118]. The setting of their work was Denmark, for the reasons given earlier in connection with adoption research. Schizophrenia being a relatively rare condition, one problem facing such a study is the selection of high-risk subjects in the first place: the group must be sufficiently large to ensure that some of its members do eventually show signs of psychiatric disorder, yet manageable enough in size to make follow-up over many years feasible. Mednick and Schulsinger solved the difficulty by capitalising on what they judged to be the firmest criterion for selection, namely genetic affinity to a known schizophrenic. In doing so they established a model for most subsequent high-risk research, which has also generally looked towards the relatives of schizophrenics for examples of individuals who should be more heavily weighted than average on the characteristics underlying the disorder.

Mednick and Schulsinger chose to study the children of mothers who had received a firm diagnosis of schizophrenia (the High Risk Group), comparing them with children with non-schizophrenic mothers (the Low Risk Group). They then set out to follow both samples into early adulthood. At initial contact all of the subjects were tested psychologically and psychophysiologically, as well as being rated for school behaviour and personality adjustment. An alarm network was set up to alert the investigators to any cases of psychiatric breakdown and, by 1967, 20 such cases had been ascertained, all from the High Risk Group. These individuals were designated a Sick Group and their past records scrutinised for any early differentiating characteristics. Various findings of interest emerged, among them being the observation in the teachers' original reports that the Sick Group subjects had been more aggressive, more disruptive, and generally more disturbed in class. Another which, as we shall see, was later to assume some significance in Mednick's work, was a tendency for the subjects to show marked autonomic instability, as reflected in certain aspects of the galvanic skin response, which had been recorded at the initial assessment.

At this point in the project it was not clear that the differences observed were *specific* to schizophrenia, a number of diagnoses being represented in the Sick Group, including personality disorder and 'borderline' psychotic states. However, in 1972 Mednick and his co-workers set out to evaluate the current life status of as many as possible of their original High and Low Risk subjects: they managed to do so in over 90 per cent of cases[119]. Part of their reassessment consisted of a thorough clinical interview leading, where appropriate, to a psychiatric diagnosis being assigned to each individual. Evaluated in this way 14 of the High Risk Group subjects were diagnosed as definitely schizophrenic, though a much larger number (29) were considered to be latent or borderline psychotics. Reporting on the premorbid characteristics of these more firmly diagnosed individuals the conclusions reached were substantially similar to those arrived at in the earlier interim analysis. Emphasis was again placed on the importance of lability of the galvanic skin response as a good predictor of later schizophrenia, especially where the subsequent illness included classic symptoms, such as hallucinations, delusions and thought disorder.

Mednick was quick to notice the relevance of this last observation to the parallel work being carried out around the same time on schizophrenics themselves, especially the research by Venables reported in the previous chapter. It will recalled that Venables and his colleagues had shown deviant patterns of galvanic skin response among schizophrenic patients and been led to interpret their results as evidence for a disorder of the brain's limbic system in psychotic illness. Mednick's similar findings on high-risk children seemed to suggest that the physiological instability that could be inferred from their galvanic skin response profiles might be present even before the onset of illness, as a characteristic feature of the nervous system of individuals predisposed to schizophrenia. On the basis of this idea Mednick, in collaboration with Venables, then launched an even more ambitious longitudinal high-risk project on the island of Mauritius, again chosen partly because of the ease with which the subjects could be followed up over many years. In this case the 'high-risk' children were selected, not on genetic criteria, but according to whether they displayed one of several defined patterns of galvanic skin responsiveness, including both the 'responder' and 'non-responder' types identified by Venables in his original studies of schizophrenic patients. As before, it is intended to follow the children through the risk period for schizophrenia.

The project having started only on 1972, it is as yet too soon to evaluate its success in predicting later psychopathology, but some interesting preliminary observations have been reported on the behaviour of the children taking part[186]. One aim of the study has been to examine how children of different psychophysiological make-up react to early social experiences and, to this end, comparisons have been made between the various response 'types' in the way they behave when exposed to a nursery school environment. The children were initially subdivided into two groups, one of which remained at home while the other attended special nursery schools set up on the island. After three years they were compared in a standard setting, using observational techniques to assess the differential effects of the nursery school experience on the two groups of children. Several differences emerged, but the one considered most salient concerned the constructive play behaviour of those, physiologically hyperresponsive, children who most resembled the subjects originally found by Mednick to be at greatest risk for schizophrenia. It was observed that such children exhibited a high level of constructive, imaginative play, irrespective of whether they had previously been to nursery school: in the other children the amount of play was very much influenced by having been to nursery school. Commenting on the result, the investigators drew upon Venables's theory, referred to in the previous chapter, that certain kinds of nervous system – typically those found in the high-risk subjects – have a greater 'openness' to environmental stimuli. They speculated that children showing the characteristic may be potentially more creative and therefore indulge naturally in more constructive play. In reaching this conclusion Venables and his colleagues were adding to an opinion which is gradually emerging, that some of the underlying features of schizophrenia may be compatible with normal, or even superior, psychological adjustment, psychiatric illness being only one of its possible outcomes. We touched briefly upon this idea of a link between creativity and schizophrenia when referring earlier to Heston's work on adopted children and will return to it at the end of the chapter.

Following the same individuals for a sufficiently long time to determine whether or not they become psychiatrically ill is a daunting prospect and many other investigators have settled for a truncated version of the strategy. This involves trying to map across from schizophrenics to their relatives, in order to see whether they share some common biological or other characteristic which might reveal an important feature of the disposition to schizophrenia. Although more limited in its objectives, this method has considerable value in discovering what have been called 'endophenotypic' indices of liability; that is, measures closer to the biology of the organism and therefore 'harder' than clinical signs. Fed back into genetics research, such measures can sharpen the investigation of the hereditary aspects of psychosis or, viewed from our present standpoint, help us to define the schizophrenic 'nervous type' more precisely. Let us look at just two examples which, in different ways, parallel important areas of research on schizophrenia itself, discussed in the previous chapter.

The first arises from the observation that the attention defect in schizophrenia appears to be demonstrable as a disorder of eye movements, specifically in the smooth pursuit or tracking movements required when following, say, a swinging pendulum. A number of studies have shown that not only schizophrenics, but often also their relatives, show such eye movement peculiarities; while twins, discordant for schizophrenia, may nevertheless be concordant for the characteristic[105]. It has therefore been suggested that eye tracking dysfunction might be a possible genetic marker of schizophrenic disposition, representing some fundamental feature of the nervous system related to attentional mechanisms. For example, Holzman, the author of several of the important studies in the field, has speculated along these lines, suggesting that the pattern of eye movement observed in schizophrenia may reflect a weakening of inhibitory controls in the brain, being just one aspect of a 'general organismic instability . . . which manifests itself as inhibition in many spheres, cognitive, perceptual, and affective'[85]. The similarity of this conclusion to some of the ideas about schizophrenia already discussed here scarcely needs underlining.

The second example of studying disposition to schizophrenia by examining relatives is more limited in the amount of data at present available, but nevertheless looks extremely promising, especially in view of the experimental findings reported in the previous chapter and other results to be described later in this chapter. The research in question concerns hemisphere function, the particular study to be quoted – as far as I am aware, the only one of its kind so far undertaken – being carried out by Green and his colleagues[79]. It followed from their earlier work which, it may be recalled, demonstrated that

schizophrenics have difficulty with auditory processing when both ears
are stimulated simultaneously, suggesting a peculiarity in the capacity
to integrate information flowing between the two hemisphere. Green
and his colleagues then went on to study performance on the same test
– interpreting stories played over earphones to both ears or to one ear –
in a group of 'high-risk' children, each of whom had a schizophrenic
parent. They found that the children also showed difficulties in
binaural relative to monaural speech comprehension, compared with a
matched group of control subjects.

The mainly biological high-risk research discussed over the last few
pages has all taken place against a background of extensive investigation into the personality characteristics of pre-schizophrenics, with the
aim of trying to identify *temperamental* variables that may help to predict
later psychotic breakdown. Here some fairly consistent, if perhaps
surprising, facts have emerged. The popular idea of pre-
schizophrenics as people who are simply shy, introverted, and
withdrawn is not, on the whole, supported by the evidence. Instead the
personality conforms more to that observed, it will be recalled, in
Mednick's high-risk sample; namely of somewhat aggressive, antisocial
children, troublesome in their relationships with their peers. Several
observers have noticed such characteristics. Robins, in a detailed
follow-up study of children earlier seen in a psychiatric clinic, found
that those who later became schizophrenic tended, when seen
originally, to present as aggressive, but also worried, brooding, restless
and irritable[142]. And Watt, enquiring into the early histories of
schizophrenics, talked of extreme 'disagreeableness' as a common
childhood trait, especially in boys[191].

Popular misconceptions about the personalities of pre-
schizophrenics probably arise from wrong use of the term 'introversion' to describe them. While intuitively it does seem likely that such
individuals *ought* to be introverted – and indeed they may show some
traits of that type – the fact is that, as normally used, the description
does not capture sufficiently strongly other important elements which
many observers have suggested predominate in schizophrenia: lack of
impulse control, for example, which is usually regarded as an
extraverted trait. Part of the confusion here is due to the various ways in
which different writers have employed the term 'schizoid', which arose
originally as an attempt to characterise the latent or pre-schizophrenic
personality. Although later diluted to signify merely 'introverted', the
description actually has a much richer meaning. In the recent
literature this has been clearly brought out in the writings of Manfred
Bleuler whose book, *The Schizophrenic Disorders*, must rate as one of the
mosy deeply insightful accounts of schizophrenia ever published[8]. The
book details a twenty-year study of over 200 schizophrenics and their

families, cared for personally by him while director of the Burghölzli Clinic in Zurich, a post held previously by his father, Eugen Bleuler. It was an extension of the latter's coining of the term 'schizophrenia' that the description 'schizoid personality' arose, taking shape (and a precise meaning), as Manfred Bleuler puts it, 'in conversations among the doctors of Burghölzli in connection with the expression "schizophrenia" around 1911'. Manfred Bleuler himself was therefore able to write directly in that tradition when he described the schizoid personality as follows:

He is taciturn or has little regard for the effect on others of what he says. Sometimes he appears tense and becomes irritated by senseless provocation. He appears as insincere and indirect in communication. His behaviour is aloof and devoid of human warmth; yet he does have a rich inner life. In this sense he is introverted . . . Ambivalent moods are more pronounced in the schizoid than in others, just as he distorts the meanings of, and introduces excessive doubts into, his own concepts. But on the other hand, the schizoid is also capable of pursuing his own thoughts and of following his own interests and drives, without giving enough consideration to other people and to the actual realities of life. He is autistic. The better side of this autism reveals a sturdiness of character, and inflexibility of purpose, an independence, and a predisposition to creativity. The worse side of it becomes manifest in a lack of consideration for others, unsociability, a world-alien attitude, stubbornness, egocentricity, and occasionally even cruelty.

Assessing his own patients according to these traits Manfred Bleuler concluded that at least half had shown some degree of schizoid tendency before their psychotic breakdown. Similar characteristics were also very noticeable, he says, in their siblings and in their offspring. Like most other writers on the topic, Bleuler is quick to point out that a range of personality types can be observed among schizophrenics and their relatives. But he leaves us in no doubt that the most important reference point for trying to gain insight into the schizophrenic personality is schizoidness, or schizoidia as it was later called; with its undertones of disharmony, self-contradiction, and ambivalence of feeling. So important for Bleuler is this notion of disharmony of personality traits that he bases his views about the inheritance of schizophrenic disposition on it. He rejects the idea that there is a *specific* genetic defect in schizophrenia, arguing instead that the underlying hereditary tendency is the appearance in some people of characteristics which, taken individually, are perfectly healthy but

which, occurring in certain disharmonious combinations, are potentially maladaptive.

The idea that some temperaments can only be understood as a
disharmony of apparently self-contradictory traits is an intriguing one
that has come up under several different guises in clinical and
observational accounts of personality. Another early writer who dwelt
on the same theme was Kretschmer. Writing in the same German psychiatric tradition as Bleuler, he was also very clear that the term
'schizoid' meant more than merely 'introverted'; referring instead to a
complex mixture of what he called a 'mimosa-like' nature coexisting
with what he described as an 'aristocratic frigidity', a mingling of
'hyperaesthetic and anaesthetic elements'[95]. 'He alone', he said, 'has
the key to the schizoid temperament who has recognised that the
majority of schizoids are not either oversensitive or cold, but that they
are oversensitive and cold at the same time, and that in quite different
relative proportions.' Interestingly, in painting his picture of the
schizoid temperament Kretschmer quotes from Strindberg who, later
to become schizophrenic, is alleged to have said of himself that 'I am
hard as ice, and yet so full of feeling that I am almost sentimental.'

Whether coincidentally or not, another, much more recent, observer
of human nature who commented in almost exactly the same vein
about these 'vulnerable toughies' was Arthur Koestler who was, of
course, especially preoccupied with the Janus-face qualities of Man.
Discussing this interest after his death, Marvin Lasky recalls how
Koestler visited a chess tournament in Iceland:

> where he, the 'passionate duffer' at chess, rushed to watch the
> Bobby Fischer–Boris Spassky championship tournament, he was
> intrigued by Fischer's personality, so tough and yet so sensitive,
> and he came up with another hybrid, the mimophant, mingling
> the touchiness of the delicate mimosa plant with the toughness of
> the thick-skinned beast[99].

Although these qualities of disharmony have been largely ignored by
academic psychologists writing about personality, it is nevertheless at
this point that we can begin to discern an historical bridge between
contemporary high-risk research on schizophrenia and work which
forms the second part of our discussion here. I am referring to
attempts that have been made, especially over the past two decades, to
arrive at an understanding of the predisposition to psychosis from the
direction of personality theory, by looking for evidence of psychotic
characteristics in normal people. The main exponent of this approach
has been Eysenck, whose work has its roots in another of the important
clinical observations made by Kretschmer: that certain features of
normal temperament can only be explained by reference to their

abnormal counterparts. Indeed, it was Kretschmer who formulated the first 'dimensional' model of personality, proposing a continuum of individual variation defined at its opposite ends by the two major psychotic disorders of schizophrenia and manic-depressive psychosis: what he called 'schizothymia' and 'cyclothymia' described their corresponding normal personality attributes. It was this theory which helped to shape Eysenck's conviction that, as with the neuroses, a dimensional approach to the psychoses was also viable.

Later experimental research by Eysenck led him to identify a third personality dimension of 'psychoticism', to sit alongside the already well-established dimensions of introversion-extraversion and neuroticism, and to develop a questionnaire scale for measuring the traits associated with it[50]. In view of our earlier discussions, it is instructive to consider what those traits are. A person obtaining high scores on the new psychoticism scale is described as follows:

... as being solitary, not caring for people, he is often troublesome, not fitting in anywhere. He may be cruel and inhumane, lacking in feeling and empathy, and altogether insensitive. He is hostile to others, even his own kith and kin, and aggressive, even to loved ones. He has a liking for odd and unusual things, and a disregard for danger; he likes to make fools of other people and to upset them ... As far as children are concerned, we obtain a fairly congruent picture of an odd, isolated, troublesome child, glacial and lacking in feelings for his fellow-beings and for animals; aggressive and hostile, even to near-and-dear ones. Such children try to make up for lack of feeling by indulging in sensation-seeking 'arousal jags' without thinking of the dangers involved. Socialisation is a concept which is relatively alien to both adults and children; empathy, feelings of guilt, sensitivity to other people are notions which are strange and unfamiliar to them[49].

Although the above characterisation misses out certain important qualities of the schizoid personality – notably the layer of hypersensitivity classically associated with it – Eysenck's thumb-nail sketch of the 'psychotic' personality does imply the same odd mingling of traits, the mixture of shy introversion and extraverted impulsivity found in descriptions of the pre-schizophrenic that have emerged from high-risk research and from other, clinical, accounts. Despite this, Eysenck's new scale has been the subject of considerable controversy and debate[25, 26]. The main criticism has been that the scale measures, not 'psychoticism' in the true sense, but is more an indicator of psychopathy, antisocial behaviour, or a general tendency to reject the accepted norms of society: the argument is based on the admitted fact that the highest scores on the scale are obtained by very socially deviant individuals, including drug-addicts, alcoholics, criminals and so on. Those who advocate that view have, however, missed the point, failing to notice the evidence referred to here, that antisocial traits actually *are* associated with schizophrenia.

How to explain the connection is another matter. One possibility rests on genetic considerations and takes into account the fact that there is a high degree of selective, or assortative, mating between psychotics and criminals: Mednick, for example, has concluded from his own high-risk studies that male psychopaths especially seem to have a strong affinity for female schizophrenics[116]. The line of reasoning would then be that some 'high-risk' families contain the genetic tendency to *both* schizophrenia *and* antisocial behaviour, but that each is inherited quite independently of the other. However, Gottesman and Shields who, as geneticists, recently examined that argument, concluded that even allowing for the complication of assortative mating, there is still good evidence for a genuine association between schizophrenia and certain configurations of antisocial or asocial traits which, in the European tradition of writers like Bleuler, can be termed 'schizoid psychopathy'[66]. Of course, as already emphasised when discussing psychopathy in a previous chapter, this does not imply that all schizophrenics are potential criminals or that all socially deviant individuals are liable to psychotic breakdown. But it does suggest that the personality characteristics which predispose to schizophrenia may sometimes be expressed in antisocial form, possibly because there is something intrinsic to them which pushes the individual towards deviant or, in extreme cases, outright criminal behaviour.

Eysenck's measure of the traits we have been discussing, and which he labels 'psychoticism', is very much an outgrowth of his own general theory of individual differences, an attempt to fill a gap in personality description not covered by his earlier dimensions of introversion-extraversion and neuroticism. However, others attempting to identify psychotic characteristics among the general population have taken a somewhat different approach; coming to the problem from the clinical end, as it were, and basing their measures more deliberately on a consideration of the symptoms of schizophrenia. A good example is to be found in the work of Loren Chapman and his colleagues, who have devised scales which they claim measure psychosis-proneness in normal people[21]. One is a Physical Anhedonia scale, so called because it is intended to measure the individual's inability to feel pleasure, which according to some viewpoints is a central feature of schizophrenia. The other is a scale of Perceptual Aberration, determining the extent to which people report unusual experiences, such as telepathy, peculiar beliefs about the world, and visual and auditory distortions of perception. Both scales have been tested against data obtained independently from clinical interviews and do indeed appear to tap related, but different aspects of psychotic tendency.

My colleagues and I have also been engaged for some years in the development of such scales[27]. In its latest version our own questionnaire consists of two parts. One, which we have called a 'Schizotypal Scale', is made up of items similar to those in Chapman's Perceptual Aberration Scale. The other measures the quality of emotional reactions towards others, especially ambivalence of feeling and particularly the degree to which the person experiences anger. The reason for constructing the questionnaire in this way will become clear in the next chapter when we come to discuss the 'borderline states'. Suffice it to say here that it has recently become possible to define more precisely than hitherto the clinical features of certain, relatively mild psychiatric conditions that appear to fall literally on the borderline between normality and the major psychoses. The symptoms of these disorders therefore seemed to us to provide a good template for devising scales which could measure similar characteristics, in an even milder form, among normal people.

The questionnaires just referred to, together with Eysenck's measure of psychoticism, are of course concerned solely with the description of rather superficial psychological traits. In use with normal subjects they have certainly demonstrated that the psychotic or schizotypal characteristics they measure can be widely observed among the general population: as such, the results obtained with them strongly support a dimensional view of psychosis. However, even more powerful evidence has come from research that has examined the biological correlates of the traits in question. That work has exactly the same logic as that followed when investigating the biological bases of other temperamental and personality dimensions, associated with the less severe disorders discussed in previous chapters. In other words, it has involved trying to determine whether some normal individuals resemble schizophrenics on certain measurements of central nervous function. Indeed, it is this search for the 'psychotic nervous type' that has preoccupied my colleagues and myself for nearly two decades. The results we have accumulated, taken in conjunction with those obtained from high-risk research on schizophrenia, now put it beyond reasonable doubt that certain kinds of normal nervous system can be said to be organised in a manner which can be described as 'psychotic' or 'schizotypal'.

The evidence for the last statement has come, in our own research, from two kinds of study. One, in the earlier phases of the work, involved examining psychophysiological variations in normal individuals selected on the basis of Eysenck's questionnaire measure of psychoticism. The guideline for that particular part of the research was the series of observations, reported in the previous chapter, on the psychophysiological responses of schizophrenic patients. It will be recalled that one of our most significant findings concerned the 'dissociative' nature of schizophrenics' reactions, as reflected in a tendency for their sensitivity to sensory stimuli to depart drastically from its predicted value at given levels of general arousal. Subsequent studies in our laboratory demonstrated that the same configuration of psychophysiological response can also be observed in certain normal people; namely individuals with high scores on the Eysenck psychoticism scale[26]. This confirmed our suspicion that the instability of brain function which we had inferred from our patient studies was not confined to the ill schizophrenic, but was actually a general characteristic of some normal nervous systems. That it has specifically to do with schizophrenia was then further supported by the results of another experiment which included some features of a 'high-risk' study, the subjects this time being selected on the grounds that they were the first-degree relatives of clinically diagnosed schizophrenics[32]. Again the same psychophysiological profile was observed, though it was rarely seen in a comparison group consisting of the relatives of neurotic patients. Interestingly, schizophrenics' relatives also had somewhat higher scores on Eysenck's psychoticism scale.

Our second line of enquiry into the nature of the psychotic nervous system has taken a somewhat different direction, though it too has used a similar strategy; namely, examining selected normal individuals to see whether on certain experimental measures they behave like schizophrenics. The focus for this research has been the extensive evidence, described in the previous chapter, that schizophrenics show unusual patterns of hemisphere organisation. Is this also true of some normal people? Recent results we have obtained suggest that it is. Here the subjects were chosen according to their scores on the new questionnaire of 'borderline' characteristics mentioned above. Comparisons made on a variety of hemisphere function tasks have demonstrated, almost without exception, that people with high scores on the questionnaire do differ in performance in a way that is compatible with their having schizophrenic-like nervous systems. Thus, a general finding that emerges is that schizotypal individuals, like schizophrenics, show weakened, or even reversed, laterality of function as measured on standard divided visual field tasks. This is particularly evident for the processing of verbal material – nonsense syllables or letters – where the left hemisphere's usual superiority is diminished in schizotypes[13, 137]. We have also found that they differ when examined in the auditory modality: the task used here was the same as that referred to earlier as showing effects in both schizophrenics and their children; namely the comprehension of stories played either to one ear or to both ears simultaneously[14].

Although these unusual brain asymmetries are most clearly observable with respect to *verbal* processing – and, for that reason, least ambiguously comparable to those found in schizophrenics – other differences in hemisphere function can also be observed among individuals who score highly on our questionnaire of 'borderline' characteristics. Thus, we have found that they differ, too, in the relative extent to which their hemispheres are engaged during simple perceptual processing; specifically when asked to do a task which requires them to process stimuli either 'locally' or 'globally'. These two abilities are known to be partly hemisphere dependent, the left brain, for example, normally being better at detailed or local analysis of a stimulus. In schizotypal individuals, however, the reverse seems to true[137]. This may be significant because several psychologists who have explained schizophrenia as a disorder of information processing have suggested that a crucial features may lie in the schizophrenic's inappropriate use of 'local' and 'global' modes for analysing perceptual data[134].

Another, as yet unpublished, set of observations on hemisphere function in normal subjects concerns a different kind of perceptual processing, the judgement of emotional expression. This line of research stems from some earlier work by my colleague, Paul Broks, showing that schizophrenics perform abnormally when asked to judge the emotions displayed in photographs of faces presented separately to each hemisphere. Following up this finding in normal subjects he has demonstrated that some show a similar pattern of performance to that found in schizophrenics. The form this takes is a reversal of the usual right hemisphere advantage for judging certain kinds of emotion, notably anger. Again the result is in line with some more general observations – the significance of which I will consider later – that schizophrenics seem to analyse other peoples' facial expressions in an unusual way[38].

A further feature of these results that should be mentioned is that the relationships between hemisphere organisation and schizotypy are seen much more consistently in male than in female subjects. At present it is difficult to say what the significance of that is for our understanding of brain function in relation to the dispositions to psychosis. Certainly women in general are known to be somewhat less strongly lateralised for important psychological functions, like language. Furthermore, the sexes do differ in their patterns of psychotic breakdown, women being more prone to depressive reactions or schizoaffective illnesses, in which the schizophrenic symptomatology is strongly overlaid with disordered emotionality. Some authors have argued that schizophrenic and affective forms of psychosis actually represent differences in hemisphere organisation[54]. It is therefore conceivable – although, as yet, there is no evidence to support the idea – that this is also reflected in the personality characteristics which, in men and women, predispose to various types of psychotic reaction.

Another, not unrelated, complication of the results described above concerns handedness. All of our research so far has been conducted on right-handed subjects, the reason being that, for simplicity's sake, we have felt it important to try to first sort out any relationships that may exist between brain organisation and personality in those people who make up the majority of the population; especially since the arrangement of psychological functions across the hemispheres in left-handers is not itself invariant – in other words, it is not in all cases merely a mirror image of that observed in the right-handed. But we can be sure that handedness will prove relevant to our understanding of the biological dispositions to psychopathology. The reason for saying this is that there is some evidence from studies of people who have already been diagnosed as psychologically disordered that patterns of handedness – and hence hemisphere organisation – do vary and, in turn, differ according to sex. This seems to be especially the case among individuals considered to have 'personality disorders', including hysterical and antisocial types. In one study, for example, mixed handedness was especially common among female hysterical personalities[52, 165]. In schizophrenia itself there is no striking relationship with handedness, except for a fairly consistent observation that left-handedness is slightly more common in young, male patients[175]. It is perhaps also of interest that Green and his colleagues, in their study of hemisphere function in high-risk children referred to earlier, noticed an unexpectedly high incidence of left-handedness among the offspring of schizophrenics.

Clearly we have a long way to go before we can arrive at a precise description of the schizotypal nervous system. But, as a *general principle*, the idea of a continuity between the normal and the psychotic – long considered likely by those outside the arena of academic debate – seems to be well supported by experimental evidence. In this respect, it is especially satisfying that at the biological level the continuity should be evident for *both* aspects of brain activity that have proved useful in describing schizophrenia itself; namely, in dynamic process variations – as reflected in patterns of psychophysiological response – and in hemisphere organisation. There is thus a remarkable similarity in the pieces of the two jigsaws – that for schizotypy, on the one hand, and that for schizophrenia, on the other. In each case we find evidence for a tendency towards instability of brain activity from which, in schizophrenia, we inferred that there may be a relative lack of homeostasis in the nervous system – both vertically and horizontally – and it seems that this might also be true, to a lesser degree, of the schizotypal or psychotic personality. At a psychological level there is also a parallel, in the normal schizotype's readiness to admit to perceptual aberrations, unusual thought styles and beliefs, openness to experiences, disharmony of personality structure, ambivalence of emotional response to others, and an uncertainty about the self-concept. All of these features could be said to mirror the 'psychotic' form of brain organisation found in the schizotype. As, extrapolating from theories about the illness itself, could other probable characteristics: an unusual sensitivity to events in the internal and external environments, a heightened awareness of the contents of consciousness, and a highly tuned selectivity of attention.

Returning to schizophrenia itself, let us now see whether it is possible to construct a plausible account of how, in this case, illness might proceed from the dispositional characteristics that underlie it. A convenient place to start is at the point of contact between the schizotypal individual and his social environment. For it is the interaction and communication with others that almost certainly place the greatest demands on the kind of nervous system just described. The idea that social, or more narrow family influences can *by themselves* cause schizophrenia now flies in the face of considerable evidence to the contrary, some of which we referred to briefly in the previous chapter. However, it *is* the case that the immediate family environment of the schizophrenic can, once the illness has started, worsen the condition and cause relapse into further psychotic episodes. This conclusion is clearly supported by the work of Leff and his colleagues, who have demonstrated that the schizophrenic is extremely sensitive to the amount of face-to-face contact and level of expressed emotion he encounters from close relatives[100, 183]. Now Leff and his co-authors studiously avoid inferring from this that similar effects may be at work *prior to* the onset of illness or that they could, through prolonged exposure to such influences, contribute to subsequent breakdown. However, I would suggest that indeed may be the case and that the overall vulnerability to schizophrenia consists of a genetic disposition, compounded by a particular form of interaction between the schizotypal nervous system and the family environment. How, in detail, might this work?

Part of the clue, on the biological side of the equation, might lie in what we have seen to be the unusual manner in which schizophrenics (and schizotypal individuals) process events around them. The way they deploy their attention is certainly odd, two particular features which I would like to emphasise here being as follows: one is the tendency to utilise local and global perceptual strategies in a peculiar fashion and probably to rely much of the time on detailed, rather than holistic, modes of analysis; the other is to do so especially in the analysis of *social* stimuli, such as facial – and therefore non-verbal – expressions of emotion in others[192]. Given that the latter are among the most elaborate stimulus configurations encountered in life – but also vital to social development – it seems probable that the schizotype, merely because of the arrangement of his nervous system, will be at greater risk of misintepreting non-verbal social signals, because of his tendency to focus on, or attend selectively to, their constituent parts rather than consider them in a total context. Put more generally, he might just have more difficulty sorting out meaning in the complicated flow of verbal and non-verbal interchange that makes up social communication, particularly if this signifies strong emotion, and especially so given the unusual organisation of both the expressive and receptive aspects of language in the schizotypal brain. Occurring from childhood onwards this form of interaction with others could exacerbate a pre-existing genetic disposition, to produce a cognitive and personality style that is vulnerable to schizophrenic breakdown.

So much for the contribution of the individual's nervous system 'type'. What about family influences that may interact with it? If, as suggested, recent work on 'expressed emotion' in schizophrenia can be generalised to childhood, we could conclude that particular kinds of family milieu, because of their emotional climate of criticism, overinvolvement and so on, might be especially powerful in bringing about the effects just described. Here, incidentally, there may be something to be said in favour of the old idea of 'double-bind', as a pathological form of communication in which the sender in a social interaction emits verbal and non-verbal messages of conflicting meaning: a typical example is the parent who, aggressively hugging the child, simultaneously says 'I love you'. The theory that such interactions by themselves can cause schizophrenia is now discredited. On the other hand, they would present to the schizoptypal child a particularly difficult example of the kind of interpersonal situation with which his nervous system is ill-equipped to deal. The double-bind aside, there is considerable evidence that the communication patterns in schizophrenics' families are abnormal[84]. Undoubtedly these partly arise as a reaction to the schizophrenic or potentially schizophrenic family member. But another important element, often overlooked, is that the parents will, through genetic affinity with their offspring, share some of the temperamental make-up of the vulnerable child and therefore some of his or her difficulties with social interaction. This would mean that communication within the family may be *mutually* ambiguous or otherwise unusual, biological and social factors operating synergistically to push the most genetically prone individual towards schizophrenia.

According to some opinion it might be said that what I have just described *is* schizophrenia, especially if one sees that condition as part of a broad spectrum of deviance. For the above account does not depart too drastically from the explanation offered by those with Laingian and other radical psychiatric views – even though it does introduce a much more biological emphasis than they would prefer. On the other hand, even they would recognise that as a full-blown illness, schizophrenia involves a very marked discontinuity of function, a recognisable break into bizarre, and apparently incomprehensible symptoms. It is therefore still necessary to explain how and why this occurs. A crucial factor here, I believe, is the other unusual feature of the psychotic brain; namely the relative instability of mechanisms responsible for central nervous arousal. As we have seen, this can result in marked shifts in physiological state which will, inevitably, cause the individual to respond inappropriately – and on occasions strongly – to situations that evoke arousal. Now it can be stated as a general principle, which applies to all organisms, that excessive arousal will disrupt psychological functions, finding the weakest point in potential sources of abnormality and throwing these into sharp relief: in the schizotypal person this would seem to be the arrangement of the higher nervous system as it relates to the organisation of language, thought, attention and social perception. It is not difficult to see how such psychological functions might become deranged under conditions of particularly acute stress. To take a highly specific example, the pre-schizophrenic's tendency to 'read' the behaviour of others in an unusual way may only take on pathological valence at times of heightened emotional arousal. Only then perhaps is he likely seriously to misinterpret and attach sinister significance to perceived non-verbal (or verbal) signals which otherwise may remain below the threshold at which they disturb consciousness: the road from there to elaboration through delusional thought is a short one.

The sources of stress which provide the background against which such effects occur are likely to be varied. The family environment is certainly one, as we have seen. Another is the experience of new, alienating environments to which pre-schizophrenics react badly. And one schizophrenic of my acquaintance traced his own breakdown to the mounting strain of maintaining a façade of 'normality' in the face of an increasing awareness, starting in his early childhood, that he was different from others. But undoubtedly an important set of triggering factors are those developmental changes associated with critical phases in the person's life. It is not without significance that the peak incidence for schizophrenic breakdown is observed in adolescence and early adulthood, and of course it is at this time that the most rapid spurts in emotional and physical growth occur, accompanied by psychic upheaval of such force that it can almost be said in itself to have the quality of temporary psychosis. The hormonal and other changes occurring in adolescence will therefore almost certainly unbalance even further the nervous system of the already vulnerable individual, making him particularly sensitive to the internal and external events that can precipitate a clinically psychotic reaction.

Another question we need to ask about is the subsequent change in the individual's personal adjustment, once the schizophrenic break with reality has occurred. The natural course of schizophrenia is very variable. In some cases it may consist of a single psychotic episode from which the person fully recovers: in others the schizophrenic will continue relentlessly down a path of social and interpersonal inadequacy, occupational disablement, and mental distress. A common picture, however, is one in which the original acute schizophrenic experience, even if reversed, seems to sensitise the person to the possibility of further breakdowns, having an accumulating effect over time. Why does this happen? There are two ways in which we can seek to answer the question. One is simply in terms of the immediate influences that tend to precipitate relapse in schizophrenics. Here we have seen that the emotional climate of the family environment is certainly important, a possible link with the biological mechanisms of the disorder having been unearthed in further work by Leff and his colleagues: they showed that in the presence of relatives judged to be high in emotional expressiveness schizophrenics tend to get physiologically more aroused – and hence go into precisely the kind of state which would be expected to revive the psychotic behaviour[171].

There is, however, a more fundamental reason why psychotic illness acts to increase future vulnerability and why, once set in motion, schizophrenia may become progressively more and more difficult to reverse. It stems from a quality that is intrinsic to the disorder, one to which I was introduced by an acquaintance who suffered schizophrenic breakdown and who, as a biologist, was able to speak with some authority on the matter. The person's experience and attempts subsequently to understand it led to what I believe is an important insight. It makes use of the idea, referred to several times, that schizophrenia really consists of two elements: temporary changes in dynamic brain processes, such as arousal, which help to precipitate and drive the person into a psychotic state; and delusional thoughts and ideas which form the permanent or relatively permanent bedrock of the schizophrenic condition. The argument is that even if the former are subdued – say, with drugs – the latter are less easily removed, being stored in memory, ready to be activated again in appropriate situations. It is therefore easy to see how, once established, schizophrenia is difficult to reverse in its entirety and why the threshold for further breakdown is lowered by each episode of illness.

Let us now turn upside down some of the questions being addressed over the last few pages and consider another set of issues raised by the continuity view of schizophrenia. If the predisposition to schizophrenia varies in a graded fashion among the general population, why is it that, relatively speaking, only a few become ill? Certainly an important factor, strongly indicated by the genetic evidence, is the difference between individuals in their degree of inherited liability to schizophrenic breakdown. Interacting with this will be their amount of exposure to critical influences that either further increase overall vulnerability or, alternatively, allow what might otherwise be a strong genetic prediposition to lie dormant. Such influences include biological hazards, like minimal brain damage at or soon after birth, life events in childhood and adolescence, and the quality of the family environment during upbringing. Another important, though less definable, factor is undoubtedly the extent to which even highly schizotypal individuals are protected from breakdown by intellectual and other personality resources – their 'ego-strengths' – which enable them to cope with, and sometimes profit from, unusual, psychotic, states of mind.

An illuminating example of this last point is Jung who, after his break with Freud just before the start of World War I, entered what can only be considered a period of schizophrenic turmoil – or, as he himself, recalling it years later in *Memories, Dreams, Reflections*, referred to as his 'confrontation with the unconscious'[87]. He describes the experience in a vivid detail that accurately recapitulates many features of the psychotic state, which he, as a psychiatrist, felt compelled to explore:

An incessant stream of fantasies had been released, and I did my best not to lose my head but to find some way to understand these strange things. I stood helpless before an alien world; everything in it seemed difficult and incomprehensible. I was living in a state of tension; often I felt as if gigantic blocks of stone were tumbling down upon me . . . But since I did not know what was going on, I had no choice but to write everything down in the style selected by the unconscious itself. Sometimes it was as if I were hearing it with my ears, sometimes feeling it with my mouth, as if my tongue were formulating words; now and then I heard myself whispering aloud. Below the threshold of consciousness everything was seething with life . . . When I was writing down these fantasies, I once asked myself, 'What am I really doing? Certainly this has nothing to do with science. But then what is it?' Whereupon a voice within me said, 'It is art.' I was astonished. It had never entered my head that what I was writing had any connection with art. Then I thought, 'Perhaps my unconscious is forming a personality that is not me, but which is insisting on coming through to expression.' I knew for certainty that the voice had come from a woman. I recognised it as the voice of a patient, a talented psychopath who had a strong transference to me. She had become a living figure within my mind.

Jung leaves us in no doubt that he was aware of the schizophrenic quality of his experience, for he goes on to note that at every stage of it he had 'run into the same psychic material which is the stuff of psychosis and is found in the insane . . . the fund of unconscious images which fatally confuse the mental patient.' Yet he had retained his sanity and indeed it was on the basis of the fantasies he encountered during that period that he went on to formulate his own, very influential, theory of the psychology of Man.

Many other passages in Jung's *Reflections*, and elsewhere in his writings, convince us that he was, in the richest sense, of schizotypal personality, though of powerful intellect and with deep inner resources, a combination which, in his case, issued not in illness but in great creativity. Which brings us to one further implication of the view of schizophrenia presented here; namely that there is an association between creativity and madness. The idea is, of course, firmly established in folklore belief, supported by observations that psychotic breakdown – or psychotic-like characteristics – seem to be common among the great thinkers in art, literature, and science; Strindberg, mentioned earlier, is just one of many examples. Are these merely special, dramatic cases, as Rothenberg[144] has suggested? Or are they genuine, albeit outstanding, instances of an inextricable link between the creative process and the process that leads to madness? On the face of it, the latter view seems absurd, since the positive qualities responsible for creative thought and those we associate with the illness of the schizophrenic seem quite incompatible; a dissonance which accounts for the understandable reluctance of many people to accept it. The difficulty disappears, however, if we consider carefully the line of reasoning that supports it.

The argument rests *not* on the suggestion that the schizophrenic state is itself conducive to creativity: even the outstanding historical figures usually quoted when debating the issue have found it difficult to work during periods of madness, though some notable exceptions are Jung, from whom we have just quoted, and some artists, like Van Gogh and the Hungarian painter, Csontváry. These examples are, however, unusual and the case for a connection between creativity and schizophrenia relies on a rather different kind of evidence. It comes from studies suggesting that among the other psychological features that are inherited as the disposition to schizophrenia, are characteristic styles of thinking which in themselves are quite normal: indeed, when utilised optimally, they enter into original thought. It is only when, in psychosis, they get out of control that the contents of consciousness to which they give rise are transformed into the *disorder* of thought by which we recognise schizophrenic illness. The evidence here has come from a number of different directions, but most obviously from studies demonstrating that individuals with schizotypal or psychotic personality characteristics show a predictably greater tendency towards the divergent and loose associative styles of thought that are formally equivalent to the 'overinclusiveness' of thinking seen in schizophrenics[199]. From another standpoint, it has also been found that, in certain important respects, the modes of attention adopted by highly creative normal people resemble those of schizophrenic patients[42]. And several studies point to these characteristics being part of the genetic disposition to schizotypy, a salient example being a finding by McConaghy, who has written extensively on the topic, that what he calls 'allusive' thinking is more frequent in the psychiatrically healthy relatives of schizophrenic patients[114]. In these results, then, there is not only further evidence for the continuity view of schizophrenia but also a clear implication that profound mental illness may spring out of the same roots as those which determine some kinds of normal, or even superior, psychological adjustment.

The above conclusion can help to answer other questions that have puzzled thoughtful observers of schizophrenia. Why, for example, does schizophrenia persist in the population, given the well-attested evidence that schizophrenics themselves have a much lower fertility rate than average? Indeed, why does it exist at all? The probable answer is that the genes for disposition to the disorder do not in themselves have any lethal significance: on the contrary, in moderate degree they may have some biological advantage in mediating qualities of creativity and so on that have survival value for the human race. Given the continuous form in which the underlying traits are inherited, and their widespread dispersion in the population, the tendency to psychotic breakdown itself is probably due to a pathological combination of the responsible genes in certain unfortunate individuals; schizophrenia being the penalty the human species pays for its unique adaptiveness and flexibility. There is an instructive parallel here with some types of physical disease, notably sugar diabetes, which, as noted earlier, closely resembles schizophrenia in showing a similar pattern of inheritance and continuous gradation of clinical symptomatology. It has been argued, at least in the case of certain forms of diabetes, that the genes implicated may also in the past have had biological advantage, allowing some animals to survive better in food-scarce environments, but that this has become *disadvantageous* under the dietary and other living conditions of modern Man[124]. If the analogy seems too strained, there are many other examples within psychiatry itself where traits that form a necessary and adaptive part of normal human variation also, in excessive degree, lay the foundation for psychopathology: anxiety is an obvious example. The difficulty with schizophrenia is discovering its precise underlying form and – to echo Venables's comments about the children currently under study in Mauritius – identifying the combination of genetic and environmental factors which may lead the schizotypal individual into schizophrenia on the one hand, or towards personal fulfillment on the other.

The picture of schizophrenia drawn over the past two chapters has highlighted as much its connection with health as its quality of illness. There is, I believe, an important lesson to be learned here about how we construe schizophrenia in future studies, and where, in our attempts to comprehend it, we focus our attention. Partly as a backlash against antipsychiatric views there has been a sharp return, over the past decade, to earlier opinion that an 'organic' cause for schizophrenia can still be discovered – without paying reference, that is, to its origins in normal brain function and behaviour. While it certainly may prove possible to trace certain forms of psychotic illness to a discrete lesion in the brain, this now seems unlikely in the majority of cases where, as we have seen, there is overwhelming evidence to the contrary. Now, one noticeable consequence of this emphasis on brain *pathology* – and one that has actually always bedevilled scientific, as distinct from humanistic, study of schizophrenia – is the tendency for research to seek evidence of the *deficits* with which it is associated, the *failures* of biological, psychological and social function to which it gives rise. This, I believe, has held us back from taking advantage of the important insights into schizophrenia which the radical psychiatrists, despite their wrongheadedness in other respects, have offered us.

Fortunately, it is now possible to detect a slowly growing awareness, even among some of those engaged in the scientific study of schizophrenia, that the obsessive search for ways of describing the psychotic person's *incompetence* is actually a serious barrier to our proper understanding of it and how it arises. In practical terms, this changing perspective is mirrored in occasional reports by experimentalists that schizophrenic patients – in whom, for obvious reasons, it is usually very easy to demonstrate behavioural deficits – are actually *superior* in some psychological functions to the control subjects with whom they are compared. A good example comes from a recent study by LaRusso demonstrating that schizophrenics are actually better than normal individuals at detecting the non-verbal cues which indicate whether other people are feeling sham or pretend, as distinct from genuine, emotion[98]. The greater sensitivity of schizophrenics found in LaRusso's experiment is, of course, a particularly good example of how a normal psychological process – in this case, social perceptiveness – can become, as Cannon from whom we quoted in chapter 1 would have said, a 'menace instead of a benefit': in real life it is presumably not conducive to mental health to be *too* attuned to other peoples' feelings! But to know something of the normal is a necessary first step to understanding its transformation into the abnormal. In this respect, schizophrenia seems no different from any other form of mental disorder. Manfred Bleuler, after a lifetime of caring for and studying schizophrenics, reached a similar conclusion:

It is possible, even probable, that schizophrenic illness is staged in the same general spheres of life where the neuroses are formed, and in which the human personality is shaped by a constant interplay between hereditary developmental tendencies and environmental experience[8].

9

On the Borderline

Repeatedly in this book we have come across psychological aberrations which, at particular points, have not fitted neatly into the main theme of the topic under discussion. They have failed to do so for a variety of reasons and in a variety of ways. Debating the concept of disease in psychiatry we were left feeling unsure whether certain disorders could properly qualify for that label; considering the relatively milder psychiatric conditions we noted some awkward differences between the neuroses proper and what appeared to look more like chronic personality disturbance; and discussing the psychoses we found the boundaries of the latter not easy to define, partly because of their evident overlap with other abnormal mental states, less serious but having a psychotic quality about them. To some extent these difficulties were resolved as we went along, partly by referring to the notion of degrees of disease or, in the terminology of physical medicine, subclinical varieties of illness that manifest themselves as mild chronic disabilities. The distinction drawn between illness and personality as predisposition to illness also helped in showing how, at the blurred edge between those two facets of aberration, symptomatic disorder and temperamental deviance almost become one, especially in cases where the person's suffering is shared as much, if not more, by others. And finally, construing the vulnerability to psychotic breakdown in dimensional terms, coupled to the genetic evidence for that view, allowed us to encompass the idea that there is almost certainly a continuity from even severe mental illness to normal personality, the space between perhaps being occupied by gross disorders of the character or temperament.

Although clarifying certain ambiguities, the points just raised and the previous discussion of them really only serve to introduce other, new questions about psychological disorders, questions that have been partly answered in earlier chapters, but which deserve more detailed consideration under a single heading. The heading chosen is that of the so-called 'borderline states'. In making that choice I have opted to enter a territory which is itself fraught with uncertainty but one where I believe some of the issues confronted in this book will eventually be settled. Even so, at the time of writing, the concept of 'borderline' – denoting, as the name implies, that there are some disorders which do not slip easily into conventional psychiatric categories – is extremely controversial. One reason undoubtedly is that the emergence of the concept has been very much connected with psychoanalytic thinking: this alone has made it distasteful to more conventional researchers and clinicians. However, as I hope to show, there are now signs that work carried out under the 'borderline' rubric is approaching the point where it is capable of being integrated with the kinds of theory and evidence that have guided discussion elsewhere in this book.

Not unconnected with the psychoanalytic origins of the borderline concept is the fact that usage of the term is very much more prevalent in the United States than in Great Britain. Psychiatrists on this side of the Atlantic, schooled more in a traditional medical framework, have been suspicious of a label which, both semantically and conceptually, challenges the integrity of their more rigid approach to classification and diagnosis. Sometimes 'borderline' even evokes downright hostility from British doctors. One psychiatrist of my acquaintance, when asked for his help in selecting suitable patients for research on borderline states, refused on the grounds that the term merely indicates a lack of certainty by clinicians in reaching a 'proper' diagnosis – a startling faith, indeed, in current nosologies and in the diagnostic acumen of his profession.

The Transatlantic division in attitude towards the borderline concept and the influence that adherence to psychoanalytic ideas has had on its acceptance are also revealed in other ways. North American psychiatric journals are currently awash with articles on the topic. On the other hand, the *British Journal of Psychiatry*, official organ of the Royal College of Psychiatrists, does not even list 'borderline' as an index entry and a recent search of its contents over the past fifteen years unearthed only five articles, three of which were written by American investigators. Of the remaining two one was a contribution from Scotland where, outside London, psychoanalysis has perhaps had its greatest influence on British psychiatry[108]. The authors of that paper, Macaskill and Macaskill, also note the dearth of interest in the borderline concept in Great Britain and report that up to the time when they were writing, 1981, they could find only four articles on it, three of which were in the *British Journal of Medical Psychology*, a strongly psychoanalytic publication. The only other paper by British psychiatrists in their own professional journal was as recently as April 1984. Significantly perhaps, this article concerned a survey of attitudes to the borderline diagnosis among clinicians at the Maudsley Hospital, the trendsetter for psychiatric practice in England[174]. The results of the enquiry are of some interest. It turns out that only about a quarter of the psychiatrists at the Maudsley use the diagnosis 'borderline' and that those who reject the borderline concept do so for one of three reasons: they are largely unfamiliar with it; they consider the kind of disorder it might cover extremely rare; or they think it has little utility, because it fails (*sic*) '...to discriminate between personality and illness'.

The difference between British and American expert opinion about the borderline concept has even penetrated the semi-popular press in the two countries. Sass, in a contribution to *The New York Times Magazine*, refers with enthusiasm to the growing interest in and increasing incidence of borderline personalities in American psychiatric practice. Referring to the common description of them as more ill than neurotics but less ill than psychotics, he writes colourfully about their manipulativeness, self-destructiveness, impulsivity, above all their unpredictability:

> 'All is caprice. They love without measure those whom they will soon hate without reason.' This observation by a 17th-century English physician was cited in *The New England Journal of Medicine* as perhaps the most succinct diagnostic statement ever made about borderline patients. Erratic and quixotic, they tend to perceive the world in extreme dichotomies of good and evil, and they are often intolerant of routine and social convention. Some say their case histories are filled with such strange predicaments and lurid details that they read like novels. . . . Well-known people to whom the label has been applied include Marilyn Monroe, Adolf Hitler, Kierkegaard, Lawrence of Arabia, Zelda Fitzgerald and the novelist Thomas Wolfe[147].

The subtitle of Sass's article is 'A new diagnosis of mental illness that is stirring up controversy in psychological circles is a metaphor for our unstable society'. The English newspaper, *The Guardian,* surveying the same scene with its usual jaundiced eye, cynically agrees, the author of its article dismissing the Americans' preoccupation with so-called 'borderline personalities' as just another example of their narcissistic hypochondriasis, the latest fashionable version of their 'me and my analyst' complex, conveniently (and lucratively) exploitable by psychotherapists[11].

Actually neither of these two writers does full justice to the borderline concept and what it implies: Brock because of his – and his professional advisors' – apparent ignorance of the topic; Sass because although better informed, his emphasis is almost entirely on psychoanalytic aspects which, while historically and clinically important, gives a highly slanted and limited view of current thinking about the borderline states. For the fact is that many of the ideas contained in the borderline concept, despite the latter's unlikely origins, converge very sharply on the very different theories of psychological disorder drawn upon here. That this has not always been immediately obvious stems not just from the unwillingness of many researchers and clinicians, especially on this side of the Atlantic, to admit into consciousness anything having a psychoanalytic taint: it also arises from the fact that the term 'borderline' has been used in a number of different ways, has often remained undefined, and just in appearance *looks* vague and unappealing to diagnosticians and scientists seeking orderliness in their descriptions of psychiatric illness. What, it may be asked, are borderline conditions borderline to? Normality, neurosis, psychosis? And do they constitute a homogeneous disorder or several distinct abnormal states? In order to see how, despite such difficulties, the literature on borderlines has come to be highly relevant to arguments of the kind being put forward here we need to examine the evolution of the borderline concept and look at some recent developments in its usage.

Although the description of certain patients as 'borderline' emerged exclusively out of the early writings of the psychoanalysts, the latter were not the only, or even the first, to recognise similar characteristics in certain individuals of abnormal personality. As Sass notes in the article cited earlier, the observation goes back several centuries. Indeed, the remoter origins of the borderline concept can be said to antedate and lie outside the purview of the psychoanalytic movement – ironically, perhaps, in the history of European psychiatry[110]. They can be discerned, for example, in the notion of 'moral insanity', coined by the early 19th-century English psychiatrist Prichard to describe individuals who, while not mad in the ordinary sense, displayed gross disorders of the character and temperament almost amounting to insanity. Later, both Kraepelin and Eugen Bleuler reinforced the idea of a possible affinity with the psychotic states, the latter in his concept of 'latent schizophrenia'. But subsequently it was largely left to clinicians of a psychodynamic bent to explore the borderlands between the well-recognised disorders. The reason for this – interesting in itself – is probably twofold. First, psychoanalysts have generally been less constrained by the need to pigeon-hole their patients and have therefore been made less anxious by the failure of certain individuals to fit predetermined and often arbitrary diagnostic categories. Secondly, although more conventional psychiatrists certainly continued to evolve schemes for *classifying* 'difficult' cases – using labels like 'hysterical personality', 'personality disorder', 'psychopathy' and so on – they almost always admitted, and still admit, defeat over explanation and therapy: with respect to the latter, for example, they have been unable to arrive at any effective physical methods, comparable to those used in the treatment of anxiety or depression. Nor, incidentally, have behaviouristically inclined clinical psychologists had much to offer in either sphere. Perhaps inevitably, therefore, it was out of a psychology which dared to explore the personality in depth that some inchoate understanding of borderline conditions emerged. The term 'border-line', in the form in which it has been most influential this century, was therefore literally conceived on the psychoanalytic couch.

From the very beginning, psychoanalysts, including Freud himself, were aware that there were certain patients who did not respond well to – indeed they could even be made worse by – their orthodox methods of free association and intensive exploration of the mental state. The study of such individuals – often observed to have severe disorders of character – assumed increasing prominence as the psychoanalytic movement diversified, Freud's ideas were taken up and modified by other workers, and the therapeutic techniques of psychoanalysis were applied to a wider variety of patients than the 'classic' neurotic conditions: a seminal example was Wilhelm Reich's description of the masochism, immaturity, narcissism and ambivalence of the 'impulsive character'[140]. The possibility that such people bordered on the psychotic was never very far from the thinking of the early writers on the topic: Reich certainly believed so. In any case the distinctions between the normal, the neurotic, and the psychotic have never been sharply drawn in psychoanalytic theory, a fact which paved the way for increasingly explicit statements, particularly by American analysts in the 1930s, that there existed a class of patients seen in clinical practice who while not overtly psychotic were sufficiently disturbed to put them outside the realms of simple neurosis and therefore too ill for classical psychoanalysis. Such individuals were admitted to be a diverse group and were variously described by different writers as including paranoid personalities, sexual perverts, psychopaths, narcissists and many other people who failed to integrate a sense of reality into their emotional lives. By the 1950s in American psychiatry the possible association with psychosis of at least some of these varied conditions had begun to be even more clearly stated, increasing use being made of terms like 'borderline schizophrenia', 'latent schizophrenia', and 'pseudoneurotic schizophrenia' to designate certain individuals who manifested their psychotic tendencies not in classic symptomatology, but as personality disorders or in a form mimicking the neuroses. It was around this time, too, that a phrase emerged which many still consider captures the essence of the temperament found in borderline individuals; namely that they are 'stable in their instability'[151].

Emerging out of this historical background, interest in the borderline states has now become, as we have seen, an important growing-point – or, depending on one's viewpoint, growth industry – in the contemporary psychiatry of North America. However, disguised to some extent in popular accounts of this phenomenon, there have over the past twenty years been increasing attempts to define the borderline concept more precisely, to bring work on it more into line with other psychiatric research effort, and generally to provide it with a firmer descriptive and empirical base. Admittedly progress has been slow, and there is still some disagreement about the meaning and usage of the term 'borderline'. Currently there seem to be four rather different, though very much overlapping ways in which it is used, each continuing a thread in the historical development of the borderline concept[104].

One form of usage, and that most directly in the psychoanalytic tradition, places emphasis less on 'borderline' as a diagnostic label, rather more on the fact that it denotes a certain kind of disordered psychic structure common to individuals who may, clinically, present with a variety of conditions, including sexual maladjustment, antisocial behaviour, drug addiction and so on[91]. The characteristic features are decribed as: a poorly integrated sense of identity, a tendency to be dominated by primary process thinking or fantasy, and a reliance on primitive defence mechanisms – especially 'splitting', a protective device which, according to psychodynamic theory, allows these typically ambivalent persons to maintain their contradictory feelings towards others or, in more severe cases, to prevent complete disintegration of the ego. Here there is a clearly implied resemblance between the psychic structure of the borderline and that of the psychotic as viewed by psychoanalysts, the main difference between the two being the former's less distorted, or even unimpaired, grasp of reality.

Other interpretations of the borderline concept have concentrated more on descriptive features than on depth analysis, though they have differed somewhat in the position taken over a possible affinity, if any, with the psychotic states. Some writers appear to reject any such association, arguing that the borderline state is a clinical syndrome in its own right, its main differentiating features being anger as the main or only affect, relationships with others that are dependent but rarely reciprocal, depressing loneliness, and a lack of self-identity[74]. However, research that has defined the borderline states in this way suggests that they cannot be completely separated from psychosis proper, even though they do show some distinctive clinical characteristics. Thus Gunderson and his colleagues, who have done considerable research on the topic from this point of view, found that patients meeting the criteria for 'borderline' described above differ from schizophrenics in a number of important respects; having, for example, more active social and sexual lives, disturbed as these may be. At the same time, it is admitted that that such individuals may suffer brief psychotic episodes, show thinking styles reminiscent of schizophrenics, and have a similarly poor work and educational history[78].

A third view of the borderline is one that more firmly continues the American tradition of defining schizophrenia itself very broadly and which argues that it is possible to recognise individuals who can literally be described as 'borderline schizophrenics', with characteristic features like strange thinking, brief cognitive distortions or 'micropsychoses', anhedonia (the inability to feel pleasure) and multiple neurotic manifestations, including severe anxiety[92]. The significant evidence quoted in support of this approach has come from genetic studies, some of which we encountered in chapter 7. Reviewing that evidence in the context of borderline research Siever and Gunderson have reached a number of firm, if cautious, conclusions[156]. In their opinion there is no doubt that some borderline conditions do have important genetic determinants, shared in some cases with chronic schizophrenia, and demonstrated in the fact that borderline characteristics are more frequently than chance found in the biological relatives of chronic schizophrenics. However, Siever and Gunderson also point to evidence that some borderline cases may be genetically related to other major psychiatric disorders, especially the affective illnesses.

Which brings us to a fourth perspective that has been taken on the borderline concept. Some clinicians have suggested that the borderline states have an affinity, not so much with schizophrenia, but with other forms of psychotic illness, namely depression and manic-depressive psychosis. Three claims have been used to support this point of view. One is that a notable feature of many borderline individuals is a disturbance of their *emotional* lives, especially a tendency towards gross instability of mood. The second is based on evidence about the treatment of borderline patients with drugs. Thus it has been said that in those cases where drugs have been used successfully it is the antidepressants, rather than the major tranquillisers employed in the treatment of schizophrenia, that have proved most effective[94]. And, thirdly, genetic evidence has been quoted, suggesting that some borderlines may have a stronger family history of affective disorder than of schizophrenia[168].

Mention of this last interpretation of 'borderline' makes it appropriate now to digress slightly and take up a question first introduced in chapter 7, but scarcely touched upon since then; namely the connection, if any, between schizophrenia and other functional psychotic states. Is manic-depression, for example, a recognisably separate illness, or merely a variant of some general psychotic condition, of which schizophrenia is the most commonly observed form? And to what extent can we look towards a similar explanation of the predisposition to affective disorder as that proposed for schizophrenia? Conventional psychiatric classifications certainly set the two apart, on the reasonable grounds that when occurring in their pure forms, each is associated with a distinctive pattern of symptomatology. But it is also true that clinicians have been forced to recognise the existence of so-called 'schizoaffective states' in which a mixture of schizophrenia and affective psychotic symptoms occurs in the same person. Formal statistical analyses of the symptoms of psychosis have tended to confirm the lack of discontinuity between schizophrenia and affective illness. For example, Brockington and his colleagues examined that very point and, finding that the two kinds of disorder 'present as a spectrum with no clear dividing line between one and the other', concluded that 'there is still no compelling evidence that the universe of psychotic patients falls naturally into these two groups'[12, 90]. Those who have looked at the same question from a genetic point of view have reached a rather different conclusion, arguing that schizophrenia and affective psychosis tend to 'breed true to type' in families[149, 181]. But careful inspection of the evidence suggests that this is by no means always observed, clear cases of manic-depression, for example, often occurring against a family background of schizophrenia, and vice versa: certainly the overlap seems to be no less than that found for the different forms that schizophrenia can take in different individuals. Finally, even the argument that the two types of psychosis are distinct because they respond to different kinds of treatment is not convincing: drug therapies found useful in affective disorder are often also beneficial in schizophrenia, and vice versa [39, 123].

It is then also of interest to consider observations that have been made concerning the *predisposing* characteristics that might underlie schizophrenia on the one hand, and affective psychosis on the other. There, too, we gain the same impression that certain features are common to both, while others are peculiar to each, allowing for the possibility that in many individual cases the predipositions are intermingled and only recognisable as distinct when they occur in pure form. This is certainly a quite explicit assumption of the way Eysenck deals with the question of prediposition to different types of psychosis[50]. For he would argue that 'psychoticism' is a *general* dimension of personality predisposing to all forms of psychotic illness, the particular direction in which disorder occurs depending on the individual's weighting on other personality characteristics, mainly introversion-extraversion. According to him schizophrenia is likely to be associated with a combination of psychoticism and introversion, manic-depression with a combination of psychoticism and ex-traversion. Since both of these dimensions are regarded as being continuously variable, many permutations are possible, giving rise, in the case of illness, to a corresponding mixture of psychotic symptoms.

As we saw in the previous chapter, Kretschmer also addressed the same question much earlier this century. Although, unlike Eysenck, he proposed a *single* personality dimension – schizothymia-cyclothymia – to encompass the normal equivalents of the two major types of psychosis, a similar theme is evident, albeit cast in slightly different form: that, lying as they do on the same continuum, there is an essential connection between schizophrenia and manic-depression. Kretschmer even went as far as to draw them together by noting that the contradictory quality of ambivalent elements which he, and others, had considered fundamental in the schizoid personality structure was also true of cycloid individuals, of whom he wrote:

> We ought not, therefore, to describe cycloid individuals, even apart from intermediate grades, as simply hypomanic, or simply depressive. For in many hypomanics there is hidden a small depressive component,and in the majority of cycloid melancholics there is a vein of humour. The hypomanic and melancholic halves of the cycloid temperament relieve one another, they form layers or patterns in individual cases, arranged in the most varied combinations[95].

Returning to the borderline states, we can now see why, when seeking a connection with the major psychoses, some writers have looked towards schizophrenia, other towards the affective disorders. But we can can also see why these are not mutually exclusive alternatives, but merely reflect the fact that the psychotic illnesses themselves are not sharply distinguishable. It now seems indisputable that many cases of borderline syndrome do have a general association with the major psychoses, forming part of the spectra of deviation which the latter describe. But it is also clear – indeed entirely predictable – that they are heterogeneous, those showing an affinity to psychosis doing so with *different* forms, according to which one they border on - and hence the one with which they share a common underlying disposition. Stone, in his eminently comprehensive text on the borderline states, reaches a similar conclusion, reminding us too of the range of abnormality which American practitioners have come to include under the description 'borderline':

> Some patients are now labelled 'borderline' for being, in effect, the casualties of our anachronistic nomenclature. Paradoxically, another group of borderline patients is the creation of our efforts, in recent years, to improve upon the older categories by creating diagnostic criteria that meet research standards. These tend to be strict; many of the cases they exclude are subsequently designated borderline according to one or another schema. . . .
> Another important group of borderline patients reflects the time

element in the unfolding of the classical schizophrenic and primary affective ('manic-depressive') illnesses: certain adolescent and young adult patients with ill-defined psychiatric disorders of moderate severity go on to exhibit clearly recognisable categories of illness (schizophrenia, bipolar manic-depression, and so forth) in their late twenties or thirties. In the meantime they are often called borderline. Besides these cases of 'incipient' schizophrenia or manic-depression are others, with attenuated forms of those disorders, who never go on to develop the full-blown condition. Many of these patients have also been called borderline, and their alleged relationship to the parent condition often represents an educated guess on the part of the clinician. In some instances this educated guess is reinforced by the presence of a family history strongly positive for one of the unequivocal forms of a functional psychosis. . . . Finally, borderline syndromes are encountered where no kinship to schizophrenia or affective illness is discernible but where psychosocial factors have been unusually adverse[169].

Given the differing uses to which the 'borderline' has been put, it is not suprising that some clinicians, intolerant of ambiguity, have reacted with irritation. However, others have been convinced, rightly I believe, that the existence of disorders which do not seem to fit conventional nosological categories is a more accurate reflection of the realities of psychological aberration; that individuals do malfunction in ways that are sometimes not easily assimilated by our preconceptions of psychiatric illness; that frequently they do so in a manner that is psychotic in quality, if not in degree; and that in consequence even the boundaries between accepted diagnostic labels, such as 'neurotic' and 'psychotic' become difficult to discern. It is these facts which the term 'borderline', as a shorthand description, has tried to articulate. There is of course a risk that it, too, can become a category – a dangerously ill-defined one – and it is probably this catch-all quality that has evoked most criticism. Many investigators are, however, aware of this problem and in recent years a great deal of thought, again mostly by American workers, has been devoted to the task of trying to define more precisely what is meant by 'borderline'.

Stone himself has made an important contribution here. He points out that there are three quite different elements, dimensions or frames of reference that in the past have been used separately, but should be used together, to describe the borderline states. One is what he calls the *constitutional* element, namely the inborn factors which predispose to the development of the major clinical syndromes like schizophrenia, affective psychosis, or a mixture of the two, and which may colour the appearance of their attenuated, or borderline, forms. A second is the *adaptation level*, which reflects the degree of personality organisation or disintegration present and which can be seen to range from the neurotic, through the borderline, to the psychotic. And, thirdly, there is the *personality type* – obsessive, hysterical, antisocial and so on – which helps to shape the behavioural and psychological style of the borderline patient.

Although in detail Stone's suggested approach to the classification of the borderline states is dauntingly 'multiaxial' – in the fashion of much current writing in American descriptive psychiatry – it does help to clarify some of the ambiguities in the borderline concept and points to places where answers about causation might be sought. Stone is well aware, for example, that psychoanalytic theory, which has tended in the past to dominate discussions of the borderline states, cannot by itself provide an adequate guideline for understanding them and that it is necessary to seek a *rapprochement* between psychodynamic explanations and those emerging from biological psychiatry; for he concludes his book as follows:

> The time seems now at hand to push on further to a psychoanalytic psychobiology – in which the newer genetic, biochemical, neuroendocrinological, and neurophysiological data are also integrated into a still broader framework. This kind of integration is particularly necessary in the realm of the borderline syndromes[169].

Stone is also one of the few contemporary American writers on the borderline states to draw upon theories of temperament and personality of the kind emphasised here. Uniquely, he even refers to Eysenck! For he acknowledges the latter's contribution in identifying dimensions of individual variation that could help to describe some features of borderline individuals, whose personality structure certainly seems to contain elements associated by Eysenck with 'psychoticism', as well as others, like impulsivity, that have also figured large in Eysenckian theory. In other words, although as far as I am aware the appropriate study has not been done, it could be confidently predicted that many borderline patients would fall at the extremes of the Eysenck dimensions, especially 'psychoticism'. Ironic as it may seem, we can therefore discern here our first likely point of convergence between the biological theories of temperament and those ideas, mainly of psychoanalytic origin, that gave rise to the borderline concept.

Although Stone's writings have clarified some of the muddled thinking that surrounds the term 'borderline', a more practical advance in terms of *classification* of the borderline states has come from work leading up to recent changes in the official American glossary of mental disorders, the *Diagnostic and Statistical Manual*. The latest revision of the manual (DSM-III) sets out explicit criteria for diagnosing borderline states, whereas in its earlier form the only reference to such conditions was under the heading 'borderline schizophrenia'. The change partly reflects a shift in American practice towards defining schizophrenia itself more narrowly than was once the case and hence the need to provide rational guidelines for diagnosing borderline syndromes, which might otherwise have remained even more vaguely specified than before.

As a basis for its revision to the *Diagnostic and Statistical Manual*, the American Psychiatric Association drew upon the findings of research it commissioned on how the term 'borderline' was used by clinicians. A crucial project was that conducted by Spitzer and his colleagues who studied the diagnostic habits of the members of the American Psychiatric Association and then went on to establish what they suggested were, and what were eventually adopted as, the definitive characteristics of borderlines[162]. From a review of the previous literature, Spitzer and his co-workers concluded that although the borderline description has been employed in many different ways, these actually reduce to *two* major forms of usage. One is applied to individuals who are thought to fall on a spectrum with, and be genetically related to, schizophrenia and who have been recognised as such on the grounds that they show attenuated schizophrenic characteristics, like cognitive disortions and so on. The other refers to a constellation of personality traits in which the emphasis has been rather more on features like impulsivity, self-damaging behaviour, hostility, and other signs of emotional instability. Starting from this observation, Spitzer and his collaborators, with the cooperation of other prominent workers in the field devised two sets of rating scale items, corresponding to the two borderline 'types' just described: these were initially designated 'schizotypal' and 'unstable'. The selected items were then cast into a single rating scale which was circulated to a very large sample of psychiatrists across the United States who were asked to apply it both to patients whom they considered typically 'borderline' and to control patients not falling into that category. A series of statistical analyses of the resulting data allowed the investigators to extract two item clusters which seemed to have good internal consistency and diagnostic validity and which eventually formed the basis for establishing, in the new DSM-III, the categories of 'schizotypal personality disorder' and 'borderline personality disorder'[40]. These are the characteristics said to describe the two kinds of borderline individual:

DSM-III Diagnostic Criteria for Schizotypal Personality Disorder

At least four of the following:

1 magical thinking, e.g., superstitiousness, clairvoyance, telepathy, '6th sense', 'others can feel my feelings' (in children and
  adolescents, bizarre fantasies or preoccupations)
2 ideas of reference
3 social isolation, e.g., no close friends or confidants, social
  contacts limited to essential everyday tasks
4 recurrent illusions, sensing the presence of a force or person
  not actually present (e.g., 'I felt as if my dead mother were in
  the room with me'), depersonalisation, or derealisation not
  associated with panic attacks
5 odd speech (without loosening of associations or incoherence),
  e.g., speeck that is digressive, vague, overelaborate, circum-
  stantial, metaphorical
6 inadequate rapport in face-to-face interaction due to con-
  stricted or inappropriate affect, e.g., aloof, cold
7 suspiciousness or paranoid ideation
8 undue social anxiety or hypersensitivity to real or imagined
  criticism

DSM-III Diagnostic Criteria for Borderline Personality Disorder

At least five of the following:

1 impulsivity or unpredictability in at least two areas that are
  potentially self-damaging, e.g., spending, sex, gambling,
  substance use, shoplifting, overeating, physically self-
  damaging acts
2 a pattern of unstable and intense interpersonal relationships,
  e.g., marked shifts of attitude, idealisation, devaluation,
  manipulation (consistently using others for one's own ends)
3 inappropriate, intense anger or lack of control of anger, e.g.,
  frequent displays of temper, constant anger
4 identity disturbance manifested by uncertainty about several
  issues relating to identity, such as self-image, gender identity,
  long-term goals or career choice, friendship patterns, values,
  and loyalties, e.g., 'Who am I?', 'I feel like I am my sister when I
  am good'
5 affective instability: marked shifts from normal mood to
  depression, irritability, or anxiety, usually lasting a few hours
  and only rarely more than a few days, with a return to normal
  mood

6 intolerance of being alone, e.g., frantic efforts to avoid being alone, depressed when alone

7 physically self-damaging acts, e.g., suicidal gestures, self-mutilation, recurrent accidents or physical fights

8 chronic feelings of emptiness or boredom

Although the solution to the classification of the borderline conditions that has come out of Spitzer's work will, for some, appear oversimplified, it does at least cut through a jungle of terminology and definition that bemuses the reader of the literature on these disorders and provides a more straightforward guide for objective study of them. An immediate question that can be, and has been, raised about the new classification is whether the two categories recognised are genuinely distinct varieties of borderline disorder, or whether they merely represent different manifestations of a common underlying 'borderline personality structure'. Part of the answer to that question can be found in the original study which led to their definition. There it was observed that there was virtually no correlation between the sets of characteristics used to define the two borderline 'types'. But this was only true when the analysis was confined to patients who had already been assigned to the *general* borderline category. When an unselected group of patients was examined – including borderlines *and* other individuals not diagnosed as such – there was a substantial correlation between the defining features of schizotypy and unstable personality. In other words, it seems that once individuals are recognised as suffering, in a broad sense, from a borderline disorder it is possible to discriminate those who are predominantly schizotypal from those who are more characteristically of emotionally unstable personality. On the other hand, it is also true that borderlines have certain underlying features in common that differentiate them from other psychiatric patients.

A further, obvious question to be asked here is how far each of the varieties of borderline disorder now identified represents a mild manifestation of the disposition towards one or other of the two major forms of psychotic illness, being genetically related to them. As we saw earlier, it has certainly been suggested that emotionally disturbed forms of borderline state – corresponding to what would now be called 'unstable personality disorder' – probably is genetically related to affective psychosis. In the case of the schizotypal form, an actual association with schizophrenia has been found in a study by Rieder[141]. Using the new criteria for schizotypal personality disorder, he reappraised the case histories of individuals who, in an earlier genetics study, had been described as 'borderline schizophrenics' and who had been found to occur frequently among the relatives of firmly diagnosed schizophrenics. Rieder observed that many such individuals met the criteria for schizotypal personality.

On clinical and genetic grounds, then, there is already good reason to suppose that the borderline states are what are sometimes referred to as *formes frustes* of the major psychotic illnesses, manifest as gross personality disorders. What other, additional, evidence do we have for that conclusion? Because of its relatively recent entry into the thinking of scientific investigators, the borderline concept is only just beginning to inspire research which would put it beyond doubt; research, say, showing a resemblance between borderline patients and psychotics on measures which would indicate that they share a similar central nervous system organisation. Indeed, a very noticeable, though in view of its strongly psychoanalytic origins perhaps unremarkable, feature of the literature on the borderline states is the almost total absence of an historical base in experimental research. As we saw earlier, Stone has commented in a similar vein, stressing the need for more research to identify measurable characteristics, including biological genetic markers, of the kind which have been so extensively studied in relation to the major psychiatric syndromes.

Despite the slow entry of research workers into the field of borderline disorders, there is nevertheless already some evidence to support the idea of a strong biological affinity with the major psychoses. Thus, in a recently reported study Braff used a laboratory procedure, derived from the experimental literature on schizophrenic cognitive disorder, to examine individuals diagnosed as showing schizotypal personality disorder according to the new DSM criteria[9]. Comparisons were made with matched groups of patients with firm diagnoses of either paranoid schizophrenia or depression. The experiment employed a technique in which the subject was required to recognise a briefly presented target stimulus quickly followed by a further powerful, but noninformational, display: the method makes it possible to access the early stages of information processing where, as we saw in chapter 7, schizophrenics seem to behave in an unusual fashion. Braff confirmed that this was so in his own sample of schizophrenics. But, more interesting, he also showed it to be true of the schizotypal borderline patients, suggesting that the latter do indeed have a similar type of nervous system.

Investigations of the kind just quoted are slowly beginning to appear in the literature on borderlines, as the DSM-III criteria begin to have their influence. This is being seen especially in high-risk research where attempts, on the one hand, to find biological markers for schizophrenia and, on the other, to describe borderline characteristics more objectively are becoming inseparably joined: an example is to be found in recent studies of eye-tracking dysfunction, a psychophysiological sign which we have seen has been extensively studied in relation to schizophrenia[157, 158]. The study of the borderline patient is therefore an inextricable part of, and cannot be dissociated from, the study of the major psychoses, the same biological and psychological mechanisms coming under scrutiny and the same forms of explanation of the abnormal behaviour observed beginning to be identified.

Recognising the borderline states as mild forms of psychotic illness is, of course, entirely consistent with the view of the latter developed over the previous two chapters. For such conditions can logically be seen as disorders sitting between full-blown psychosis and the personality variations that predispose to them. The connections linking these three domains of investigation – personality, illness, and the predisposition to illness – are now becoming increasingly evident. For example, the Eysenckian dimensions look as though they probably define, at one and the same time, characteristic features of borderline personality structure and traits predisposing to psychosis. And an even firmer bridge is evident in work we described in the previous chapter on individual differences among normal subjects in the extent to which they can be found to show explicitly defined 'borderline' characteristics. Here it is worth reiterating that the questionnaire for assessing borderline traits described there was deliberately fashioned after the the DSM-III criteria shown earlier. Indeed, by referring back to those criteria it is possible to get a good idea of the kinds of characteristic examined in our new questionnaire. It will also be recalled that the most significant result we have obtained using the questionnaire concerns differences between individuals on tests of hemisphere function, differences that closely resemble those observed in schizophrenic patients. We also noted the possible consequences of having such a 'schizotypal' central nervous system: how the unusual perceptual, attentional and language processing with which it is associated might sensitise the person to environmental events which, under some circumstances, could predispose to psychotic modes of responding, even psychotic illness. It is, of course, not difficult to extrapolate these ideas to an understanding of how the same characteristics might lead to psychological and social aberrations which stop short of frank psychotic breakdown, occurring instead in an intermediate form, as the partially disintegrated, unstable and ambivalent personality structure observed in borderline patients.

More generally, it is also now possible to fill in some of the other gaps left in our discussion, not only in the last two chapters, but also from the very beginning of this book. The apparent coexistence of psychotic and anti-social personality traits, for example, becomes explicable; for the characteristics that define the borderline states are frequently indistinguishable from those used to describe other forms of deviant personality and often lead to similar forms of socially maladaptive behaviour, such as drug addiction, aggression and disturbed interpersonal relationships. The reason labels like 'psychopathy', 'hysterical personality', 'character disorder' and so on often seem fuzzy is also elucidated. Unless carefully defined to describe forms of abnormality that really do fall outside the psychological domain of the psychotic – as indeed is sometimes the case – such terms can refer to disorders that are truly borderline. Finally, the difficulty of defining psychosis itself, evident even in the first chapter here, can be accepted as a genuine question, to be answered not by seeking (except for practical diagnostic purposes) arbitrary points of discontinuity, but by recognising the natural spectrum of behaviour that runs from the normal, through the borderline, to the psychotic.

One consequence of accepting the borderline concept that deserves further comment is the implication that there is no clear dividing line between the neuroses and the psychoses. The idea is, of course, perfectly acceptable to psychoanalysts. Indeed, as we have seen, that strand of theorising about the borderline disorders which has its origins in psychoanalytic thought quite firmly sees them as constituting a halfway stage in the disintegration of personality. Even Stone, a more eclectic writer, has incorporated this idea into his own account of the borderline syndromes, with his suggestion that 'adaptation level' is one of the dimensions along which psychiatric disorders vary, determining the degree to which, and the ways in which, a common underlying psychopathology can manifest itself, both temporally and structurally. This does not mean, to re-emphasise an earlier point, that *all* forms of neurosis are merely lesser manifestations of psychosis: it is a perfectly familiar idea, even in physical medicine, that quite different aetiologies give rise to similar superficial symptomatologies, forming the final common path for causal influences which are themselves highly specific. But it should caution us against accepting uncritically the conventional wisdom which sets the discussion of neurosis apart from the attempt to understand psychosis; or, looked at another way, we should not be too quick to reject some of the more valuable ideas contained in psychoanalytic theory.

Before leaving this topic it is worth noting that psychoanalysts or others recently contemplating the borderline concept are not the only modern writers to argue against the current tendency to separate the psychoses from other mental illnesses. Foulds, a psychologist whose work we came across in a different context in chapter 1, took a similar view[58]. Concerned more with classification and diagnosis than with causation, he proposed a schema which was essentially hierarchical, the major psychiatric syndromes being arranged in a descending order of severity, downwards from the most disintegrative forms of psychosis to the mild neuroses. The hierarchy was considered to be non-reflexive, patients being assigned to their place on it according to the symptoms of the most serious illness from which they suffered; but this did not preclude them from receiving subsidiary diagnoses located lower down the hierarchy. Use of the system in practice proved it to be highly accurate and able to accommodate a number of important clinical facts, such as the coincidence of neurotic and psychotic syndromes in the same individual; the tendency for neurotic symptomatology to herald schizophrenic breakdown; or, alternatively, the uncovering of neurotic disorder by treatment for acute psychosis. Foulds's thoughts about underlying mechanisms were confined to a proposal that shifts up and down his descriptive hierarchy reflect changes in an individual's ability to maintain satisfyingly mutual personal relationships with other people; otherwise he had little to say. This neglect of aetiological considerations – the failure, for example, to explain why some, but not other, patients progress to more severe illnesses – is clearly a weakness in Foulds's model. But his writings deserve more attention than they have received, if only because he was one of the few clinical psychologists, soberly and without fuss, to challenge successfully an assumption on which a great deal of current psychiatric research is based.

Returning finally to the borderline states, it is my conviction that the area of research they encompass could hold the key to many puzzling and as yet unsolved problems in psychiatry, including some that have surfaced in this book. People who fit the description 'borderline' extend our attempts to understand personality to its limits, presenting, as they do, an ambivalent mix of emotional tendencies and an uncertainty about the nature of their own selves as puzzling as any seen in schizophrenia. Yet as Sass, whom I quoted earlier, points out, they need not necessarily be found as psychiatric patients or clients – and certainly need not be regarded as schizophrenic, in the conventional sense. Yet their mental turmoil seems not far away from the psychotic. A case as typical as any – which helps to draw together several of the themes of this chapter – is that of Edie Sedgwick: Andy Warhol superstar, golden girl of the 1960s, Vogue model, and drug addict whose short, bright, sad life (and death) were recently chronicled through extensive interviews with her relatives and friends[166]. Born into a privileged background, with a heritage of mental illness (her father was manic-depressive) and considerable creativity, Edie Sedgwick emerged, as one acquaintance put it:

> as a caterpillar that had turned into a butterfly . . . All of a sudden the spotlights were on her and she was being treated as something very, very special, but inside she felt like a lump of dirt. Then when she was being paid less attention to, she didn't know who she was. That possibility of destruction was built into the

weakness of her personality. We have to get used to the reality that we're alone. If you can't get used to it, then you go mad. And she went kind of mad . . . She was very nervous, very fragile, very thin, very hysterical. You could hear her screaming even when she wasn't screaming – this sort of supersonic whistling.

Another friend described her in a similar vein:

She could be quite a different person from hour to hour. What sort of creature am I today? Am I like this? Am I like that? Very mercurial: she could be immensely difficult or very sweet; she could be creative and sculpt and have an organized week; or she could retreat and be chaotic and not do anything. That was part of her charm – that she was so unpredictable.

Some talked of there being 'so much anger involved' in her personality; others of how 'underneath there was an incredible dark fear'. Her brother Jonathan spoke of her exquisite sensitivity:

Edie had this other trick of being able to talk your sentences as you said them . . . . Did it blow my mind! I couldn't get my words out fast enough. I couldn't beat her! . . . With Edie there was no time between feeling and thought . . . I just didn't like being read that closely.

Edie Sedgwick died at the age of 28 from an overdose of barbiturates. Which of her qualities finally destroyed her is difficult to say, but retrospectively labelling her 'borderline' (unhelpful and unnecessary in itself) is at least an invitation to try to understand.

10

Reflections

For the readers of this book the perspective taken on personality and mental disorder may have emerged as an uneasy eclectic mix, a gritty amalgam of the digestible and the unpalatable. Few will surely have needed persuading of the idea that some forms of psychological abnormality   notably the classic signs of anxiety and certain manifestations of antisocial behaviour – stem from, indeed may be said to be in some sense continuous with, normal variations in temperament or personality. But the emphasis on biological, even genetic influences in such conditions may have been less convincing for those whose preference is for social, sociological and environmental explanations. Hopefully not too controversial has been the insistence on resting the conclusions reached on the findings of studies in experimental psychology and experimental psychopathology – despite the fact that the subject matter of those disciplines has less intrinsic appeal, compared with the exotic attractions of psychodynamic or other loosely arranged styles of studying human behaviour.

In the case of the more serious, psychotic types of disorder it is for other reasons that the arguments here have departed from some currently received wisdom. A genetically based biological influence on their aetiology can now scarcely be disputed, though exactly how we should conceptualise it is more open to question than many, schooled in the strict medical traditions of psychiatry, would have us believe. Here it has been argued that the psychotic states are really no different from those conditions that we are accustomed to label 'neurotic', in the sense that like the latter they too represent a maladaptive or disabling transformation of elements that make up the human personality. The fact that in the psychotic states the break into illness involves a greater discontinuity of function, while important to our understanding, should not distract us from seeing their essential continuity with normality and health, a connection highlighted by the evident biological and phenomenological overlap between the lesser and the more serious types of mental disorder.

The ideas developed over the previous chapters were arrived at by cutting across some established polarities of opinion, in the process of which we discovered some unexpected alignments of viewpoint. For example, we found that Eysenck and the antipsychiatrists agree in criticising the use of a medical framework for studying mental illness. Their solutions are different, of course, and both are wrong in rejecting outright the concept of disease in psychiatry. For we have seen that there are many points at which we can perceive a resemblance between psychological disorders and certain kinds of physical disease, where the criteria for defining the ill state can be equally arbitrary. This is not to deny that the disease label contains a greater element of social comment when applied to psychological abnormality – inevitably so because disturbed behaviour does not occur in isolation from its social context and can scarcely escape the evaluative actions of others. But in recognising this important difference between physical and mental disease we should not, like Szasz and other antipsychiatrists, overreact into excluding from consideration one of the strongest points of similarity, namely the grounding of psychological abnormality in the biology of the organism. In that respect Eysenck is much closer to conventional psychiatry, a fact which has however, generally been ignored by psychiatric writers. This is perhaps because psychiatry too has created its own false dichotomies. Apart from some speculations about the neuropharmacology of anxiety it has remained fairly silent about the biology of the less serious disorders. Generally it has left that furrow to be ploughed, with a few notable exceptions, by non-medical psychophysiologists having an interest in personality. Where it has sought a theoretical perspective of its own it has relied on a mishmash of ideas borrowed from psychoanalysis, sociology and, more recently, some parts of behaviourist psychology. In contrast, the stance of conventional psychiatry towards the more serious disorders has been quite thoroughly organic, though its preference for the classic approach of neuropathology – a formula that so outraged Szasz – carries a serious danger: that the vision of its research on diseases like schizophrenia may be so narrowed that it succeeds in explaining only those untypical examples where a discrete brain lesion can be demonstrated. It now seems unlikely that this will apply to the majority of cases and that, if we are to refer our explanations of such disorders to brain biology, then we need to do so in a broader research context which embraces the psychogenetics, psychophysiology and neuro-psychology of normal as well as abnormal personality.

I suspect that as criticisms some of the above remarks apply less to the psychiatry of North America than they do to that of Great Britain. This may be due to the stronger influence on American psychiatry of the psychoanalytic doctrine, which has conferred on it several powerful benefits: more flexibility of thought about mental disorder, a readier acceptance of the ambiguous boundaries between illness and health, and, most importantly, a greater preparedness to see even the most severely disturbed individual, not merely as an object of disease, but as a suffering person whose psychology, as well as biology, is important. Admittedly, some of these advantages have brought with them an occasional tendency to indulge in theoretical speculations so florid as to cause others to react with incredulity – and academic psychology to turn its back entirely on the psychoanalytic movement. On the other hand, psychoanalysis and its offshoots have helped to keep open a concern with the humanistic aspects of personality while others of more experimental bent pursued their goal of objective measurement of Man's behaviour. The academic community in psychology may yet have cause to be grateful for that fact and eventually come to recognise the potential advantages to be gained from conjoining facts obtained in the clinic and those gathered in the laboratory. Already, as observed in the previous chapter, we find an American writer calling for, and seeing the possibility of, an integration between psychoanalytic and biological conceptions of mental illness; though it has to be said that that is the kind of interdisciplinary comment unlikely to be voiced in the British psychiatric or psychological literature.

Following, to some extent, from the last comment, it will also have been evident that in proceeding through the book it has proved necessary to move on, sometimes quite quickly, from the relatively simplistic biological theories of temperament with which we started, in order to try to account for facets of human personality and mental illness which 'nervous type' models in their classically stated and current form do not begin to explain. This is not to argue that biological researchers should try to put more psychological flesh on their theoretical skeletons by seeking a particular affinity with psychoanalysis. More important is the general point: that there is a need to break down some of the conceptual barriers that have so far prevented psychiatry and abnormal psychology arriving at a more complete biopsychology of human personality. For example, a prominent theoretical and empirical anchor for our discussions here has been psychophysiology, a discipline whose expressed aim is to bridge the gap between the psychological and the biological. It must be admitted, however, that to date psychophysiological research has concentrated mainly on the *physiological* side of the equation. On the psychological side it has been principally concerned with rather superficial, broadly defined characteristics, such as mood states, personality traits and diagnostic groupings, and has been content to seek correlations between them and physiological variables. The explanatory models of psychophysiology reflect this emphasis, being unashamedly conceptual *nervous system* models which rarely get to grips with the fine detail of psychological data and which, to the outside observer, must appear at times to offer a somewhat impersonal, robotic view of Man, as a creature driven – sometimes to distraction – by his biological make-up. That impression is no doubt reinforced by the fact that when psychophysiology has departed from the mere correlational and descriptive, and tried to give an account of 'psychological mechanisms', it has tended to take a thoroughly behaviouristic perspective on the matter. A good example in the abnormal field is the conditioned response explanation of neurotic phobias, linked to the idea of individual differences in physiological reactivity.

Although that approach has certainly been successful in accounting for certain narrow aspects of psychiatric disorder, its limitations quickly become apparent once one moves on to consider more complex types of psychological dysfunction or those features that do not easily fit behaviourist paradigms. The mechanisms of conversion hysteria, for example, remain an enigma; while conditioned response explanations of schizophrenia have been a lamentable failure. The fact is that the real stuff of psychopathology is experiential, hidden from view, consisting of images, thoughts, ideas, motives, attitudes, expectations, and the causes of irrationality – all of the things which behaviourism, already virtually defunct anyway in general psychology, finds difficult to investigate and explain. That being so, scientific researchers in abnormal psychology should, I believe, pay more deliberate attention to evidence gathered by the methods of introspection, trying to build a more substantial bridge between their models of the nervous system and psychological data which up to now they have been shy of, or even downright hostile to, investigating.

The inclusion of a studied introspectionism among its methods would actually not be a new venture for experimental psychopathology: it would merely be a return to its origins. For there was a time when 'introspectionism' was a less disreputable term, even in academic psychology. Thus, much of the latter's early methodology relied on the subject's self-report: indeed, to some extent, it still does – for even the simplest psychophysical procedure, such as the determination of a sensory threshold, forces the investigator to enter, if only in the most elemental sense, the private world of the individual he is studying. The subsequent rise of behaviourism, however, inhibited experimental psychologists from going further than that. An additional factor was undoubtedly the divorce of academic psychology from real-life concerns, especially those encountered in the clinical setting. At the turn of the century there were some clinicians who attached themselves to the newly emerging disciplines of experimental psychology and psychophysiology, using its methods as a way of exploring the mental state of their patients: Jung's early application of the word-association technique to the study of schizophrenic thought is a good example.

These two influences – the retreat into the laboratory and a behaviouristic preoccupation solely with observable action – were to the detriment of psychology, limiting it to narrow and esoteric concerns and creating for it a public image which it is only now, slowly, beginning to reverse. In this respect it is an irony that Pavlov is mostly remembered for his work on the conditioned reflex and for, unwittingly, helping to create the school of mechanistic thought in psychology which powerfully shaped fifty years of its history. Even the influence of Pavlov's ideas about temperament, less well-known in any case, stopped short, at least in the West, at his early theory based on animal experimentation. Yet he himself, as we saw when discussing his writings on the topic, clearly recognised that it was necessary to introduce new concepts into nervous typological theory, in order to take account of the higher mental functions peculiar to Man and to explain the personality differences to which these give rise.

At this point it is worth pausing to speculate, with the benefit of several intervening chapters since discussing Pavlov's work, how, in outline, future nervous type theories of personality might start to take shape and how they might be able to incorporate data that have previously been regarded as outside their scope of explanation. It may be recalled that Pavlov devised the twin notions of first and second signal systems to account for, respectively, the affective and ideational processes which, according to their relative imbalance or equilibrium, determine the behavioural and psychological expression of more basic biological processes that underlie different types of temperament. In contemporary thinking about the brain the idea that Pavlov was groping for finds a rough parallel in work on the functional relationship between the two cerebral hemispheres. For, as shown here, we can now be reasonably sure that an important biological substrate for personality, both normal and pathological, probably does consist of variations in cerebral organisation of the kind revealed in hemisphere research. Further exploration of that possibility is therefore likely to be one of the most fruitful growing-points in research on the biology of personality over the next decade. This means that it will necessary to find ways of integrating ideas from what have historically been two different routes to the construction of a conceptual nervous system for Man: one, psychophysiological, with its emphasis on low-level brain structures and on dynamic neural processes; the other, neuropsychological, concerned with the exploration of the functional properties of anatomically defined regions in the higher nervous system. Here it is worth reminding ourselves of the two reasons why the latter approach is likely to become increasingly important in personality research. One is that neuropsychology offers the possibility of substituting the real brain for the 'black box' models of the nervous system found in cognitive psychology, another area of research which, as we have seen, has contributed in its own right to our understanding of many forms of psychopathology, such as depression and schizophrenia. The other, more general, reason is that neuro-psychological investigations (of, say, hemisphere organisation) are able to probe quite directly at the interface between the nervous system and those aspects of mental activity – language, perception, memory and feeling – which lie at the heart of personality: in the abnormal states they also suggest ways in which we might match brain to mind in our attempts to understand the mechanisms of symptom formation. In short, they promise a convenient route through which to explore the neurobiological correlates of consciousness – and of the unconscious – and a way of handling much that in the past has been relegated to introspectionist psychology.

None of this should be taken as minimising the continuing importance of the strictly psychophysiological approach. The latter is ideal for studying, in the intact human subject, the spatial, temporal and other features of basic physiological processes, like inhibition and excitation, which modulate activity at all levels in the nervous system and which, as we have seen, are in themselves a major source of individual differences. Psychophysiology also provides an increasingly sophisticated technology for the fine-grain analysis of biological signals, especially in the EEG, that accompany mental events. Nervous typological researchers of the future will undoubtedly combine, more often than they do now, the methodologies of both disciplines; to put it in a practical context, recording psychophysiological variables while simultaneously probing the brain with divided field and other techniques derived from neuropsychology. Used together in this way it should then be possible to arrive at conceptual nervous system models that have a more 'psychological' content, closer to the data which our introspections quite firmly tell us are there but which have so far eluded, or not interested, biological workers in personality research.

Contemplating the likely nature of such models, it is probable that many of the conclusions about personality already reached by those working in the classic tradition of nervous type theory will still stand. For there is too powerful a body of evidence to reject the view that individuals differ according to certain fundamental nervous properties, probably genetically determined, which underlie temperamental qualities like reactivity, sensitivity, attentiveness, and ability to regulate the demands of the environment. An important common feature of these properties seems to be the role they play in maintaining, or failing to maintain, an excitatory-inhibitory balance in the nervous system. It is conceivable that the relative strengths of 'excitation' and 'inhibition' are constant for the individual, being ultimately dependent on some characteristics of neuronal activity, and manifest in different forms at various levels of central nervous organisation, from the microscopic to the macroscopic, and represented in both the upper and lower brain. Whether or not that proves to be the case, it seems certain that the general notion of excitation-inhibition will remain a central guiding principle in nervous typological theory.

It will then be necessary to graft on to that principle other facts about the biological differentiation of the human organism, such as variations in lateralisation and specialisation of psychological functions, especially language. These individual differences are also probably under some genetic control, though possibly inherited quite independently of the other more dynamic nervous properties referred to above. During development, however, the two sources of variation are bound to be inextricably interactive: for example, the degree to which some linguistic functions become established in the dominant hemisphere may well partly depend on the quality of excitatory and inhibitory influences that operate both vertically in the nervous system and horizontally, across the corpus callosum. Looking at this interaction from a more general viewpoint, the extent to which thresholds vary for the triggering of excitation and inhibition in the brain almost certainly helps to determine, through the attentive mechanisms, the contents of consciousness. The latter consist, of course, not only of events in the external environment, but also of stored memories, affects and images that may motivate internal as well as observable responses. The latter, in their turn, may alter the physiological state associated with and partly helping to produce them. It is at this triple interface − between psychological content, neurophysiological process and functional anatomical organisation of the brain − that new insights will be required. It seems to me that they are unlikely to be reached without developing in personality research a more elaborated 'scientific introspectionism', suitably adapted to the experimental method, but capable of going beyond the simple verbal responses which at present pass as self-report.

It is probably evident that the above speculations were very much guided by the conclusions about personality that have been reached in this book from work on the psychotic states. For some that may seem a rather odd source from which to seek inspiration. Although in earlier times the psychology of disorders like schizophrenia was of great concern to clinicians and other observers, more recently interest in the form and quality of the psychotic experience has greatly receded, taking with it a relative disregard for anything other than the underlying biology. Exceptions, of course, are psychoanalysts, radical writers like Laing who, in the 1960s, formed the 'unacceptable face' of psychiatry, and a few experimental psychologists who, during the same period, attempted to translate the self-reports of schizophrenics into the attention theories of the time. Currently even these influences have waned and the predominant emphasis among those shaping public opinion is strictly neuropathological, helping to bring about the separation, which I have challenged here, of the study of psychosis from that of normal personality. Of course, it could be argued that preoccupation with the introspective data of schizophrenics is no great loss; that ideas about the probable continuity between the psychotic and the normal *have* continued to develop, albeit unnoticed – in, for example, Eysenck's dimensional theory of personality. The irony is, however, that it is precisely in trying to gain insight into the nature of psychotic characteristics that we are brought up against the limitations of current models of the Eysenckian type; not, I should stress, because their dimensional assumptions about psychosis are wrong – the evidence strongly suggests otherwise – but because the bare psychophysiological concepts the models contain are inadequate to explain psychotic forms of temperamental make-up.

It is here that a defence of introspectionism, of the validity, for example, of the schizophrenic's self-report, and of the need for new conceptual nervous models in personality theory take on relevance. It is clear – and I would suggest we only know this from the psychotic's introspections, extrapolated to our own experiences – that the core feature of schizophrenia is a profound disturbance of consciousness. Schizophrenia is, in other words, the prime example of a mental state that is relatively inaccessible to the methods on which much current nervous typological theory is based. That would not matter much (for our present argument, that is) if we could be sure that the state were merely a bizarre epiphenomenon of some underlying neuropathology having no likely reference point in normal consciousness. But, as evidence for the continuity model demonstrates, this is manifestly not the case. The proposal here for a conjoining of psychophysiological and neuropsychological ideas about the brain therefore assumes special significance when we turn our attention to the understanding of the psychoses, their borderline variants, and the normal personality styles associated with them. The particular possibility that a crucial and common biological feature of all of these is the organisational arrangement of the cerebral hemispheres makes the suggestion even more relevant in the light of conclusions, drawn for example from split-brain research, that therein lie the clues to some important riddles that have so far defied explanation: the mechanisms of unconscious influences on behaviour, the nature of self-identity, and the parallel linguistic and non-linguistic modes by which the individual internalises a representation of the outside world. The introspections of schizophrenics tell us that it is indeed in some of these respects that they are confused, as also seems to be the case in some 'borderline' individuals, whose ambivalence of feeling and attitude to others – so salient a feature of that personality type – probably has a similar explanation. As we have seen, there is a remarkable match between the experimental evidence and these introspections. This should encourage biological researchers to take more account of such data in formulating their personality theories. The fact that we are led to this conclusion from the study of the psychotic states is in itself interesting and suggests, unlikely though it may seem, that it is from there that some of our most profound insights about mind/brain relationships will come.

Changing direction somewhat, let us now consider a different set of topics; namely the several major omissions that will have been apparent in this book. One is the little reference made here to evidence obtained from animal research. This has been deliberate because it was felt that a coherent enough story could be told about personality and mental disorder on the basis of what we already know from studies of human subjects. The contribution of animal research to the field must nevertheless be acknowledged. Indeed, the human studies and the biological theories of personality drawn upon here, especially in earlier chapters, owe a great deal to such research, Pavlov's pioneer observations being the notable example. And, more generally, our knowledge of the brain – vital to an understanding of the biology of personality – has depended, and will continue to depend, on research strategies for studying the nervous system that cannot be used in Man. The limitations of those strategies must also be recognised, however; not merely in the trite comment that extrapolating across species is hazardous, but in a deeper sense. Clearly there are certain features of personality which we can be sure are impossible to model in animals and others that are extremely difficult to do so: these are of course the very same features that pose the problems for human research that we have just been discussing. It is therefore necessary to ask what are the real limits of animal experimentation in the field and what form it might take in the future.

Animal research on personality is inevitably confined to modelling some human characteristic that finds a parallel in the objectively observable behaviour of a lower species. The most successful examples – anxiety is one – involve some feature, or set of features, that has a very clear and universally recognisable counterpart in the animal. Even in those cases the replica is quite incomplete, but at least a sufficiently large part of it is patent enough for even the casual observer to be persuaded. The problem for the animal researcher comes when he attempts to go beyond that. He is then faced with the unenviable choice between a slippery slide into the swamp of anthropomorphism or the sterile safety of analogical reasoning that offers little in the way of a next practical step to knowledge about the human state. Sometimes the conflict is resolved by virtually abandoning the original animal model. An instance of the latter is the 'learned helplessness' explanation of depression, to which the initial animal observations were probably irrelevant for arriving at the subsequent cognitive theory. The danger, of course, is that, once set in motion, animal research inspired by some question in human psychology, takes on an impetus of its own, is conducted for its own sake, and the long-term aim is forgotten. That criticism is more serious for psychology – especially for the psychology of personality – than it is for other life sciences because we know from the very beginning that there are some insights into human nature that we can never gain by turning to animals. The question for us here is really whether animal experimentation has now done its admittedly very useful job of helping to point research on the biology of personality in the right direction and contributing to its broad theoretical structure. To jump to such a drastic conclusion would be to underestimate the complexity of those problems where animal research has been and can continue to be of value. But it is possible that the time has now come to re-evaluate the form of its contribution in the future (here, of course, I am not referring to work in the general field of animal neurophysiology, but to research which has the specific aim of elucidating human individual differences).

In trying to answer the question just posed it is perhaps worth reminding ourselves of how, if our earlier supppositions are correct, research utilising *human* subjects will develop in the future. It was suggested it might do so by seeking a closer connection between experiential psychology, psychophysiology, and the neuropsychology of higher nervous function. Clearly animal experimentation is at a disadvantage here. Animals cannot tell us what is going on in their heads; nor do they have the highly developed and differentiated cortical structures that make that possible. They do, however, show *psychophysiological* responses which, as far as we know, are biologically continuous with those of man, at least up to the point at which the development of their nervous systems ceases. Therein perhaps lies the clue to the future role of animal research in the study of personality. Animal researchers could, with advantage, seek a different kind of bridge with human psychology – looking not for similarities in gross behaviour (these rapidly reach their upper limits of extrapolation to Man) but for parallels in psychophysiological responses that can be precisely specified. They could then exploit the one respect – the functional properties of the nervous system – in which different species do appear to show biological continuity. An example of this strategy was the study of 'augmenting-reducing' in cats reported in chapter 3, where we saw that it is possible to reproduce in animals certain EEG correlates of human temperament. But it is again schizophrenia research which illustrates the point best, since it is there that the difficulties of finding an animal model for the human condition are most clearly highlighted.

I think it must now be clear that a *complete* animal model of schizophrenia is impossible: the crucial role played by language and thought disturbance in the condition makes it so. While recognising this to be the case, animal researchers have nevertheless frequently sought a crude analogue in lower species, usually motivated by the search for the biochemical 'cause' of schizophrenia. Essentially what they have done is to try to identify some piece of behaviour which they believe is fundamental to schizophrenia and which, because it is observable, can be reproduced in animals: commonly it takes the form of stereotyped movements or other glaring abnormalities of response, often induced with massive doses of drugs, such as amphetamine[44]. Actually, the parallel with schizophrenia is remarkably unconvincing in its inability to capture the essence of the human disorder. One reason is simply that amphetamine is a poor choice of drug with which to model schizophrenia (As I have argued elsewhere, LSD, for example, would be much better[24].) However, a much more telling reason is that the rationale for most studies of 'schizophrenia' in animals is unsound. For such experiments rest on the assumption that between animals and Man there is some kind of unchanging continuum – of 'schizophrenicity' – which can, as it were, be scaled down to simple behavioural elements, yet retain its essential similarity. (The assumption, a legacy of early behaviourism, commonly forms the basis of animal modelling, not only in psychiatry but also in psychology.) There is, however, an alternative to this approach that differs from it in subtle but important ways, and which is illustrated in attempts by human psychophysiologists to find parallels between their own observations on schizophrenics and those made by animal investigators engaged in direct study of the brain itelf.

A good example of the strategy just described is to be found in the writings of Venables, whose work was mentioned in an earlier chapter as of considerable significance in demonstrating marked instability of the galvanic skin response among schizophrenics, especially their tendency to show extreme patterns of either excessive underreactivity or excessive overreactivity. It may be recalled that Venables interpreted this finding as evidence of instability in the brain's limbic system. What is of interest here is that he was then able to support that intepretation by referring to work showing that identical instabilities of galvanic skin responding can be induced in animals (monkeys, in this case) in whom parts of the limbic system had been lesioned experimentally. The point about these observations is that they make no pretence that what is being modelled in animals is *schizophrenia* (indeed the experiments Venables quotes were carried out for a quite different purpose). Instead, they merely help to identify, in a way that is impossible from research on Man, the neurophysiological mechanisms that might be responsible for certain dynamic brain processes which appear to be disturbed in human psychosis; forming only one, probably low-level, part of its biological correlates. Although more narrowly focused and more limited in what it can tell us about schizophrenia, such exchange of information between the human and animal researcher actually takes us closer to an understanding of the disorder than studies which, motivated by the search for a single 'cause', attempts to find some convincing analogue of psychosis in the behaviour of a lower species.

The study just quoted is, I believe, generalisable to other animal research on personality and mental disorder. For it illustrates how, instead of looking for what are often more and more strained parallels with human behaviour, such research might do better to seek a closer *rapprochement* with human psychophysiology, sharing data with the latter and trying to answer incisive questions about nervous typological processes which species have in common but which, for a variety of reasons, can be better examined in animals. Actually, what is being suggested here is in the spirit of the original Pavlovian tradition in this field, though turned on its head. Just as the growth of modern biological theories of personality depended on the application to humans of ideas about the nervous system obtained from animals, so there would now seem to be a case for animal researchers deriving their experiments more directly from evidence about nervous system differences that has accumulated in the meantime from psychophysiological studies of human subjects. The questions asked would then be different, often having only a slender reference point in human personality in its fullest sense. But the questions may be more pertinent and their answers more helpful to those working with human subjects.

The perspective on animal research just outlined might appear to undermine its importance, relegating it to a secondary place in relation to human research. To some extent that is true – inevitably so, since with the exception of those few who find animal temperament intrinsically interesting, the ultimate purpose is to understand the *human* personality. On the other hand, many problems remain where animal research can make an important contribution. It is simply that they would be solved more quickly if animal experimentation were viewed as a tool of human psychology, necessary but economically used.

Not entirely unconnected with the neglect of animal research here is another omission, namely the lack of reference to the biochemical correlates of individual differences. Actually, the field of biochemistry – and here I am referring strictly to brain biochemistry – is highly specialised and technical, and already so extensive that any attempt to give a sensible and comprehensive account of its subject matter would have imparted a style and purpose to the book which was not intended. In any case it is doubtful whether the conclusions reached about personality and mental disorder would have been substantially different. Neurochemical techniques are just another tool for filling in detail at the biological end of the spectrum, incapable of answering purely psychological questions but potentially very useful for the fine-grain analysis and quantification of those brain processes that underlie behaviour. Biochemical models of the brain – and that is all they are at the present time – are therefore no different from, and no substitute for, other more macroscopic conceptual nervous system models: they are merely constructed lower down the hierarchy. Nevertheless, for completion some comment is necessary about the contribution of biochemistry research to the topics we have been discussing here. In doing so it is worth noting that there are three rather distinct senses in which biochemical data could be said to have been relevant to the subject matter of this book.

One, explicitly medical, application of neurochemistry is an inextricable part of the attempts just mentioned in relation to animal research to trace the origins of disorders like schizophrenia to a single biochemical anomaly, which can then be construed as the cause of the illness. This endeavour has a long history in psychiatric research, which has gone through the whole gamut of brain chemicals, hailing each new one that is discovered as a possible cause of schizophrenia. The most popular recent version of the hypothesis, however, has been that implicating the neurotransmitter, dopamine. Pursuit of the 'dopamine hypothesis' has stimulated a vast amount of research effort[80, 120]. Part of that work has sustained, and been sustained by, the animal models of schizophrenia criticised earlier: the argument is that the drugs producing the 'psychotic' behaviour patterns in animals do so by influencing dopamine sensitive neurones in the brain. Unfortunately, even though the pharmacological part of the reasoning there may be correct, the methodology, as we have seen, is vitiated by the disastrous fit of the animal model to the clinical condition. Testing the hypothesis in humans has involved assaying the metabolites of dopamine in the blood, urine or cerebrospinal fluid, often after appropriate experimental manipulations, such as adminstering drugs; or, in the search for more direct evidence, examining the chemical content of the autopsied brains of deceased schizophrenics[37]. The latter, 'lemon-squeezer' approach to the problem is crude in the extreme, the people whose autopsied brains are studied having lived through a long period of chronic illness and drug administration – factors which usually have not been, or cannot be, properly controlled for in selecting comparison groups. Furthermore, the rationalé of the method is as suspect as that of many animal models of schizophrenia, in failing to match the biological conception to the complex psychology of the clinical condition and in not fully recognising that any neurochemical changes observed may be as much an epiphenomenon of the psychotic experience as vice versa.

The dopamine hypothesis is also very weak when looked at from a purely biochemical viewpoint. For it almost certainly tells only part of the story. True, we can now be fairly sure that dopamine *is* involved in schizophrenia, if only because it is an important neurotransmitter in the limbic system, a brain circuit which, as pointed out many times here, probably does help to mediate some of the psychological processes that underlie the disorder. But that is different from saying that there is anything *exclusive* about the supposed disturbance of dopamine metabolism in schizophrenia, let alone it being the 'cause' of the disease. Much more likely, extreme functioning of the limbic system – and hence dopamine pathways – forms part of a widespread abnormality involving the whole brain, and hence all neurotransmitters. Indeed, precisely that conclusion was reached recently by Oades, after surveying neurochemical and neurophysiological research on schizophrenia[126]. Actually, Oades confined his brief much more narrowly: to an attempt to explain just one aspect of schizophrenia, disordered attention. Even there, it was clear from his review that an equally convincing – or unconvincing – story about schizophrenic attention could be constructed around each of the known chemical transmitters in the brain and the neural circuits where they act. In other words, at the present time, from a *biochemical* point of view schizophrenia looks no different from what it does psychologically, neuropsychologically or psychophysiologically: a disorder of the whole person, to the understanding of which biochemistry has a relevance or irrelevance, depending on one's construction of Man.

The last remark brings us to the second, rather different sense in which neurochemical studies of behaviour might be considered relevant to the subject matter of this book. I am referring to the use of biochemical measurements as a substitute for, or alongside, grosser indices of physiological activity, like EEG and galvanic skin response, in research trying to identify the biological correlates of normal individual differences in temperament: a recent prominent example of this application is to the study of the biochemical basis of 'sensation seeking[202]. The reasoning here is that compared with more conventional psychophysiological techniques, such methods provide more 'fundamental' data about the nervous system; which is true, in so far as they take us literally nearer to the nerve cell. But there are dangers in this approach to the biology of temperament. One entirely practical problem is that given our very incomplete knowledge of the neurochemistry of the brain, attempts to evaluate its individual differences *and* simultaneously try to relate these to personality is probably an exercise of illusory exactitude, biochemical conceptual nervous system models being, if anything, even less well-grounded than those based on other, psychophysiological, forms of measurement. A more serious hazard, however, is being led into a crude reductionist philosophy of human personality, a belief that greater precision of measurement will lead to greater understanding of Man's psychology. For there is a temptation, when taking such a downward facing perspective on behaviour, to lose sight of other very important questions about mind and brain that need to be answered and which I have argued here would require that study of the biology of personality develop in a quite different direction – towards the investigation of psychological variations as they relate to the functional properties of the higher nervous system.

A third kind of application of biochemical research techniques that is of interest here is again somewhat distinct from the other two, though it can be said to converge on both of them, in each case for a different reason. It concerns the measurement in blood or other biopsy material of biochemical substances in order to try and find biological markers for mapping out the *genetics* of mental disorder[17]. Being reasonably close to the genotype such markers should, when discovered, have a greater precision than more macroscopic indices, derived from, say, psychophysiology and are certainly more exact than the crude criteria based on clinical symptoms that genetic researchers have had to rely on in the past. Depending on one's viewpoint on psychiatric disorder, biochemical research of this type can be interpreted in one of two ways. On the one hand, it can be seen merely as an offshoot of the kind of work just mentioned; that is, as an attempt to apply biochemistry to specifically genetic aspects of normal temperamental differences – and hence, by extrapolation, to the hereditary basis of *predispositions* to mental illness, viewing the latter as continuously variable characteristics. Alternatively, from a more medical viewpoint, it can regarded as the first stage in a search for specific major genes which, in a more discontinuous sense, might define an individual's liability to diseases like schizophrenia or manic-depressive psychosis. As we have seen, for many varieties of even serious mental disorder the former seems likely to be the actual outcome of such research; but either way there is no doubt that the use of biochemical techniques will take us nearer to the answer.

A third topic that has received almost no attention in this book is the *treatment* of mental illness. The reasons for this omission are perhaps plain, the purpose here being to concentrate on the origins of personality and its disorders, rather than their modification. Nevertheless, the views expressed do have some consequences for treatment that deserve comment – and here the term 'treatment' will be used in its very broadest sense, to mean any attempt that society makes to modify or prevent behaviour which it, or the individual, considers unpleasant or undesirable.

The starting-point to be taken here is the implied constraints on behavioural and psychological change which seem to follow from several of the observations about personality made in previous chapters. Without entering at this stage the argument to which that statement can give rise (I shall do so later), it is possible to suggest that for whatever reason – constitutional or otherwise – adult individual temperaments do seem to contain certain elements which, even in the person's own judgement, are difficult to alter. Some of these elements, if they are extreme, may cause personal psychological pain and often simultaneously evoke distress in others: almost always they potentially threaten the individual's ability to adapt to, or live happily, in some social group, whether the immediate family circle or society at large. Others may lead the individual, perhaps despite himself, to behave in ways which he later regrets. Whether or not there is guilt, those around the person will disapprove of the actions as being contrary to the agreed set of social rules that pertain in the social group to which he belongs. Occasionally the person may appear to be deficient in a sense of the emotional quality and significance of his actions: in the most extreme case, as in the severe psychotic states, that 'insight' may be eclipsed entirely.

What I have just done, of course, is to describe in summary form part of the range of human temperament, some of the ways in which people do seem to differ profoundly and which set the style of their maladjustment if they are judged psychiatrically disturbed or socially deviant. On asking whether these individual differences are alterable we naturally have to conclude that in a sense they are. Society, through its treatment and corrective agencies, *does* bring about change in the sick, unhappy or deviant person: the psychiatrist lifts the psychotic's temporary loss of insight with drugs; the behaviour therapist extinguishes the anxiety neurotic's phobic reaction; the social worker relieves the domestic burdens of the depressed housewife; and the prison authorities limit the psychopath's repertoire of actions. But in none of these cases, if we are honest, is there a pretension that the remedies are anything other than palliative, or that the underlying temperamental dispositions are essentially altered. Even the most medically orientated psychiatrist would not claim that he has 'cured' the schizophrenic, while the very rationale for developing deconditioning techniques in clinical psychology was the belief that it is merely necessary to modify superficial behaviours. Social workers, for their part, are only too painfully aware that, try as they might, the personal vulnerabilities of their clients constrain their efforts to bring about change. Finally, and in its most explicit act of despair about the apparent fixedness of the human condition, society finds it necessary to resort to total restriction on the freedom of some of its members.

The existence of these differences in human temperament clearly presents society with a serious dilemma: how to balance a respect for individuality, however painfully revealed, against the need to eradicate the sometimes unpleasant consequences of extreme temperamental aberration. One solution we can sweep away immediately is a 'biological' answer to the question. Nervous typological theory might seem to raise, if only futuristically, the entirely repugnant vision of genetic engineering, the selection of 'desirable' nervous types; or the permanent modification of extreme psychophysiological status with drugs – already too close for comfort in the pharmacological straitjackets that constrain many schizophrenic patients. These remedies are neither a sane application of the principles of a biological theory of personality, nor are they sound scientifically – even, if some were tempted to suppose that they were, in the case of the more severe, psychotic forms of aberration. For, as we saw in a previous chapter, in the genetic substrate of schizophrenia might indeed lie the springs of some of Man's most desirable qualities. What, then, is the answer?

One possibility is for society to look for alternative ways in which the aberrant individual can express his temperamental dispositions. After all, temperament does not provide a blueprint for behaviour as such, only for *styles* of behaviour, similar temperaments finding expression in quite different ways. The evidence for this is all around us: the hysteric and the actress, the obsessive and the librarian, the schizoid and the Oxford don are often seen to come from, respectively, the same temperamental bags. In a similar vein, one may recall the remarks of an Israeli army psychiatrist, commenting in the wake of his country's invasion of Lebanon, that heroes in war and psychiatric casualties are frequently made of the same stuff. The point is most clearly brought out, however, in Cleckley's book on psychopathy, *The Mask of Sanity*, in which clinical case-histories sit comfortably alongside descriptions of the psychopath 'as businessman', 'as man of the world', 'as gentleman', 'as scientist', 'as physician', and 'as psychiatrist': to which we could add politician, bishop, soldier and lawyer, television personality, and university professor[33]. The desirable, the admired, the powerful, the successful and the apparently healthy do indeed spring from the same temperamental sources as the feared, the rejected, the downtrodden and the manifestly sick.

The possibility of explicitly utilising that fact in a treatment situation came to me some years ago when I was involved in the behaviour modification of compulsive gamblers. At the time I was employing an unsatisfactory therapeutic mixture of deconditioning, amateur psychotherapy and exhortation. Finally, faced with one particularly intractable case I decided, in desperation, to try a different strategy. The man in question had previously been a fairly successful entrepreneur who had, however, squandered away on the racecourse most of the proceeds from his various business interests. In personality he was, like many compulsive gamblers, a risk-taking, impulsive, sensation-seeking man – and I told him so. I explained bluntly that there was not very much he could do about his temperament but that he could exploit his disposition to gamble in life by directing it towards more personally (and financially) satisfying ends, such as trying to reconstruct his businesses, before it was too late. Strangely, no one among the many professionals from whom he had sought advice had suggested to him that slant on his problem; yet it proved very effective as a 'cure' for his gambling, turning an otherwise psychologically and domestically destructive tendency into a personally fulfilling and socially acceptable form.

Society, of course, already implicitly exploits temperamental differences in its choices, approvals and tolerances, and through social class and other institutions that mould the ways in which individual temperaments find expression. It already does so, too, in its more thoughtful use of psychiatric treatments. When applied intelligently, drug administration is always seen as an adjunct or preliminary to other therapies aimed at bringing about more permanent readjustment: in the schizophrenic in order to re-establish psychological contact and in the less serious disorders as a way of breaking through the vicious circle set up by anxiety or depression. True, in some forms of treatment – psychoanalysis and similar methods derived from depth psychology – the expressed purpose is to try and bring about fundamental changes in the individual's personality. However, it is doubtful whether psychoanalysts could, or would wish to, claim that they significantly shift their clients along the parameters of temperament referred to in this book. What they may do is to succeed in re-directing the individual's personality resources or bring the person to terms with his or own frailties. Unfortunately, even this is difficult – as witness the inordinate length of psychoanalytic therapy – and it has to be acknowledged that once adult behaviour patterns are well established they do become quite resistant to change. In some fairly straightforward cases, like my gambling man, it clearly is possible, and there are other instances where an application of knowledge about the individual's temperament could form a basis for treatment; for example, the exploitation, to the person's benefit, of obsessional, exhibitionist or assertive traits.

The main relevance of nervous typological theory to this field, however, lies in its implications for *prevention*. Existing models and policies in preventive psychiatry take two forms. One, applied to the severe psychotic states, is narrowly genetic with presumed practical implications in genetic counselling. The other concentrates on social, educational and other environmental factors, the alleviation of which will, it is hoped, bring about an improvement in mental health, if not in this at least in the next generation. Neither takes any account of biologically based individual differences of the kind emphasised here. Yet there would seem to be considerable scope for doing so, specifically in the context of social and environmental models, as part of the search for the optimal conditions under which persons of different constitutional make-up can express their individuality. For example, we still have little idea why children seemingly at equal genetic risk for schizophrenia differ vastly in their adult adjustment, from chronic disability to creative eccentricity. To posit other hereditary modifying variables is certainly a possibility, but that is pure conjecture. Equally likely are some subtle intra-family influences, or even broader sociological factors associated with economic status or social class. Take, too, those with psychopathic tendencies in their temperament. Such individuals who express their disposition in an acceptable, even socially revered, form surely do so, in part, because of the more privileged background from which they come compared with others, of a similar temperament, exposed to the life experiences of deprivation or even the positive encouragement of a criminal subculture. Yet solving such problems in sufficient detail to formulate positive policies of prevention in the field of mental care will only come about if, as is rarely the case, biological theorists and social theorists see themselves as in cooperation, rather than in opposition, seeking interactive instead of mutually exclusive solutions.

The foregoing remarks bring me naturally to one final topic: the broader social and political implications of the ideas presented in this book. There are good reasons for ending the book on such a note. I am aware that the emphasis placed here on the genetic and biological influences in behaviour has taken on unfortunate connnotations. Historically it has given the deranged an excuse for proposing, and indeed instituting, hideous eugenic policies for eradicating the biologically 'unfit'. More recently it has spawned arguments about racial differences that would be merely silly if they were not so inflammatory. Politically, stress on biological differences has sometimes become associated with downright Fascist ideology. In an allegedly more liberal guise, it has been exploited in spurious support of the neo-conservative free-for-all philosophy that social progress comes about by encouraging an unrestrained Darwinian competitiveness. Much of the debate has focused in the last few years on the question of inherited factors in intelligence. But that has not always been the case and the issues involved have a wider relevance, including genetic influences on other forms of individual variation that enter into social competence. The potential exploitation of that evidence for political purposes cannot therefore be ignored.

The same points have recently been made at much greater length – and with considerable emotional force – by Rose, Kamin and Lewontin in their book, *Not in Our Genes*[143]. It is an irony, however, that they have been led to do so as part of a wholesale attack on research into genetic influences on behaviour: this would certainly include all of the studies quoted here. Their argument seems to be that anyone who conducts such research is *inevitably* driven by a belief in a crude biological determinism – and hence motivated by a need to bolster right-wing ideologies. In putting their case, it is important to note, they do not deny the existence of genetic effects, since they also reject – though with noticeably less conviction – alternative, antipsychiatric, sociological, or other entirely environmental explanations of behaviour. What, then, are they saying? Frankly, it is sometimes difficult to tell, except that after several false starts in the book, they eventually appeal to an elaborated, very generally stated form of interactionism between genes and environment, a perspective which few serious thinkers about the problem would wish to challenge. The result is that the authors leave us with the impression of three people sitting around talking excitedly to one another – and to the straw man they wish to demolish!

One problem with the viewpoint adopted by Rose and his co-authors is that they are entirely negativistic, and very selective, in how they present evidence about genetic influences on individual differences; as well as being not only blinkered in their own intepretation of it, but also quite presumptuous in the way they construe the conclusions drawn by others, including those who have actually carried out the research. True, they are able to construct a sensational argument by appealing to dramatic, special or historical cases. In debating the genetics of intelligence, for example, they naturally revive the disreputable spectre of Sir Cyril Burt; while in addressing the very complex question of schizophrenia, they rely on an outdated view of the disorder, discussing twin and family adoption studies quite out of context to the real issues that are at stake. Of course, to expose bad science or overenthusiastic interpretation of its findings is as important in psychogenetics as elsewhere. But it is also wrong to misrepresent the *total weight* of scientific evidence in a particular field in order to support what in their case is an equally political point. For the fact is that genes *are* important in behaviour, as the authors of *Not in Our Genes* agree – though how they know this without referring to studies of the kind they attack so violently (and many others they do not mention) is difficult to fathom! As a scientific question, as Rose and his co-authors quite rightly state, the real problem is finding a suitable conceptual framework for understanding how genetic and environmental influences mutually interact. But surely one can only do that by conducting research which, however far from the ideal in its methodology, at least tries to address the issue: it is not helpful, even though it may be less exhausting, to sit on the sidelines and criticise.

If there is a message to be taken from *Not in Our Genes* it is in warning us against the danger of people with political power arriving at half-truths on the basis of incomplete knowledge of the results of genetic research; as well as reminding scientists who conduct such research of their responsibilities towards those whose views they might, unwittingly or otherwise, influence. In this respect Rose, Kamin and Lewontin are quite correct to direct their attack where they do; for, unlike alternative political philosophies, that of the New Right partly depends for its justification on biological deterministic principles of the crudest kind, principles which it is only too easy to find 'evidence' for by distorting genetic facts. The fallacy that helps to drive such opinion lies in misrepresentation of the power of genes to shape behaviour. Gene action is actually very distant from its phenotypic expression, offering a variety of outcomes that are as much dependent on autonomous social processes as they are on the biological disposition to respond to the environment in particular ways. In the case of temperament, as emphasised here, genetic tendencies to aggression, anxiety, sociability, schizotypy and other traits may issue in behaviours that vary considerably in their content and direction depending on the environmental influences at work. Cognitive ability is equally variable in its manifestation, its real-life expression being influenced by numerous factors such as personality, encouragement, social opportunity and so on. It is also dependent on so many component skills that even if, in some individuals, inherited factors can be said to place some theoretical upper limit on their development, the genetic question is so complex that at our present stage of knowledge it becomes a purely hypothetical one. Certainly, to equate cognitive capacity narrowly with the ability to perform on conventional IQ tests is entirely misleading, and to introduce such information into political discussions is quite mischievous.

Even at their best, the conclusions reached about the role of genetic influences in shaping social phenomena are quite naive and here I must disagree, for example, with the view put forward by Eysenck in his book *The Inequality of Man*, that social class mobility can be almost entirely explained on the basis of genetic principles[48]. The argument is that although social class and intelligence are related, there is still hope for the poorer members of society because the population genes for intelligence are constantly being reshuffled, leading to upward and downward changes in class position. Yet apart from shifts at the two extremes – where it is hardly of any significance – and with the exception of the odd blueblooded outcast or lucky road-digger's son, such mobility is manifestly not the case: it is certainly not enough to satisfy any genuine social reformer. For even if in some remote way social hierarchies, and changes in them, do partly derive from biological qualities – and here surely we must include personality as well as intellect – the divisions they create quickly take on self-perpetuating properties of their own which have nothing to do genetic inheritance. In short, biological hereditarianism has a way of becoming social hereditarianism, with its inherent Catch-22: even the able and the assertive may be defeated in their attempts to achieve fulfillment if they do not already possess the privileges that surround the positions to which they aspire.

The foregoing comments are not mere polemic. They are supported, at least as far as Great Britain is concerned, by the results of social mobility research, especially the carefully conducted studies recently reported by Goldthorpe and his colleagues[65]. These authors draw an important distinction, often ignored, between *absolute* and *relative* social mobility, or what they occasionally refer to as 'fluidity' between the social classes. They point out that over the past several decades there has indeed been considerable upward mobility – due to an expanding economy since the Second World War and the creation of many new service occupations. But in *relative* terms, measured as true movement between the classes, mobility has remained static, perhaps even declined. They put it as follows:

> However, the results of our enquiry . . . lead clearly to the conclusion that . . . no significant reduction in class inequalities has in fact been achieved. Systematic shifts are evident in the pattern of absolute mobility rates, of a kind that would be expected from the nature of the changes occurring in the occupational structure. But relative mobility rates, which we take as our indicator of the degree of openness, have remained generally unaltered; and the only trends that may arguably be discerned (apart from over the early stages of the life-cycle) are indeed ones that would point to a widening of differences in class chances.

The authors then go on to discuss the reasons for this social class rigidity in British society, in doing so being led firmly to reject a 'biological' explanation:

> Furthermore . . . we have shown that the pattern of relative mobility chances – or, in other words, of social fluidity – that has been associated with the British class structure over recent decades embodies inequalities that are of a quite striking kind. In particular, an enormous discrepancy emerges if one compares the chances of men whose fathers held higher-level service-class positions being themselves found in such positions rather than in working-class ones with the same relative chances of men who are of working-class origins. Where inequalities in class chances of this magnitude can be displayed, the presumption must be, we believe, that to a substantial extent they do reflect inequalities of opportunity that are rooted in the class structure, and are not simply the outcome of differential 'take-up' of opportunities by individuals with differing genetic, moral, or other endowments that do not derive from their class position. At all events, this is the interpretation that must stand, at least until some latter-day Social Darwinists or Smilesians are able to offer some alternative account of an empirically credible kind.

Another distasteful feature of political hereditarianism – and one that paints it in its true colours – is the exclusive concentration on the advantages acceptance of its arguments can confer on the *well-endowed* – the supposedly genetically gifted, fit and mentally sound. It does so under the guise of the deceptively seductive meritocratic principle. Admirable though it may be to argue that people should be rewarded for their differing personal qualities, meritocracy actually reduces to elitism, backed up by an appeal to 'genetics' and given a liberal facade in platitudinous statements that inherited differences do not imply inequalities of opportunity, legal right and so on. Never does the political hereditarian consider the implications of even his own principles for social reforms that might benefit the potentially *less* able and the potentially *less* stable. Yet it could be equally well argued that such individuals require and deserve the special attention of society, aimed at offsetting the disadvantages of their allegedly poor genetic endowment: after all, following the hereditarian's line of reasoning, the genetically bright and aggressive should already be well equipped to take care of themselves!

The point is, of course, that the joining of genetics to politics in this way is entirely spurious and distracts from the real questions that face the social reformer: how to establish *genuine* equality of opportunity;

how to find the right balance between individual freedom and common good; how to distribute social, medical, educational and economic resources according to need; essentially how to provide environments that maximise each person's intellectual and emotional resources, without elitist value judgements as to their worth. The fact of genetic diversity does not conflict with these aims; it is merely irrelevant to them. For the manner of achieving them, and the sentiments behind wanting to achieve them, ultimately go beyond what science can say, drawing upon values such as care and concern, on gut feelings of the kind that led Orwell to exclaim: 'Socialism is such elementary common sense that I am sometimes amazed that it has not established itself already'[128].

It is again Orwell, in his *Nineteen Eighty-Four*, who, with equal honesty but perhaps less hope, draws our attention to a much more real political implication of the ideas discussed in this book. We have seen that normality and abnormality are not always sharply distinguishable and that even when, as in the psychotic, they appear to be, the divisions and boundaries actually become unclear on close inspection, our medical and legal classification having no absolutes, but serving more to reinforce a comfortable illusion that we know the difference between the ill and the not ill, the good and the bad, the acceptable and the unacceptable. We have also seen that the same temperament can express itself in diverse ways. Of all of the temperaments considered here, that belonging to the psychopath (however defined) is perhaps the most intriguing (and the most frightening): because of its supreme inherent flexibility, its superficial plausibility, its occasional penchant for violence, its Machiavellianism, its tendency to border on the mad – but above all because of its appearance, often unrecognised as such, in all walks of life. There is possibly a lesson here for the political observer interested in the psychology of power: that such aberrations do not merely lead to the clinic or the prison cell but are more than occasionally found among people in high places, with a disproportionate influence on the course of events and sometimes with unpleasant consequences for Mankind. Whatever the shade of our political opinion, we might do well to reflect soberly on that fact.

References

1 ABRAMSON, L. Y. and SELIGMAN, M. E. P. Learned helplessness in humans: critique and reformulation. *Journal of Abnormal Psychology*, 1978, *87*, 49-74.

2 AMES, D. Self-shooting of a phantom head. *British Journal of Psychiatry*, 1984, *145*, 193-194.

3 BEAUMONT, J. G. and DIMOND, S. J. Brain disconnection and schizophrenia. *British Journal of Psychiatry*, 1973, *123*, 661-662.

4 BECK, A. T. *Cognitive Therapy and the Emotional Disorders*. New York: International Universities Press, 1976.

5 BEECH, H. R. (Ed) *Obsessional States*. London: Methuen, 1974.

6 BERLYNE, D. E. *Conflict, Arousal and Curiosity*. New York: McGraw-Hill, 1960.

7 BIGELOW, L. B., NASRALLAH, H. A. and RAUSCHER, F. P. Corpus callosum thickness in chronic schizophrenia. *British Journal of Psychiatry*, 1983, *142*, 284-287.

8 BLEULER, M. *The Schizophrenic Disorders. Long-term Patient and Family Studies.* (Translated by S.M. Clemens.) New Haven: Yale University Press, 1978.

9 BRAFF, D. L. Impaired speed of information processing in nonmedicated schizotypal patients. *Schizophrenia Bulletin*, 1981, 7, 499-508.

10 BROADBENT, D. E. *Perception and Communication*. Oxford: Pergamon, 1958.

11 BROCK, P. Profits and loss in the borderline cases. *The Guardian*, 22 June 1983.

12 BROCKINGTON, I. F., KENDELL, R. E., WAINWRIGHT, S., HILLIER, V. F. and WALKER, J. The distinction between the affective psychoses and schizophrenia. *British Journal of Psychiatry*, 1979, *135*, 243-248.

13 BROKS, P. Schizotypy and hemisphere function. II. Performance asymmetry on a verbal divided visual-field task. *Personality and Individual Differences*, 1984, *5*, 649-656.

14 BROKS, P., CLARIDGE, G., MATHESON, J. and HARGREAVES, J. Schizotypy and hemisphere function. IV. Story comprehension under binaural and monaural listening conditions. *Personality and Individual Differences*, 1984, *5*, 665-670.

15 BROWN, G. W. and HARRIS, T. *Social Origins of Depression*. London: Tavistock Publications, 1978.

16 BUCHSBAUM, M. Average evoked response and stimulus intensity in identical and fraternal twins. *Physiological Psychology*, 1974, *2*, 365-370.

17 BUCHSBAUM, M. S. and HAIER, R. J. Psychopathology: biological approaches. *Annual Review of Psychology*, 1983, *34*, 401-430.
18 BULMER, M. G. *The Biology of Twinning*. Oxford: Clarendon Press, 1970.
19 CANNON, W. B. *Bodily Changes in Pain, Hunger, Fear, and Rage*. Boston: Charles C. Branford, 1953.
20 CHAPMAN, J. The early symptoms of schizophrenia. *British Journal of Psychiatry*, 1966, *121*, 225-253.
21 CHAPMAN, L. J., EDELL, W. S. and CHAPMAN, J. P. Physical anhedonia, perceptual aberration, and psychosis proneness. *Schizophrenia Bulletin*, 1980, *6*, 639-653.
22 CLARIDGE, G. S. *Personality and Arousal*. Oxford: Pergamon, 1967.
23 CLARIDGE, G.S. The schizophrenias as nervous types. *British Journal of Psychiatry*, 1972, *112*, 1-17.
24 CLARIDGE, G. S. Animal models of schizophrenia: the case for LSD-25. *Schizophrenia Bulletin*, 1978, *4*, 187-209.
25 CLARIDGE, G. S. Psychoticism. In R. LYNN (Ed) *Dimensions of Personality. Papers in Honour of H.J. Eysenck*. Oxford: Pergamon, 1981.
26 CLARIDGE, G. S. The Eysenck Psychoticism Scale. In J. N. BUTCHER and C. D. SPIELBERGER (Eds) *Advances in Personality Assessment*, Vol 2 Hillsdale: Lawrence Erlbaum, 1983.
27 CLARIDGE, G. S. and BROKS, P. Schizotypy and hemisphere function. I. Theoretical considerations and the measurement of schizotypy. *Personality and Individual Differences*, 1984, *5*, 633-648.
28 CLARIDGE, G. S., CANTER, S. and HUME, W. I. *Personality Differences and Biological Variations. A Study of Twins*. Oxford: Pergamon, 1973.
29 CLARIDGE, G. S. and CLARK, K. Covariation between two-flash threshold and skin conductance level in first-breakdown schizophrenics: relationships in drug-free patients and effects of treatment. *Psychiatry Research*, 1982, *6*, 371-380.
30 CLARIDGE, G. S., DONALD, J. R. and BIRCHALL, P. M. A. Drug tolerance and personality: some implications for Eysenck's theory. *Personality and Individual Differences*, 1981, *2*, 153-166.
31 CLARIDGE, G. S. and MANGAN, G. L. Genetics of human nervous system functioning. In J. L. FULLER and E. C. SIMMEL (Eds) *Behaviour Genetics. Principles and Applications*. Hillsdale: Lawrence Erlbaum, 1983.
32 CLARIDGE, G. S., ROBINSON, D. L. and BIRCHALL, P. M. A. Psychophysiological evidence of 'psychoticism' in schizophrenics' relatives. *Personality and Individual Differences*, 1985, *6*, 1-10.
33 CLECKLEY, H. *The Mask of Sanity*. St Louis: C. V. Mosby, 1976.
34 COLBOURN, C. J. Divided visual field studies of psychiatric patients. In J. G. BEAUMONT (Ed) *Divided Visual Field Studies of Cerebral Organisation*. London: Academic Press, 1982.
35 CONNOLLY, J. F., GRUZELIER, J. H., MANCHANDA, R. and HIRSCH, S. R. Visual evoked potentials in schizophrenia: intensity effects and hemisphere asymmetry. *British Journal of Psychiatry*, 1983, *142*, 152-155.
36 COOPER, J. E., KENDELL, R. E., GURLAND, B. J., SHARP, L., COPELAND, J. R. M. and SIMON, R. J. *Psychiatric Diagnosis in New York*

and London. A Comparative Study of Mental Hospital Admissions. Maudsley Monograph No 20 Oxford: Oxford University Press, 1972.

37 CROW, T. J., BAKER, H. F., CROSS, A. J., JOSEPH, M. H., LOFT-HOUSE, R., LONGDEN, A., OWEN, F., RILEY, G. J., GLOVER, V. and KILLPACK, W. S. Monoamine mechanisms in chronic schizophrenia: post-mortem neurochemical findings. *British Journal of Psychiatry*, 1979, *134*, 249-256.

38 CUTTING, J. Judgement of emotional expression in schizophrenics. *British Journal of Psychiatry*, 1981, *139*, 1-6.

39 DELVA, N. J. and LETEMENDIA, F. J. J. Lithium treatment in schizophrenia and schizo-affective disorders. *British Journal of Psychiatry*, 1982, *141*, 387-400.

40 DSM-III. *Diagnostic and Statistical Manual of Mental Disorders.* (Third Edition). American Psychiatric Association, 1980.

41 DUSTMAN, R. E. and BECK, E. C. The visually evoked potential in twins. *Electroencephalography and Clinical Neurophysiology*, 1965, *19*, 570-575.

42 DYKES, M. and McGHIE, A. A comparative study of attentional strategies of schizophrenic and highly creative normal subjects. *British Journal of Psychiatry*, 1976, *128*, 50-56.

43 EAVES, L. and YOUNG, P. A. Genetical theory and personality differences. In R. LYNN (Ed) *Dimensions of Personality. Papers in Honour of H.J. Eysenck.* Oxford: Pergamon, 1981.

44 ELLINWOOD, E. H. and KILBEY, M. M. Chronic stimulant intoxication models of psychosis. In I. HANIN and E. USDIN (Eds) *Animal Models in Psychiatry and Neurology.* Oxford: Pergamon, 1977.

45 EYSENCK, H. J. *Dynamics of Anxiety and Hysteria.* London: Routledge and Kegan Paul, 1957.

46 EYSENCK, H. J. Classification and the problem of diagnosis. In H.J. EYSENCK (Ed) *Handbook of Abnormal Psychology.* (1st Edition.) London: Pitman, 1960.

47 EYSENCK, H. J. *The Biological Basis of Personality.* Springfield: Charles C. Thomas, 1967.

48 EYSENCK, H. J. *The Inequality of Man.* London: Temple Smith, 1973.

49 EYSENCK, H. J. and EYSENCK, S. B. G. *Manual of the Eysenck Personality Questionnaire.* London: Hodder and Stoughton, 1975.

50 EYSENCK, H. J. and EYSENCK, S. B. G. *Psychoticism as a Dimension of Personality.* London: Hodder and Stoughton, 1976.

51 FENTON, W. S., MOSHER, L. R. and MATTHEWS, S. M. Diagnosis of schizophrenia: a critical review of current diagnostic systems. *Schizophrenia Bulletin*, 1981, 7, 452-476.

52 FLEMINGER, J. J., DALTON, R. and STANDAGE, K. F. Handedness in psychiatric patients. *British Journal of Psychiatry*, 1977, *131*, 448-452.

53 FLOR-HENRY, P. Psychosis and temporal lobe epilepsy: a controlled investigation. *Epilepsia*, 1969, *10*, 363-395.

54 FLOR-HENRY, P. Laterality, shifts of cerebral dominance, sinistrality and psychosis. In J. GRUZELIER and P. FLOR-HENRY (Eds) *Hemisphere Asymmetries of Function in Psychopathology.* Amsterdam: Elsevier/North-Holland, 1979.

55 FLOR-HENRY, P., FROM-AUCH, D., TAPPER, M. and SCHOPF-LOCHER, D. A neuropsychological study of the stable syndrome of hysteria. *Biological Psychiatry*, 1981, *16*, 601-626.
56 FOULDS, G. A. *Personality and Personal Illness*. London: Tavistock, 1965.
57 FOULDS, G. A. Personality deviance and personal symptomatology. *Psychological Medicine*, 1971, *1*, 222-233.
58 FOULDS, G. A. and BEDFORD, A. Hierarchy of classes of personal illness. *Psychological Medicine*, 1975, *5*, 181-192.
59 FREEDMAN, D. G. An ethological approach to the genetical study of human behaviour. In S. VANDENBERG (Ed) *Methods and Goals in Human Behaviour Genetics*. New York: Academic Press, 1965.
60 FRITH, C. D. Consciousness, information processing and schizophrenia. *British Journal of Psychiatry*, 1979, *134*, 225-235.
61 GALIN, D. Implications for psychiatry of left and right cerebral specialisation. *Archives of General Psychiatry*, 1974, *31*, 572-583.
62 GARMEZY, N. Children at risk: the search for the antecedents of schizophrenia. Part I: Conceptual models and research methods. *Schizophrenia Bulletin*, 1974, No 8, 14-90.
63 GARMEZY, N. Children at risk: the search for the antecedents of schizophrenia. PartII: Ongoing research programmes, issues, and intervention. *Schizophrenia Bulletin*, 1974, No 9, 55-125.
64 GIBSON, E. J. and WALK, R. D. The visual cliff. *Scientific American*, 1960, *202*, 64-71.
65 GOLDTHORPE, J. H. *Social Mobility and Class Structure in Modern Britain*. Oxford: Clarendon Press, 1980.
66 GOTTESMAN, I. I. and SHIELDS, J. *Schizophrenia: The Epigenetic Puzzle*. Cambridge: Cambridge University Press, 1982.
67 GRAY, J. A. *Pavlov's Typology*. Oxford: Pergamon Press, 1964.
68 GRAY, J. A. The psychophysiological basis of introversion-extraversion. *Behaviour Research and Therapy*, 1970, *8*, 249-266.
69 GRAY, J. A. *The Psychology of Fear and Stress*. London: Weidenfeld & Nicolson, 1971.
70 GRAY, J. A. *Pavlov*. London: Fontana, 1979.
71 GRAY, J. A. *The Neuropsychology of Anxiety*. Oxford: Oxford University Press, 1982.
72 GREEN, P., HALLETT, S. and HUNTER, M. Abnormal interhemispheric integration and hemispheric specialisation in schizophrenics and high-risk children. In P. FLOR-HENRY and J. GRUZELIER (Eds) *Laterality and Psychopathology*. Amsterdam: Elsevier/North-Holland, 1983.
73 GREEN, P. and KOTENKO, V. Superior speech comprehension in schizophrenics under monaural versus binaural listening conditions. *Journal of Abnormal Psychology*, 1980, *89*, 399-408.
74 GRINKER, R. Diagnosis of borderlines: a discussion. *Schizophrenia Bulletin*, 1979, *5*, 47-52.
75 GRUZELIER, J. H. A critical assessment and integration of lateral asymmetries in schizophrenia. In M. MYSLOBODSKY (Ed) *Hemisyndromes. Psychobiology, Neurology, Psychiatry*. New York: Academic Press, 1983.

76 GRUZELIER, J. and MANCHANDA, R. The syndrome of schizophrenia: relations between electrodermal response, lateral asymmetries and clinical ratings. *British Journal of Psychiatry*, 1982, *141*, 488-495.

77 GRUZELIER, J. H. and VENABLES, P. H. Skin conductance orienting activity in a heterogeneous sample of schizophrenics. *Journal of Nervous and Mental Disease*, 1972, *155*, 277-287.

78 GUNDERSON, J. G. Characteristics of borderlines. In P. HARTOCOLLIS (Ed) *Borderline Personality Disorders*. New York: International Universities Press, 1977.

79 HALLETT, S. and GREEN, P. Posssible defects of interhemispheric integration in children of schizophrenics. *Journal of Nervous and Mental Disease*, 1983, *171*, 421-425.

80 HARACZ, J. L. The dopamine hypothesis: an overview of studies with schizophrenic patients. *Schizophrenia Bulletin*, 1982, *8*, 438-469.

81 HARE, R. D. *Psychopathy. Theory and Research*. New York: Wiley, 1970.

82 HERNÁNDEZ-PEÓN, R., CHAVÉZ-IBARRA, G. and AGUILAR-FIGUEROA, E. Somatic evoked potentials in one case of hysterical anaethesia. *Electroencephalography and Clinical Neurophysiology*, 1963, *15*, 889-892.

83 HESTON, L. L. Psychiatric disorders in foster home reared children of schizophrenic mothers. *British Journal of Psychiatry*, 1966, *112*, 819-825.

84 HIRSCH, S. R. and LEFF, J. P. *Abnormalities in Parents of Schizophrenics*. London: Oxford Univerisity Press, 1975.

85 HOLZMAN, P. S. Cognitive impairment and cognitive stability: towards a theory of thought disorder. In G. SERBAN (Ed) *Cognitive Defects in the Development of Mental Illness*. New York: Brunner/Mazel, 1978.

86 HUGDAHL, K., FREDRIKSON, M. and OHMAN, A. 'Preparedness' and 'arousability' as determinants of electrodermal conditioning. *Behaviour Research and Therapy*, 1977, *15*, 345-353.

87 JUNG, C. G. *Memories, Dreams, Reflections*. London: Fontana, 1967.

88 JUNG, C. G. *Psychological Types*. The Collected Works of C. G. Jung , Vol 6, London: Routledge and Kegan Paul, 1971.

89 KENDELL, R. E. A new look at hysteria. In A. ROY (Ed) *Hysteria*. Chichester: Wiley, 1982.

90 KENDELL, R. E. and BROCKINGTON, I. F. The identification of disease entities and the relationship between schizophrenic and affective psychoses. *British Journal of Psychiatry*, 1980, *137*, 324-331.

91 KERNBERG, O. The structural diagnosis of borderline personality organisation. In P. HARTOCOLLIS (Ed) *Borderline Personality Disorders*. New York: International Universities Press, 1977.

92 KETY, S. S., ROSENTHAL, D., WENDER, P. H. and SCHULSINGER, F. The types and prevalence of mental illness in the biological and adoptive families of adopted schizophrenics. In D. ROSENTHAL and S. S. KETY (Eds) *The Transmission of Schizophrenia*. Oxford: Pergamon Press, 1968.

93 KETY, S. S., ROSENTHAL, D., WENDER, P. H., SCHULSINGER, F. and JACOBSEN, B. The biologic and adoptive families of adopted individuals who became schizophrenic: prevalence of mental illness and other characteristics. In L. C. WYNNE, R. L. CROMWELL, and S.

MATTHYSSE (Eds) *The Nature of Schizophrenia. New Approaches to Research and Treatment.* New York: Wiley, 1978.

94 KLEIN, D. F. Pharmacology and the borderline patient. In J. E. MACK (Ed) *Borderline States in Psychiatry.* New York: Grune and Stratton, 1975.

95 KRETSCHMER, E. *Physique and Character.* (Translated by W.J.H. SPROTT.) London: Kegan, Trench, and Trubner, 1925.

96 LADER, M. H. and WING, L. *Physiological Measures, Sedative Drugs and Morbid Anxiety.* Oxford: Oxford University Press, 1966.

97 LANDAU, S. G., BUCHSBAUM, M. S., CARPENTER, W., STRAUSS, J. and SACKS, M. Schizophrenia and stimulus intensity control. *Archives of General Psychiatry*, 1975, *32*, 1239-1245.

98 LARUSSO, L. Sensitivity of paranoid patients to non-verbal cues. *Journal of Abnormal Psychology*, 1978, *87*, 463-471.

99 LASKY, M. Remembering. Interview with Diana West, reprinted in: The life and death of Arthur Koestler. *Encounter*, 1983, *61*, 45-64.

100 LEFF, J. Schizophrenia and sensitivity to the family environment. *Schizophrenia Bulletin*, 1976, *2*, 566-574.

101 LERNER, H. E. The hysterical personality: a 'woman's' disease. *Comprehensive Psychiatry*, 1974, *15*, 157-164.

102 LEWIS, C. S. *A Grief Observed.* London: Faber, 1961.

103 LEWIS, E. G., DUSTMAN, R. F. and BECK, E. C. Evoked response similarity in monozygotic, dizygotic and unrelated individuals: a comparative study. *Electroencephalography and Clinical Neurophysiology*, 1972, *32*, 309-316.

104 LIEBOWITZ, M. R. Is borderline a distinct entity? *Schizophrenia Bulletin*, 1979, *5*, 23-38.

105 LIPTON, R. B., LEVY, D. L., HOLZMAN, P. S. and LEVIN, S. Eye movement dysfunctions in psychiatric patients: a review. *Schizophrenia Bulletin*, 1983, *9*, 13-32.

106 LUKAS, J. H. and SIEGEL, J. Cortical mechanisms that augment or reduce evoked potentials in cats. *Science*, 1977, *198*, 73-75.

107 MACALPINE, I. and HUNTER, R. A. (Eds) *D. P. Schreber: Memoirs of My Nervous Illness.* London: William Dowson, 1955.

108 MACASKILL, N. D. and MACASKILL, A. The use of the term 'borderline patient' by Scottish psychiatrists: a preliminary survey. *British Journal of Psychiatry*, 1981, *139*, 397-399.

109 MACDONALD, N. Living with schizophrenia. *Canadian Medical Association Journal*, 1960, *82*, 218-221.

110 MACK, J. E. Borderline states: an historical perspective. In J.E. MACK (Ed) *Borderline States in Psychiatry.* New York: Grune and Stratton, 1975.

111 MANGAN, G. *The Biology of Human Conduct.* Oxford: Pergamon, 1982.

112 MARKS, I. M. *Fears and Phobias.* London: Heinemann, 1969.

113 MAXWELL, A. E. Difficulties in a dimensional description of symptomatology. *British Journal of Psychiatry*, 1972, *121*, 19-26.

114 McCONAGHY, N. The use of an object sorting test in elucidating the hereditary factor in schizophrenia. *Journal of Neurology, Neurosurgery, and Psychiatry*, 1959, 22, 243-246.

115 McGHIE, A. and CHAPMAN, J. S. Disorders of attention and perception

in early schizophrenia. *British Journal of Medical Psychology*, 1961, *34*, 103-116.

116 MEDNICK, S. A. Berkson's fallacy and high-risk research. In L. C. WYNNE, R. L. CROMWELL and S. MATTHYSSE (Eds) *The Nature of Schizophrenia. New Approaches to Research and Treatment*. New York: Wiley, 1978.

117 MEDNICK, S. A. and McNEIL, T. F. Current methodology in research on the aetiology of schizophrenia: serious difficulties which suggest the use of the high-risk-group method. *Psychological Bulletin*, 1968, *70*, 681-693.

118 MEDNICK, S. A. and SCHULSINGER, F. A learning theory of schizophrenia: thirteen-years later. In M. HAMMER, K. SALZINGER and S. SUTTON (Eds) *Psychopathology. Contributions from the Social, Behavioural, and Biological Sciences*. New York: Wiley, 1973.

119 MEDNICK, S. A., SCHULSINGER, H. and SCHULSINGER, F. Schizophrenia in children of schizophrenic mothers. In A. DAVIDS (Ed) *Childhood Personality and Psychopathology: Current Topics, 2*. New York: Wiley, 1975.

120 MELTZER, H. Y. and STAHL, S. M. The dopamine hypothesis of schizophrenia: a review. *Schizophrenia Bulletin*, 1976, *2*, 19-76.

121 MERSKEY, H. *The Analysis of Hysteria*. London: Balliere Tindall, 1979.

122 MOSS, P. D. and McEVEDY, C. P. An epidemic of overbreathing among schoolgirls. *British Medical Journal*, 1966, *2*, 1295-1300.

123 NAYLOR, G. J. and SCOTT, C. R. Depot injections for affective disorders. *British Journal of Psychiatry*, 1980, *136*, 105.

124 NEAL, J. V. The genetics of diabetes mellitus. In R.A. CAMERINI DAVALOR and H. S. COLE (Ed) *Early Diabetes*. New York: Academic Press, 1970.

125 NEBYLITSYN, V. D. Current problems in differential psychophysiology. *Voprosy Psykhologii*, 1971, No 6, 13-26.

126 OADES, R. D. *Attention and Schizophrenia*. Boston: Pitman Advanced Publishing Program, 1982.

127 ÖHMAN, A., ERIXON, G. and LÖFBERG, I. Phobias and preparedness: phobic versus neutral pictures as conditioned stimuli for human autonomic responses. *Journal of Abnormal Psychology*, 1975, *84*, 41-45.

128 ORWELL, George. *The Road to Wigan Pier*. London: Gollancz, 1937.

129 ORWELL, George. *Nineteen Eighty-Four*. London: Secker and Warburg, 1949.

130 PAVLOV, I. P. *Lectures on Conditioned Reflexes*. (Translated by W.H. GANTT.) New York: Liveright Publishing Corporation, 1928.

131 PAVLOV, I. P. *Selected Works*. (Translated by S. BELSKY.) Moscow: Foreign Languages Publishing House, 1955.

132 PAYNE, R. W., MATTUSEK, P. and GEORGE, E. I. An experimental study of schizophrenic thought disorder. *Journal of Mental Science*, 1959, *105*, 627-652.

133 PETERSON, D. (Ed) *A Mad Peoples' History of Madness*. Pittsburgh: University of Pittsburgh Press, 1982.

134 PLACE, E. J. S. and GILMORE, G. C. Perceptual organisation in

schizophrenia. *Journal of Abnormal Psychology*, 1980, *89*, 409-418.

135 PROPPING, P. Genetic control of ethanol action on the central nervous system. *Human Genetics*, 1977, *35*, 309-334.

136 RANDALL, P. L. A neuroanatomical theory on the aetiology of schizophrenia. *Medical Hypotheses*, 1980, *6*, 645-658.

137 RAWLINGS, D. and CLARIDGE, G. S. Schizotypy and hemisphere function. III. Performance asymmetries on tasks of letter recognition and local-global processing. *Personality and Individual Differences*, 1984, *5*, 657-663.

138 RAY, J. J. and RAY, J. A. B. Some apparent advantages of subclinical psychopathy. *Journal of Social Psychology*, 1982, *117*, 135-142.

139 REED, G. F. 'Underinclusion' – a characteristic of obsessional personality disorder: I. *British Journal of Psychiatry*, 1969, *115*, 781-785.

140 REICH, W. *Character Analysis*. New York: Orgone Press, 1949.

141 RIEDER, R. O. Borderline schizophrenia: evidence of its validity. *Schizophrenia Bulletin*, 1979, *5*, 39-46.

142 ROBINS, L. N. *Deviant Children Grown Up*. Baltimore: Williams and Wilkins, 1966.

143 ROSE, S., KAMIN, L. J. and LEWONTIN, R. C. *Not in Our Genes*. Harmondsworth: Penguin, 1984.

144 ROTHENBERG, A. *The Emerging Goddess*. Chicago: University of Chicago Press, 1979.

145 SARGANT, W. *Battle for the Mind*. London: Heinemann, 1957.

146 SARGANT, W. *The Unquiet Mind*. London: Heinemann, 1967.

147 SASS, L. The borderline personality. *The New York Times Magazine*, 22 August 1982.

148 SCARR, S. Environmental bias in twin studies. In S.G. VANDENBERG (Ed) *Progress in Human Behaviour Genetics*. Baltimore: Johns Hopkins Press, 1968.

149 SCHARFETTER, C. and NUSPERLI, M. The group of schizophrenias, schizoaffective psychoses, and affective disorders. *Schizophrenia Bulletin*, 1980, *6*, 586-591.

150 SCHMAUK, F. J. Punishment, arousal and avoidance learning in sociopaths. *Journal of Abnormal Psychology*, 1970, *76*, 325-335.

151 SCHMIDEBERG, M. The treatment of psychopaths and borderline cases. *American Journal of Psychotherapy*, 1947, *1*, 45-70.

152 SELIGMAN, M. E. P. Phobias and preparedness. *Behaviour Therapy*, 1971, *2*, 307-320.

153 SELIGMAN, M. E. P. *Helplessness*. San Francisco: W.H. Freeman, 1975.

154 SHIELDS, J. *Monozygotic Twins Brought Up Apart and Brought Up Together*. Oxford: Oxford University Press, 1962.

155 SHIMKUNAS, A. Hemispheric asymmetry and schizophrenic thought disorder. In S. SCHWARTZ (Ed) *Language and Cognition in Schizophrenia*. Hillsdale: Lawrence Erlbaum, 1978.

156 SIEVER, L. J. and GUNDERSON, J. G. Genetic determinants of borderline conditions. *Schizophrenia Bulletin*, 1979, *5*, 59-86.

157 SIEVER, L. J. and GUNDERSON, J. G. The search for a schizotypal personality. *Comprehensive Psychiatry*, 1983, *24*, 199-212.

158 SIEVER, L. J., HAIER, R. J., COURSEY, D., SOSTEK, A. J., MURPHY, D. L., HOLZMAN, P. S. and BUCHSBAUM, M. S. Smooth pursuit eye tracking impairment. *Archives of General Psychiatry*, 1982, *39*, 1001-1005.

159 SILVERMAN, J. Variations in cognitive control and psychophysiological defense in the schizophrenias. *Psychosomatic Medicine*, 1967, *29*, 225-251.

160 SMOKLER, I. A. and SHEVRIN, H. Cerebral lateralisation and personality style. *Archives of General Psychiatry*, 1979, *36*, 949-954.

161 SPERRY, R. W. Lateral specialisation in the surgically separated hemispheres. In F. O. SCHMITT and F. G. WORDEN (Eds) *The Neurosciences: Third Study Programme*. Cambridge, Mass.: MIT Press, 1974.

162 SPITZER, R. L., ENDICOTT, J. and GIBBON, M. Crossing the border into borderline personality and borderline schizophrenia: the development of criteria. *Archives of General Psychiatry*, 1979, *36*, 17-24.

163 SPOHN, H. E. and PATTERSON, T. Recent studies of psychophysiology in schizophrenia. *Schizophrenia Bulletin*, 1979, *5*, 581-611.

164 SPRINGER, S. P. and DEUTSCH, G. *Left Brain, Right Brain*. San Francisco: W.H. Freeman, 1981.

165 STANDAGE, K. F. Observations on the handedness preferences of patients with personality disorders. *British Journal of Psychiatry*, 1983, *143*, 575-578.

166 STEIN, J. *Edie*. London: Panther Books, 1984.

167 STERN, D. B. Psychogenic somatic symptoms on the left side: review and interpretation. In M.S. MYSLOBODSKY (Ed) *Hemisyndromes. Psychobiology, Neurology, Psychiatry*. New York: Academic Press, 1983.

168 STONE, M. H. The borderline syndrome: evaluation of the term, genetic aspects, and prognosis. *American Journal of Psychotherapy*, 1977, *31*, 345-365.

169 STONE, M. H. *The Borderline Syndromes*. New York: McGraw Hill, 1980.

170 STRELAU, J. *Temperament and Type of Nervous System*. (2nd Edition.) Wroclaw: Zaklad Naradowy Im. Ossolinskich, 1974.

171 STURGEON, D., KUIPERS, L., BERKOWITZ, R, TURPIN, G. and LEFF, J. Psychophysiological responses of schizophrenic patients to high and low expressed emotion relatives. *British Journal of Psychiatry*, 1981, *138*, 40-45.

172 SZASZ, T. S. *The Myth of Mental Illness*. New York: Harper and Row, 1974.

173 SZASZ, T. S. *Schizophrenia*. Oxford: Oxford University Press, 1976.

174 TARNAPOLSKY, A. and BERELOWITZ, M. 'Borderline personality': diagnostic attitudes at the Maudsley Hospital. *British Journal of Psychiatry*, 1984, *144*, 364-369.

175 TAYLOR. P. J., DALTON, R., FLEMINGER, J. J. and LISHMAN, W. A. Differences between two studies of hand preference in psychiatric patients. *British Journal of Psychiatry*, 1982, *140*, 166-173.

176 TEASDALE, J. Negative thinking in depression: cause, effect, or reciprocal relationship? *Advances in Behaviour Research and Therapy*, 1983, *5*, 3-25.

177 'Wrong' to send mentally ill to jail. *The Guardian*, 26 October 1984.

178 THOMAS, A. and CHESS, S. *Temperament and Development*. New York: Brunner/Mazel, 1978.

179 THOMAS, A., BIRCH, H. G., CHESS, S., HERTZIG, M. E. and KORN, S. *Behavioural Individuality in Early Childhood*. New York: New York University Press, 1963.

180 TRASLER, G. Relations between psychopathy and persistent criminality - methodological and theoretical issues. In R.D. HARE and D. SCHALLING (Eds) *Psychopathic Behaviour*. Chichester: Wiley, 1978.

181 TSUANG, M. T., WINOKUR, G. and CROWE, R. R. Morbidity risks of schizophrenia and affective disorders among first-degree relatives of patients with schizophrenia, mania, depression, and surgical conditions. *British Journal of Psychiatry*, 1980, *137*, 497-504.

182 VANDENBERG, S. G. Hereditary factors in normal personality traits (as measured by inventories). In *Recent Advances in Biological Psychiatry* (Vol 9). New York: Plenum, 1967.

183 VAUGHN, C. E. and LEFF, J. P. The influence of family and social factors on the course of psychiatric illness. *British Journal of Psychiatry*, 1976, *129*, 125-137.

184 VENABLES, P. H. Input dysfunction in schizophrenia. In B. MAHER (Ed) *Progress in Experimental Personality Research*. New York: Academic Press, 1964.

185 VENABLES, P. H. Input regulation and psychopathology. In M. HAMMER, K. SALZINGER, and S. SUTTON (Eds) *Psychopathology. Contributions from the Social, Behavioural, and Biological Sciences*. New York: Wiley, 1973.

186 VENABLES, P. H., MEDNICK, S. A., SCHULSINGER, F., RAMAN, A. C., BELL, B., DALAIS, J. C. and FLETCHER, R. P. Screening for risk of mental illness. In G. SERBAN (Ed) *Cognitive Defects in the Development of Mental Illness*. New York: Brunner/Mazel, 1978.

187 VOGEL, F., SCHALT, E., and KRUGER, J. The electroencephalogram (EEG) as a research tool in human behaviour genetics: psychological examinations in healthy males with various inherited EEG variants. II. Results. *Human Genetics*, 1979, *47*, 47-80.

188 VOGEL, F., SCHALT, E., KRUGER, J., PROPPING, P. and LEHNERT, R. F. The electroencephalogram (EEG) as a research tool in human behaviour genetics: psychological examinations in healthy males with various inherited EEG variants. I. Rationale of the study, materials, methods, heritability of test parameters. *Human Genetics*, 1979, *47*, 1-45.

189 WALKER, V. J. and BEECH, H. R. Mood state and the ritualistic behaviour of obsessional patients. *British Journal of Psychiatry*, 1969, *115*, 1261-1268.

190 WATSON, J. B. *Behaviorism*. Chicago: University of Chicago Press, 1924.

191 WATT, N. F., STOLOROW, R. D., LUBENSKY, A. W. and McLELLAND, D. C. School adjustment and behaviour of children hospitalised for schizophrenia as adults. *American Journal of Orthopsychiatry*, 1970, *40*, 637-657.

192 WEINMAN, J. A. and FERDOWSKI, S. The processing of facial information in schizophrenia. *British Journal of Psychiatry*, 1982, *140*, 206.

193 WEXLER, B. E. Cerebral laterality and psychiatry: a review of the literature. *American Journal of Psychiatry*, 1980, *137*, 279-291.

194 WEXLER, B. E. and HENINGER, G. R. Alterations in cerebral laterality during acute psychotic illness. *Archives of General Psychiatry*, 1979, *36*, 278-284.

195 WHITMORE, R. *Mad Lucas*. North Hertfordshire District Council, 1983.

196 WIDOM, C. S. A methodology for studying non-institutionalised psychopaths. In R.D. HARE and D. SCHALLING (Eds) *Psychopathic Behaviour*. Chichester: Wiley, 1978.

197 WILLIAMS, J. M. G. *The Psychological Treatment of Depression*. London: Croom Helm, 1984.

198 WOODRUFF, R. A., GOODWIN, D. W. and GUZE, S. B. Hysteria (Briquet's syndrome). In A. ROY (Ed) *Hysteria*. Chichester: Wiley, 1982.

199 WOODY, E. Z. and CLARIDGE, G. S. Psychoticism and thinking. *British Journal of Social and Clinical Psychology*, 1977, *16*, 241-248.

200 WORLD HEALTH ORGANISATION. *The International Pilot Study of Schizophrenia*. Geneva: WHO, 1973.

201 ZUCKERMAN, M. *Sensation Seeking*. New York: Wiley, 1979.

202 ZUCKERMAN, M., BALLENGER, J. C., JIMERSON, D. C., MURPHY, D. L. and POST, R. M. A correlational test in humans of the biological models of sensation seeking, impulsivity, and anxiety. In M. ZUCKERMAN (Ed) *Biological Bases of Sensation Seeking, Impulsivity, and Anxiety*. Hillsdale: Lawrence Erlbaum, 1983.

Index